Modern/Postmodern

Modern/Postmodern

Off the Beaten Path of Antimodernism

Eric Mark Kramer

PRAEGER

Westport, Connecticut
London

Library of Congress Cataloging-in-Publication Data

Kramer, Eric Mark.
    Modern/postmodern : off the beaten path of antimodernism / Eric
Mark Kramer.
      p. cm.
    Includes bibliographical references and indexes.
    ISBN 0–275–95758–6 (alk. paper)
    1. Postmodernism.   2. Civilization, Modern.   I. Title.
B831.2.K73   1997
149—dc20   96–41392

British Library Cataloguing in Publication Data is available.

Library of Congress Catalog Card Number: 96–41392
ISBN: 0–275–95758–6

First published in 1997

Praeger Publishers, 88 Post Road West, Westport, CT 06881
An imprint of Greenwood Publishing Group, Inc.

Printed in the United States of America

The paper used in this book complies with the
Permanent Paper Standard issued by the National
Information Standards Organization (Z39.48–1984).

10 9 8 7 6 5 4 3 2 1

To my mother, Helen Kramer

Contents

Preface

The two most fundamental media are time and space. The human creates these as formal expressions. They are the result of disintegration. There are many styles of division. Time and space are articulated in every contingent gesture. The comparative study of civilizations reveals the various styles of expression, the various kinds of time and space. These fundamentally presupposed dimensions affect other values, hopes, dreams, identities, and expectations (or lack thereof).

CULTURE AS EXPRESSION

In the human world, the space/time unity forms warps called ''mood,'' which are variances in style of communicating and comportment—in a word, attitude or feel. We even speak of the ''gravity'' of a situation or event. Mood is ''global.'' For instance, the mood of an entire situation changes when a group of teenagers is invaded by a parent, when a person gets or loses a job, when a student gets a good or bad grade, when the weather changes, when one is told that one has a deadly disease, when lovers ''break up,'' when someone smiles, and so forth. Mood saturates all human experience and it is expressed, which means that it is articulated in the form of interior and exterior design, hair and clothing styles, odor, music, styles of walking and talking, and so forth. A space and time can be altered by perfume or lighting.

Human beings create mood by altering the valence of space and time, that is, the way space and time are combined/created. The human, as an individual, group member, or anonymous ''I'' (not ''me''), is created by the culture. To call this relationship a dialectic of self/other, individual/group, culture/nature (and so on) is just one way to express the ontogenetic process of permanence and flux and presence and absence. Space and time are the necessary conditions for formative expression. But an expression, the formative and transformative style of articulation, also creates space and time as qualities. Formative, contingent expression is a necessary condition for the existence of transcendental dimensions. The transcendent and immanent are co-constituting phenomena: neither exists without the other; neither has ontic priority. The immanent is meaningful only as it relates to the transcendent, and vice versa. They exhibit simultaneous ontogenesis. This is the meaning of co-constitutional genesis (Kramer, 1993). They always appear together. In some cultures space and time is articulated as a point-like unity (the magic world), or as a polarity that is ambiguously defined (the mythic world), or as a sharply demarcated duality (the perspectival world), or as an integral transparency of identity and difference (the aperspectival world). Thus, some cultures have a faster rhythm than others, and each culture creates different spaces for habitation. Even the space and time of conflict, like war-making, varies across cultures. These variances in spatio/temporal valence are what make cultures different, identifiable.

The idea that humans ''create'' and are created by the complex of expressive activity called culture may sound arrogant, but the point is that the formal awareness of these dimensions is a consequence of human activity—transformational articulation. Dimensions are always only given with each contingent expression. The generalized or transcendental conceptualization of a dimension, *sui generis*, is not exactly an extrapolation ''from'' given, ''concrete'' experience, but a recognition of the transcendent in the immanent. But such conceptualization is always already presumed as soon as one talks about ''givens,'' or a ''given'' (or perhaps better, an appearing). Each civilization is recognizable by the different formal qualities its expressions articulate, including, in a few modern instances, dedication to quantification. In short, some cultures quantify, or establish a quantifiable type of space and time, while other cultures establish (through their expressions) spaces and times that are qualitatively different. Leonardo da Vinci did not ''discover'' three-dimensional depth-space, as if it were somewhere or somewhen else. Rather, he established it by articulating it. There is nothing ''behind'' expressions, which include architectures, religions, philosophies, modes of transportation and communication, entertainments, and so forth. Dimensions pervade all contingencies. Expressions like rituals, sciences, highways, art works, utensils, and leisure activities all present styles of configuring space and time—moods or modes of being.

Some cultures present an atomistic, fragmentary mode of being, while others present a more animistic and fluid world. For example, the North American game of ''football'' presents very different types of space and time than ''soccer.'' The American football game articulates a cultural obsession with measurement of all kinds (which expresses linear space) and preconceived planning/simulation (which expresses linear time), both of which manifest atomism. Unlike the soccer field, the North American football field is a giant ruler with intervals of yardage units painted on its surface, and numbers that indicate position relative to a goal line. Every player is also assigned a number which, by convention, indicates his position, unless the player reaches an emotional status known as star stature so that the number is "retired" when the player quits because the number and player have become (magically) identical. When this happens, the player is said to "embody" or "personify" the game. Otherwise, players are interchangeable (uniform) in a standardized fashion. A coach simply plugs players into functional positions that constitute the structure of the play (spatio-temporal events). Even though fans become very attached to teams, in professional football the attachment or identity of teams to cities is not inherent but conventionally tenuous.[1] The team and the city are mirror images in that both (like the player) are marginally relevant to each other—contingent. To be contingent, or to be a contingent, signifies being a standard movable part of a larger assemblage, a detachment.

In American football, measurements are laboriously and religiously taken so that statistics can be calculated for every conceivable aspect of the game. Dedicated fans memorize them. There are officials called "linesmen" who dutifully keep the measure and who are often called onto the field to assure precision of ball placement, which means to locate the official "line of scrimmage," the point of contact between opposites, the definitive boundary between defense and offense. Tackles, passes, catches, fumbles, and so forth are categorized and counted. The identity of the player is the sum of his measures. Occasionally the character of a player will stand out as flamboyant or troublesome. This is tolerable if and only if he has good statistics, otherwise "character" is "bad." Everything is seen through the measures. Offense and defense are clearly demarcated, with different players taking the field for each mode of play. The team that has "possession" of the ball has only four tries to move it "forward," toward the goal line, at least ten yards. Failure to do so results in loss of "possession." The action is very often interrupted by "huddles," which are team meetings to discuss tactics and "call" the next plan of attack. The movement of players, such as blocking assignments and pass receiver "patterns," are choreographed ahead of time and simulated in topographic imagery (diagrams).

Soccer, by contrast, presents a much less structured spatial and temporal configuration. It also tends to present a much more emotional mood evinced by numerous and often deadly riots during matches. Soccer play is a continual flow without constant measurement or meetings to discuss the "play book." In soccer, there is no central authority like the quarterback in American football. The linear hierarchy of authority ("chain" of command) in American football is very clear from the head coach down. Soccer is less preplanned, and involves less officiating. For these reasons it is more volatile and emotional. Soccer and American football manifestly express two different civilizational valences. They do not "represent" any thing or absolute, but articulate two different styles of being/communicating.

Space, time, and mood do not exist "behind" or "before" the stylistic form that expressions articulate. Dimensions are not separate from expression. Space is not a spatial thing, nor is time a temporal phenomenon. They do not exist elsewhere or elsewhen. They are, in phenomenological terms, "eidetic" or "transcendentally" "essential." They articulate dimensions which are necessary conditions for contingencies to exist. However, they are not given "separate from" or "before" contingencies, but always and only together with them. This is the postmodern thrust of Husserlian phenomenology. The transcendent and immanent are conceivable but always given together. The transcendent and the immanent are separable only in abstract, dissociated experience which is unique to only one mode of consciousness-structure, the perspectival. Thus, Edmund Husserl's (1962) insistence that consciousness is always consciousness of some phenomenon, like a dream, a rock, a feeling, or whatever. This is why Jean-Paul Sartre (1956) concluded that pure (empty) consciousness would be "nothing." Pure dimensionality, without warping, would be utterly invisible. The ability to think about transcendental phenomena, as such, like a Newtonian constant, is a dissociative and abstracting mode of thinking. But the category cannot exist (appear) without the case. In fact, the term "contingent," as a category applicable to an infinite number of cases, is itself a transcendental concept. This ability to abstract is, by definition, a necessary condition for explanation of contingent cases, and it may be the defining quality of the human species. To define, is, by definition, objectifying. That is, humans, unlike other animals, appear to be unique in their ability to live categorically, and therefore generalizably beyond the here and now, where animals appear to be trapped. Animals are very "empirical" and sensate; humans are not. Indeed, the philosophy of empiricism itself, which argues for the existence of only the physically here and now, is a transcendental concept. But this is merely a problem of ideology (metaphysics). No matter how abstract an idea may be, it is sensical only through the experience of a dream, a sensate rock, an imagined rocket going the speed of light, and so forth. The case and category are co-constituting phenomena regardless of their metaphysical qualities. There are any number of things which may be called "empirical." The quality empirical is itself not an empirical thing, but a category of being, a set of qualities like spatial extension and temporal duration, that constitute a definition, an identity, which enables one to say that such-and-such individual experience is not a dream but an empirical object. Thus a person may identify this phenomenon (a box) as an empirical phenomenon, unlike the dream of a box. For perspectival people, identity exists by definition. For instance, despite my race, language, color, creed, gender, or other so-called inherent identifiers, I am an American citizen by (legal) definition.

Like time, which is not a temporally locatable object, the concept of "space" is not spatially localized. It makes no sense to ask how big the concept "space" is, or how durable "time" is. The medium is always and only given with that which is mediated, and vice versa. Hence, the qualities of space, time, and mood are given in the style of a culture's expressions which are usually variants of a more pervasive civilizational style. Such differences appear as respective modes of interacting or communicating, including manufactured environments, pace of life, and configurations of production, wealth, education, age, and so forth. One cannot understand behavior without understanding the most fundamental presuppositions the actor presumes (either knowingly or not, makes no difference). These presuppositions are given in the behavior and artifacts themselves. They are not somewhere ''else'' in some mysterious metaphysical realm beyond ''direct experience'' (the only kind).

DIMENSIONAL ACCRUAL/DISSOCIATION

This book presents a theory of social interaction/communication which suggests that as dimensional awareness accrues, so too dissociation increases. When one communicates, one may or may not exchange or establish an empirical thing but most certainly always exchanges, shares, and establishes an idea, want, value, and/or capability. For example, I may give Joe a bicycle or a tie; the contingent thing is variable, but in either case it is much more, it is a gift. The theory of dimensional accrual/dissociation can be used to explain any social behavior/communication including other theoretical artifacts, even the bewildering array of other conflicting theories of communication (from rhetoric to information theory and deconstruction) that now populate the modern academy.

Following from the work of Jean Gebser (Ger. 1949/Eng. 1985), it has been argued that there are basically four types of expressivity (Kramer, 1993; Kramer & Ikeda, in press). The first type is magic/idolic, the second type is mythic/symbolic, the third type is perspectival/signalic-codal, and the fourth type is an emergent integral style which this book only begins to explore. Idolic being/communicating is univalent, symbolic communication is bivalent, and perspectival perception is trivalent. As dimensionality increases, so too does dissociation in all its forms, including emotional and semantic detachment from concrete expression.

The magical world is articulated by a predominance of idolic communication/interaction.[2] Idolic communication is one-dimensional, univalent. In the magic world, there is practically no dissociation or detachment of emotional commitment between what an expression means and its concrete presence. For instance, if I steal an idol, I have stolen a god. In many parts of the world, people regularly remove gods from their temples or shrines and take them for a circuitous procession through the neighborhoods they protect, finally returning them to their ''houses.'' Examples include the ''Bai Bai'' festivals for Matsue and other deities throughout Asia. In order to become the tiger, to manifest her fierce qualities, I must eat her flesh and drink her blood. Then I become not just tiger-like, but tiger. Magic identity is collectivistic to the extreme. Who am I? I am part of an extended family. As dissociation increases, identity shrinks ''down'' through the fragmented ''extended'' family (thinkable as such only from the perspectival attitude) to the ''nuclear'' family, to the subatomic family, and finally to the modern Hobbesian world of everyone for him- or herself. While the magic world is a womb of belonging and sharing where blood ties take precedence over all other criteria (sometimes called corruption and nepotism by perspectival persons), the perspectival world is one of individual rights and responsibilities (merit and independence). In a magic world, identity can be so closely guarded through the purification of blood that many royal families have experienced symptoms of in-breeding. By contrast, in the perspectival world, identity is arbitrarily defined by legal code so that one can be a United States citizen with no regard to race, color, creed, or even language. In an environment of arbitrary identity one finds much more ''mixing'' of types of people than in magic cultures with collectivistic identities. Democracy presumes a universe of interchangeable, equal units that have no inherent qualities of differentiation. In most cultures, ''equality'' is a farfetched idea that is not supported by experience. People within the group manifest different qualities, not e-quality.

With magic idolic communication, meaning is not a problem. It cannot be ''lost,'' misinterpreted, or misconstrued. The magic world does not suffer from the threat of nihilism (and so perhaps this, along with extended shame, may be why suicide is practically unknown in most ''traditional'' societies). In the magic world, there is no semantic space between the expressed and the expression. In the magic world, activity is often less extravagant than in the ''modern'' perspectival world because the magic world is animistic. The magic world is full. Everything is interchangeable with everything else. The magic world is spaceless and timeless, so that a curse or blessing can be bestowed immediately no matter how far away the person cursed or blessed is, even if they are dead or not yet born. The magic world is filled with vital force or energy such as *mana*, *karma*, or *chi*. Everything is alive including the sky, water, mountains, rocks, sun, moon, and so on. Because the world is full of life or ''spirit,'' one must be very careful what one does. If I move this mountain, the consequences are immediately felt on the other side of the cosmos and at every point in between. Therefore, an abiding concern for harmony and serenity are understandable. Caste systems can be understood as a concern to maintain proper place. Under such conditions an appeal to harmony can have great hegemonic force stifling ideas of reorganization like reform and revolution (Kramer & Ikeda, in press).

The fact that the magic world is thoroughly unified may help us understand why many cultures have shown little or no interest in technological development in the Western-modern style or social reorganization. From the modern perspectival worldview, such cultures seem ''stagnant,'' ''backward,'' stuck in the ''Stone Age,'' ''simple,'' ''savage,'' ''lazy,'' pathetically satisfied. For magic people, the world is not only full, but it is finished and perfect. In such a world, ideas like improvement, development, progress, and correction are profane, if even thinkable. Some of the best analyses of magical being/expression have been done by Clifford Geertz (1973), Georges Bataille (1955, 1989), and Alphonso Lingis (1983).

With the accrual of another dimension, the mythic world is recognizable by two-dimensional expressions. The mythic mode of being/communicating is symbolic. A symbol indicates a nascent dissociation or separation between the expressed and the expression. The mythic world is am-bivalent. A symbol, like a metaphor, has two sides, the literal and the figural. Meaning, *sui generis*, comes into being, and so too the tragedy of nihilism. The conflict of interpretations is a defining aspect of the mythic world. Communication, as such, becomes a problem so that reflective thinking begins to appear as with the study of rhetoric and hermeneutics. The mythic world is a world of stories which open up to multiple interpretations. The "reader" is no longer imposed upon by unambiguous reality or "signs of nature" like animal footprints, but gains critical power by interpreting (reflecting upon and making) symbols. The reader becomes a metawriter—a critic. While claiming to rely on the unambiguous and intolerant sign for legitimacy, the mythic interpreter is also extending his or her will by extending ("illuminating") the "full" or "true" meaning of the text. Magic sign unfolds into mythic symbol.

Unlike an idol, if I steal a symbol of a god, like a crucifix, I have not stolen god. There may be a great deal of emotional attachment to the symbol, and therefore anger toward me as a thief, but there is no magical identity. In the mythic world, the word expresses the power to emotionally move people but not to literally transform them, as happens when a person who has the "vested power" (a magician) and knows the proper incantation can proclaim one no longer a bachelor but a spouse, no longer an alien but a citizen, no longer a civilian but a soldier, and so forth. After such a transformative ritual occurs, including oath taking and pledges, the identity of the person literally changes, and simultaneously so too does his or her orientation to the world. In short, magic incantation changes everything. By contrast, divorce indicates the contingency of marriage. The ancient marriage magic is loosing its power in an increasingly perspectival world. Divorce is a modern phenomenon that expresses individual independence and a perspectival valence.

Compared with magic incantation, mythic words are less "direct" or identical with action. In magic incantation, one must know the singularly correct words to make something happen. Without the words, nothing happens. By contrast, mythic communication may be emotionally powerful but yet interpretable—ambivalent. And yet it is not totally arbitrary. A metaphor can be "inappropriate." Thus, I can say the Sumo wrestling champion bulldozed his way across the ring, but not that he tricycled his way. Some of the best analyses of mythic communication include the many works of Carl Jung and Joseph Campbell, and more specifically Kenneth Burke (1941, 1962), Mircea Eliade (1963), and Tzvetan Todorov (1982).

With the accrual of a third dimension, emotional detachment and semantic dissociation is increased. Language becomes a mere instrument among others. As described by perspectival theorists like Ferdinand de Saussure (1974), Karl Popper (1959), and Claude Shannon and Warren Weaver (1949), communication is based on totally arbitrary signs and codes like the zero/one of computer language. Communication is the transfer of information across empty space. The perspectival world is very different from the magic world. While the magic world is alive and full, the perspectival world is a dead void. Therefore, the perspectival human has little or no moral or spiritual compunction to move mountains and recombine atomic bits like genetic material into any desired configuration. Quality vanishes and truth becomes detached and disinterested. Everything becomes spatialized, and as such, available for unitization. Each part is identical and therefore interchangeable with each other part. This is the perspectival law of equivalences that grounds the democratic attitude expressed in modern science, jurisprudence, religion, mass production, and politics. To say that all things or even all people are equal is extremely abstract and ideal, quite at odds with direct experience. This is why direct personal experience designated as "subjective" is rejected by the perspectival dissociation designated as "objectivism." Detachment is a necessary condition for the principle of equivalences. Thus, all people are equal in the eyes of God, blind justice, and the blind referee. Universalism and fundamentalism are expressed by the objectification of things and people from "on high." This indicates the visiocentric bias of the perspectival world (Kramer, 1993, 1994). The world becomes standardized and available for rearrangement. The metaphysics of the will, as Arthur Schopenhauer (1966) called it, takes the form of engineering. Everything, including life itself, because it is ultimately made of dead "building blocks" like molecules of acids, becomes engineerable. Quality, meaning, and identity are not regarded as "inherent," but arbitrary and willable. In the future, "people" (or perhaps products) will have no parents. The genetic material used for their origin may be manufactured. The definition of "parent" may come to signify those who selected the characteristics they wanted from a menu at a laboratory, or via e-mail. Children may complain that they don't like the name their parents chose for them, but in the future they may discover that they don't like the phenotype their "parents," or selectors chose. The child will be the embodiment of the "parents'" tastes, values, and perhaps financial wherewithal, as well as the engineer's capabilities. With increased freedom comes expanding responsibility and guilt. The individual must shoulder the burden of the world which he/she has made. This will be the ultimate rhetoric. The identity of the "child" and "parent" will be flexible. Indeed, I will be solely responsible for my own identity.

While the magic world is one where everyone is the same, a member of an extended family, as in prewar Japan, the modern world makes identity arbitrary and based on codes like the legal and genetic codes. Yesterday I was innocent, but with the stroke of a pen, today I am a criminal. Even personality types may be "selected for." In the magic world identity is based on membership in groups, and group "identity" is based on inherent qualities (from origin) like race, sex, age, and ethnicity that are identical in each member. Such are the magical qualities that differentiate one group from another, and as such must be defended to the death. Hence, the intensity of emotion. But if I can change my nose, sex, or complexion, then they lose their inherent "attachment." Race becomes contingently meaningless, so who would care to fight and maybe kill and die for a transient condition?

Magic identity is not bounded by space or time. Consequently, the children can be and are held responsible for the sins of the parents. White Euro-Americans living today may be held responsible for the enslavement of Afro-Americans a century before, solely on the basis of their racial membership. But from a perspectival attitude, ''I,'' as an individual, had nothing to do with slavery and therefore I do not owe anyone anything. For the perspectival modern, history is bunk and so is historical identity and context. This indicates the desire to become a rock, an object with no interest, history, culture, language—in a word, no prejudice. In late (hypertrophic perspectival) modernity, everything is arbitrary except this state of being arbitrary. Flux is a permanent condition. Even the master narrative history is conditional. All that is, is what is knowable through direct personal experience, the narrow world of the here and now which is never here or now. Hence Jacques Derrida's (1973) phenomenology of endless traces of things never really present but spoken. Postmodern magic is the claim that being is always becoming, the temporalization of time ''itself.'' Times change.

In the interest and values of predictability and control, the perspectival trivalent world attempts to push randomness and uncertainty further back into the shadowy corner of the bygone days of superstition. Thus, dissociation serves the will-to-power. The perspectival world is spatial and thus linear. Time is a fixed line segmented into three parts: past, present, and future. Free of a past that no longer is, and a future that is not yet, the late modern can do what he or she wills. Such ''a'' person sees him- or herself as a detached object, a mere trace or echo of a never-present self. There is no extended responsibility, as in ancestor worship or future reincarnation. The modern perspectival individual is relatively free of such mythic cyclical obligations, free of mythical and magical spaces and times. But the ''other side'' of freedom is loss—being al-one. Such a person has no possessions and cannot be possessed. They claim to not speak of ''my team'' or ''my city'' or ''my race'' or ''my country'' or ''my language.''

REAL PEOPLE

Humans formalize time in many ways, such as clocks and calendars, histories and prophecies. Similarly, spaces are sculpted with architecture and dance, phenotypic aesthetics and maps. For instance, well before Einstein's concept of a unified field theory, modern transportation combined space and time in expressions like miles per hour and minutes of longitude. These relatively ''mundane'' syntheses made it possible for him to think as he did.

We idolize the wanderers of space/time from Alexander the Great to Marco Polo, Eric the Red, Christopher Columbus, and the astronauts. Wandering is a lust. Where were they going? Nowhere known. They explored, just as modern (not ''post'' modern) deconstructionists trace semantic paths that amble aimlessly, shedding meaning. The "path" is the space and time and meaning generated by the finger tracing across the map or calendar. Modern identity is a location. Postmodern "identity" is nonlocalizable, and therefore often seen as nonidentity.

The signitive gesture constitutes a reason, "the way," an association of previously unrelated points, through the desert, over the mountains, across the initially boundless seas and skies. Like the nomadic Mongols living on the "plain," on the horizon line between sky and earth, the great Polynesian explorers were surface dwellers too. The Mongol lived "off the land." The Mongol could, from his saddle, pluck deer and rabbits for lunch like the mariner fishes from the side of his boat. Neither could go very far up or down.

Then the universe became spherical, and now exploration goes in all "directions." The "aim" is not so sure as an arrow pulled for a meal, because modern exploration discovers what did not exist as a target. Artists explore and scientists (of which there are fewer and fewer—not engineers) search and research. In wondering and wandering, the value is in the promenade which happens upon the unsought or the unexpected, not the redundancy of having. Humans are intelligent creatures. They create to avoid boredom.

While Newton saw lines everywhere, Faraday saw fields. The difference expresses a fundamentally different world experience. Newton was modern, Faraday articulates the cusp of the postmodern. Interest in the invisible, whether it be Maxwell's hypothetical "ether" or "electromagnetic spectrum," or waves that travel best in a vacuum, is essential to discovery. The substanceless substance that is odorless, colorless, tasteless, invisible, and silent like gravity, which passes through you without sensation, became the quarry of the postmodern scientist. The new exploration was into the nonempirical, no-thing field.

The world is undergoing a major qualitative shift. Quantitative changes are noninformative redundancies, relatively boring. An earlier shift was marked by Petrarch's new way of seeing when he climbed Mount Ventoux and became aware of a new "shocking" awareness which he recorded in the first letter of his *Familiari*, vol. 4, 1336. In that letter he described his encounter with a new reality. He was one of the first to breech a psychological barrier that remained fairly intact until the last 100 years. Up to the mid-1800s, the world over, practically no one climbed peaks, even in the European Alps. A few Incan "priests" may have climbed a peak in the Andes for sacrificial rituals as much as 500 years ago, but other than that, most climbing was for military purposes, and it did not go beyond the clouds. Petrarch, the great romantic individualist, had been "shaken by the unaccustomed wind and the wide, freely shifting vistas, I was immediately awe-struck. . . . Suddenly a new thought seized me, transporting me from space into time [*a locis traduxit ad tempora*]" (quoted in Gebser, Ger. 1949/Eng. 1985: 14).

A very similar shift in attitude has been facilitated by the first photographs of the earth from "outer" space. Without exception, the astronauts who have achieved enough "distance" to concretely experience the earth as a small isolated orb have attempted to articulate a profound change of mind not unlike Petrarch's uncomfortable announcement of the new modern world of space and time as isolated dimensions (*sui generis*). The postmodern ''space'' travelers have experienced a space-free and time-free awareness that is aperspectival. The spherical nature of the planet that moderns coped with by relativizing time into spatial ''zones'' was a modern disintegration that is now, from such a great distance, losing its meaning. Suddenly, all the modern systematizing divisions and subdivisions disappear. The view has shifted. Attitude is very important. When it changes, everything changes. Consequently, a new truly postmodern integral awareness is dawning which can see the limitations of nationalism, racism, sexism, ageism, regionalism, all ''isms'' as such.

But still the old age holds inertial force. The old age is the age of engineering, the age of problems. It is physically practical and utilitarian. Under such a view, there is no hesitation or respect for things as they are. Instead, boldness and aggression are valued. Problem solvers are handsomely rewarded. They service the metaphysics of the will. I want mass production, which engenders huge concentrations of labor and the growth of the urban world. So we engineer huge machine factories, the likes of which have heretofore not been seen. I need to stack the workers up, so engineers invented the skyscraper, an architecture hardly imaginable in the previous aeons of human existence. The new labor power needs to be conveyed quickly to and from work, so we invent massive communication and transportation systems. The will marks the face of the earth.

The particular attitude, perspective, philosophy, prejudice, or bias that identifies the modern Western world is that everything is perceived as either a problem or a solution. We may take a comparative position outside of this world to help us see it. In the Hindu world, for instance, there is a qualitative difference between *darsana* (philosophy), which is any chosen point of view, and *sadhana*, which Franklin Edgerton (1944: 179), in his commentary on the *Bhagavad Gita*, has described as its ''curious many-sidedness, tolerance, or inconsistency.'' Troy Organ (1970: 76) has called the *Gita* the gem of *sadhana*, which means that it cannot be read as a single message. Likewise, the *Upanisads* offer no system, but instead encourage absorption of even contradictory ideas. Many schools of thought find their source in the *Upanisads*. ''The typical Hindu manner of thought is an exploration of possibilities rather than a reaching of conclusions. The Hindu specializes in hypothesis formation, and does not push a single hypothesis into the role of the solution of a problem'' (Organ, 1970: 76). Hinduism, and in fact most cultural activities, are not ''pragmatic'' by modern Western standards. There is no concluding absolution. In short, there is no single best or correct interpretation (solution) of the world. It certainly is not a problem to be solved once and for all like a mathematical puzzle. There is no ''solution'' to life. It is to be lived.

But, for the modern Westerner, the world is full of problems in need of (ab)solution. As the modern term for prisons makes clear, everything is in need of ''correction.'' The world needs to be ''well adjusted,'' ''developed,'' and "improved." Yet we are not sure what the norm is, which way adjustment should go. The West feigns value-freedom and defers to the determinism of the statistical mean. Yet the West is the most aggressive civilization in terms of managing, manipulating, developing, and changing the face of the planet. The West strives to cure or erase the boundary between life and death. The Western problemistic philosophy posits a world of disease that must be purified. Everything is problematic, and every problem has a solution. The world needs to be resolved, focused, and predicted—controlled.

The greatest disease is chaos. Terrorism means lack of understanding, and standing under means control. As Pascal said, Hell itself is the impossibility of reason. There are the good, who are arranged, and there are the bad, who are deranged. The goal is to get everything scheduled/prioritized according to Western time (production) and ordinated spatially (measured and recorded), to be put into its "quadrant" in an appointment book in order to achieve, as Stephen Covey (1989) puts it, "private victory." The modern West is obsessed with ordination, laws, rules, in a word system with feedback control, as in self-monitoring and self-management.

Literacy means literality. Under the conditions of absolute literacy, figurative ambiguity is not tolerable. Subjective flux must be domesticated and transformed so that figures come to mean fixed unambiguous "values," numbers. The modern West has attempted to exterminate symbolism in favor of monosemantic codal informatics; "either/orism" as Kierkegaard (Dan. 1843/Eng. 1944) put it; no maybes, or both, or none.

In the modern West, uncertainty equals anxiety. I show up for my appointment, and you are 70 minutes late. I have timed you. "Where were you?!" "I thought we understood each other, that there was no (semantic) room for mistake." Jean Gebser (1949 Ger./1985 Eng.) has called this condition of semantic and temporal uncertainty "temporal anxiety." It is anxiety over meaning and its transient nature. Better communication is supposed to "fix" this problem by "bringing minds together," by thinking with "one mind," coming to congruence about a shared single meaning. Hence, communication, *sui generis*, has become the watchword for the modern era, but it has been reduced to informatics, input/output with no ambiguity or redundancy. Interpretation is the bane of good communication. Good communication solves problems (interpretation) and facilitates confident action. Communication is everything. The fastest-growing sector of the economy is "communication." Communication is shrinking the globe, erasing spatial, temporal, and cultural boundaries, which means to erase space, time, and culture. It is modern magic.

Ironically, however, without problems, the engineer is out of business. Anxiety is her necessary condition, just as dissatisfaction is the friend of the marketer. But engineering "solutions" do not put the engineer out of business because the solutions resolve old problems. Instead, they generate new ones. For instance, we can now safely abort fetuses. This raises the agonizing question for many: should we? Technology enables us to keep people "alive" much longer now. So the boundary between alive and dead becomes very fuzzy, and we are forced to make decisions about if and when to pull the plug on the "life support" machines. Technology gives us weapons of immense destructive capabilities, and we become paralyzed by the options. Soon genetic engineering will force freedom of choice upon us in the form of options that were unthinkable not so long ago.

Modernity is marked by hypertrophic individualism on one hand, so that even our soldiers are called "privates," and dehumanizing systematization on the other, insuring that each private, or "hand," or "grunt," is interchangeable with any other.

WHAT "I" AM

According to neurophysiologists like Charles Woody (1986), you and I are the algebraic summations of our neurotransmitters. According to neo-Heiddeggerians, like Michel Foucault and Jacques Derrida, you and I are language and text. According to the Bible, the *Upanisads*, the Koran, and Torah, you and I are moral beings with "souls." According to (the early, naive) John Locke, we are lumps that "shit happens" to. According to Karl Marx, you and I are expressions of class-specific ideology and material products. According to Aristotle, we are rational animals. According to the Dadaists, we are the chaotic animals. According to Ernst Cassirer, we are symbol makers. According to classical, neotheological (as in Thomas Aquinas) behaviorism, we are the effects of previous causes. According to G. W. F. Hegel, we are the extensions of the Absolute striving through teleological history for self-actualization (entelechy). According to measurers, we are the sum total of our measurements. According to Sigmund Freud, we are psychic systems, much like the thermodynamic model from which he borrowed the tripartite structure (psychic energy can be neither created nor destroyed, just repressed and sublimated, and hence it squeezes out of the cracks in our personalities in inconvenient ways). According to Gottfried Wilhelm Leibniz, we are "windowless monads." According to David Hume, Jean-Paul Sartre, and Zen, we are nothing but an empty stage where associations just happen. According to Jean Jacques Rousseau, we are fallen savages. According to Charles Darwin, we are random organizations (something of an oxymoron) of protoplasm struggling to survive. According to Marshal McLuhan, we are self-extenders; to Abraham Maslow, we are self-actualizers. According to Jack Cooper, Floyd Bloom, and Robert Roth (1996), we are really biochemical reactions (neuropharmacological entities). We are souls, neuromotors, hinges between stimuli and responses, "feeling tones" located in the limbic system, "naked apes," and so on.

In his book *Ideas* (Ger. 1913/Eng. 1962), Husserl recognized that the academy was fragmenting into "regional ontologies." Each specialty claimed to be the ultimate ground of reality (including the other disciplines), and each was therefore mutually excluding. If you want to study the spin of electrons, you cannot do it in the sociology department, and alienation and politics does not exist in chemistry textbooks. The chemist tells the sociologist that he is really about seven cents worth of chemicals, while the sociologist argues that the chemist is a consequence of his enculturation and the ideology of science—he is really a social animal. So knowledge of reality is falling apart; becoming absurd. How could I be both really a 2.5-pound glob of electrified jelly (as I have heard neurophysiologists refer to our brains) and also really a pile of randomly vibrating atoms, and also really a rational being? I can calculate the probability of a random universe, but the mathematical statistics I presume, I do not claim to be only probably correct. Which is it? Which reality? Is reality stratified? Is it social or biological? Macro or micro? Cultural or natural? Cognitive or concrete? Which department is really the most correct and therefore "important"? Physics? History? Communication? Medicine? Philosophy? The physicist can do the physics of history (books are really . . .), and the historian can do the history of physics (physics is really . . .).

Perhaps it is the de-part-ments that teach contingent but vocationally rewarding skills like business management, law, journalism, and engineering. Maybe money is the only really real thing. They (the experts) continue to diverge, speaking different languages, and seemingly living in parallel universes except when they leave their offices and reenter what Husserl called the "lifeworld" of mundane concerns and activities, the background to all foregrounds.

AUTHOR-ITY?

Years ago, while a graduate assistant and doctoral student in mass communication, I worked on a course entitled "Television Criticism" with Professor Hal Himmelstein. Professor Himmelstein knew a great deal about film and television history, various theories, production techniques, methods of investigation, aesthetics, and so forth. But in this class it seemed very difficult to establish any criteria of authority. What is more, although the students had watched thousands of hours of television, they did not seem to see what we had seen. How could it be?

Professor Himmelstein would point out how a show was actually a parody of another series. For instance, the television series *Maverick* was a parody of the cowboy genre in general, and *Gunsmoke* in particular. *Mary Hartman, Mary Hartman*, was a primetime parody of daytime "soap operas" and their attendant advertisements. Although the creators of such series had admitted as much, students (being accidentally sophisticated about how authorial intent does not count anyway) were not so sure.

When he pointed out that Matt Dillon's woman companion, "Kitty," was actually an aging prostitute turned pimp ("madam"), this too was met with doubt. He would point out how advertisements often make allusions to symbols found in great poetry and art. Despite all his knowledge, popularity, and goodwill, there still remained a sense that it was all just his interpretation, his opinion.

How can authority be rhetorically powerful when interpretation is inevitable? Or is authority nothing but the brutality of facts, described or generated? Facts speak for themselves. Has the ''author'' vanished, replaced by databases and processing units? Is what is ''entered'' at all a judgement? Are the printouts without doubt self-evident as to what they mean?

Other researchers simply survey audiences—market research of a sort. The truth is whatever the majority says it is. It is what Jules Henry (1963) called ''pecuniary truth.'' Truth is what sells. Thus, we have a sort of consensus of the masses (valued because they are what broad- and cablecasters create in the form of audiences and then sell to advertisers), a social construction of reality with the inertia of numbers. But, after all, the basis of measurement is totally arbitrary anyway, so what the reality scales generate is merely conventional, a social construct too. If most people do not perceive the trend of happy widowers on television (*My Three Sons*, *The Courtship of Eddie's Father*, *Family Affair*, *Bonanza*, *Sanford and Son*, *Empty Nest*, *Mayberry RFD*, *The Rockford Files*, *The Beverly Hillbillies*, *Black's Magic*, *The Fugitive*, etc.) then it is not significant, it does not exist. Could it be that such a scenario allows the fictional world to be patriarchal, for ''the man'' like the ''Equalizer,'' ''Stingray,'' James Bond, Captain Steubing on *The Love Boat*, Duncan McCloud on *Highlander*, Captain Kirk, Marshal Dillon, Sheriff Andy Taylor, Hogan on *Hogan's Heroes*, McHale on *McHale's Navy*, ''Hawkeye'' Pierce on *M*A*S*H*, Bronson on *Then Came Bronson*, Kane on *Kung Fu*, Richard Kimble on *The Fugitive*, *The Man From U.N.C.L.E.* (later followed by the ''girl''), *The Bionic Man* (later followed by the ''woman''), *Quantum Leap*, *I Spy*, *Blue Thunder*, *Kojak*, *Knight Rider*, *Stingray*, *It Takes a Thief*, *The Cat*, *The Saint*, *The Hulk*, *Have Gun Will Travel*, *Mr. Lucky*, *The Lazarus Man*, *Branded*, *The Blue Coronet*, *Fantasy Island*, and so on, to be the father of an entire ship or town, to never change diapers, and to pursue romance and adventure at will? Otherwise, even ''conventional families'' tend to be headed by males such as Dick van Dyke, Robert Young, and Bill Cosby. This trend is evident even when the family is the audience, as with ''Captain Kangaroo'' and ''Mr. Rogers.'' And when women had extraordinary powers, as in *I Dream of Jeannie* and *Bewitched*, they were controlled by men through devotion.

Do these shows have anything to do with our modern attitude toward domesticity, the ''traditional'' (two-parent) family, or commitment? Do they express a high-tech vigilantism? Even *Perry Mason*, *Ironside*, and the lead characters on *Miami Vice*, *Hawaii Five-O*, *Route 66*, and *The Wild Wild West* never had lasting relationships except with male colleagues. Why are so many named after guns like Cannon, Magnum, and Beretta? Does not their redundancy indicate an almost insatiable appetite for such stories?

At most, all that can be said is that there are X number of leading characters, but to even try to categorize them in this way is already subjective nonsense; it presumes a category that enables one to recognize a case when one sees it. In fact, what constitutes ''leading'' is not demonstrable without a shared set of criteria (value judgements). Therefore, to hazard an explanation of what such a "categorical trend" might (if it existed) mean, is off-limits as unfalsifiable and therefore senseless. If the majority does not perceive it, it is not the case. Thus, the only sense is the "common" sense. The one or few who may have exceptional insight, even when masses of people are exposed to the very same stimuli, are, by definition, too far out on the bell curve to "count." They are cut off as being too deviant. Neither geniuses nor morons are statistically significant. They don't buy in enough quantity to matter.

This book suggests a relative relativism. Authority abounds and clashes, splinters, and passes into illegitimacy. Systems fail. Maybe confusion and argumentation are not so bad. Maybe the absurdity of multiple truths is simply the truth, the "case." But yet, worlds endure. Cultures, civilizations, societies hang together as they change. As an opening confession, I believe that without truth there can be no liars, and I believe in the existence of liars.

NOTES

1. Although fans (by definition) are emotionally attached to, meaning to magically identify with, "a" team, in fact players constantly come and go. This is even true of professional franchises, as when the Cleveland Browns moved to Baltimore in 1995. For the owners, location is arbitrary, something Karl Marx understood. Owners are perspectival individuals who calculate the profitability of a team as a business like any other, irregardless of city or fan identification. While kings must inherit a throne and are royal by bloodright, chief executive officers such as presidents of countries and companies come and go, even switching from one product or service to another because the contingency is irrelevant to filling the position. When American football teams are treated this way, fans become angry. Their emotional investment, their allegiance and support, are ultimately irrelevant. While the fans speak in sympathetic terms such as "my team," the legal code recognizes only one owner—an individual or consortium of a few persons.

2. The qualifier "predominance" is used because every culture this author has studied manifests all three modes of expression, but in various intensities.

REFERENCES

Bataille, G. (1955) *The Birth of Art: Prehistoric Painting*. Lausaunne, France: Skira.
———. (1989) *The Tears of Eros*. San Francisco: City Lights Books.
Burke, K. (1941) *The Philosophy of Literary Form: Studies in Symbolic Action*. Baton Rouge: Louisiana State University Press.
———. (1962) *A Grammar of Motives and a Rhetoric of Motives*. Cleveland: World.
Cooper, J., F. Bloom, and R. Roth. (1996) *The Biochemical Basis of Neuropharmacology*. New York: Oxford University Press.
Covey, S. (1989) *The Seven Habits of Highly Effective People: Restoring the Character Ethic*. New York: Simon & Schuster.
Derrida, J. (1973) *Speech and Phenomena*. Evanston, IL: Northwestern University Press.
Edgerton, F. (1944) *The Bhagavad Gita: Translated and Interpreted*. Harvard Oriental Series, Vols. 38, 39. Cambridge: Harvard University Press.

Eliade, M. (1963) *Myth and Reality*. New York: Harper and Row.

Gebser, J. (German 1949; English 1985) *The Ever-Present Origin*. Athens: Ohio University Press.

Geertz, C. (1973) *The Interpretation of Cultures*. New York: Basic Books.

Henry, J. (1963) *Culture Against Man*. New York: Vintage.

Husserl, E. (1962) *Ideas*. New York: Collier.

Kierkegaard, S. (Dan. 1843/ Eng. 1944) *Either/Or*. Princeton, NJ: Princeton University Press.

Kramer, E. M. (1992) "Gebser and Culture." In *Consciousness and Culture: An Introduction to the Thought of Jean Gebser*, edited by E. Kramer. Westport, CT: Greenwood Press (pp. 1–60).

―――. (1993) "The Origin of Television as Civilizational Expression." In *Semiotics 1990: Sources in Semiotics, Vol. XI*, edited by J. Deely et al. Lanham, MD: University Press of America.

―――. (1994) "Making Love Alone: Videocentrism and the Case of Modern Pornography." In *Ideals of Feminine Beauty* by K. Callaghan. Westport, CT: Greenwood Press (pp. 79–98).

Kramer, E., and R. Ikeda. (in press) "Japanese Clocks: Semiotic Evidence of the Perspectival Mutation." Forthcoming in *The American Journal of Semiotics*.

Lingis, A. (1983). *Excesses: Eros and Culture*. Albany, NY: State University of New York Press.

Organ, T. (1970) *The Hindu Quest for the Perfection of Man*. Athens: Ohio University Press.

Popper, K. (1959) *Logic of Scientific Discovery*. New York: Basic Books.

Sartre, J. P. (1956) *Being and Nothing*. New York: Simon & Schuster.

Saussure, F. de. (1974) *Course in General Linguistics*. London: Fontana.

Schopenhauer, A. (1966) *The World as Will and Representation*, Vols. 1 and 2. New York: Dover.

Shannon, C., and W. Weaver. (1949) *The Mathematical Theory of Communication*. Urbana: University of Illinois Press.

Todorov, T. (1982) *Theories of the Symbol*. Ithaca, NY: Cornell University Press.

Woody, C. (1986) *Neural Mechanisms of Conditioning*. New York: Plenum Press.

Modern/Postmodern

Introduction:
Living Off the Grid

I seem to be a verb.

—R. Buckminster Fuller

TRANSVALUATING OPPOSITIONAL REALITY

This book is about communication at the most general level. Practically every "thing" is a relationship, meaning that the world is a complex of communication. Every "thing" is a value. For example, money, which materialists worship, is nothing without exchange. Money is magical in that it is transformable, transactional, transferrable. It is transcendental value. Money can take many forms and exchange for almost anything, hence its "liquidity." It is magical in its extreme ambiguity. It has identity in the sense that it can be equated with almost anything. What something is "worth" is not an inherent material dimension. Rather, worth, or value, is determined only through exchange.

Different worlds are discernable by their different modes of communicating. The magical world is essentially one of symbiotic idolatry. The mythic is essentially one of symbolic ambivalence. In the mythic world there are things money cannot buy, like emotions and values, and the sacred and/or profane. The modern is essentially signalic and values monosemantic, intolerant codes. It is quantitative. The modern world believes that the one best way, the singular perspective, can and should dominate all modes of being. The one best way means the most efficient in terms of producing/amassing material wealth/victory. In the modern world, any path is appropriate. "Good" equals the accomplishment of the goal, the want. Everything is arbitrary, and conventional/instrumental. "Truth," is permanently provisional. Everything is for sale.

To negotiate is to be "reasonable." Where one confronts that which is not negotiable or for sale, such as principle (the sacred), one is outside the domi nation of "utility" and "pragmata." Under such conditions one is confronting "dogma," strong emotional commitment. This is the realm of magic and myth, identity and emotion. Utility and pragmatism are guided by modern materialism. The "unreasonable" person of principle literally says, "no *matter* what, I will not budge." Magic and myth are alive and well in the most modern of industrial countries, although many may prefer to proclaim their extinction. Despite modern rationality, we are still "emotionally attached," albeit mostly to material things.

The modern world is obsessed with the method of fragmentation. According to modernism, the best way to solve problems is to first break them down into pieces (their "component parts," as if everything was made on an assembly line). Thus, causation is a binary phenomenon of prior cause and subsequent effect, adapted to human beings in the formulation of stimulus-response. However, as David Hume demonstrated, cause/effect (stimulus responsiveness) remains complex. Therefore, the sensorium was dissected by the German physiologist Johannes Muller in the early 1800s. He isolated the five senses from each other, thus abandoning the synthetic complexity of the synergistic "lifeworld." Neurophysiologists are just now trying to put it back together by attempting the Kantian effort of trying to understand how the whole of experience is more than the sum of sensory data, memory, association, imagination, emotion, and so on. We now admit that moods, for instance, affect how things look and sound, taste and smell, and feel, and that seeing what one smells affects the smell, and so forth (Pribram, 1971; Ackerman, 1990).

Since the modern (which is practically synonymous with "Western") perceives the entire world as problematic (what Peter Sloterdijk, 1987, has called "problemaholism"), whereby problems are identified and then solutions engineered, and since the best way to solve problems is to break them down into smaller bits, then the world must be reduced, atomized, in order to really grasp it. This is the essence of the mechanical view of the world. This gaze is anything but disinterested. It sees (presumes) problems awaiting "solution," "improvement," "development" everywhere it looks. Now some may protest this characterization of the West. But "development" and "modern" are very often used to claim that market economies, mass production, and, of course, mass consumption (without which mass production could not be sustained) are hallmarks of the "West." The Western view tends to see markets and labor rather than people. According to Peter Drucker (1942: 8), the best-selling author of management texts and advice, "Indeed, scientific management is all but a systematic philosophy of worker and work. Altogether it may well be the most powerful as well as the most lasting contribution America has made to Western thought since the Federalist Papers."

Drucker is a bit too nationalistic in his rendition of both history and "scientific management." However, the systematization of work, the tyranny of the clock manifested as efficiency and "performance" are indeed the essential contribution of Western culture to the rest of the world. This is the essence of "modernization" and "development" toward Western values and behavior patterns. "Corrections" is the watchword. Since the Renaissance, manuals have proliferated, showing the step-by-step (one) best way to do things. This is the modern way of communication. It is reductionistic (manipulative), linear (spatial), and dissociating (instrumental). In a word, it is systematic, usually in the service of power interests and values that attempt to define themselves as the "natural," "best," and "inevitable" way (goal orientation).

A good example is the modern way of production. Labor management is a modern phenomenon. The rationalization of work, meaning the dissection of it in the interest of external control, began with assembly lines and "scientific management." "Scientific management," especially time and motion studies, which are the most pure form of behaviorism, began with Hugo Munsterburg's work *Psychological and Industrial Efficiency* (German, translated in 1913). The modern world values efficiencies in commercial and military might. The fact that Ford's mile-long Willow Run factory could turn out a bomber an hour during World War II is one example of the mixture of the two worlds. During the 1950s, automobile styling became a central marketing tool. Every three years cars changed. From the mid-1950s on, automobile styling took its cues from military aircraft design.

Later, the automobile industry, led by General Motors, promoted an entire lifestyle of individualism by tearing up trolley car tracks around America at its own expense, to assure that public transportation could not compete with private commuting. Then the largest private sector institutions in the world promoted the largest publicly funded engineering project in history, the interstate highways and "defense roads," to further promote the automobile. Tenant eviction became a major source of contention as entire neighborhoods were demolished to make way for the new super highways. Suburbia is the consequence of the automobile. With nothing within walking distance, the car became a necessity (which challenges isolated elderly persons and others who cannot drive). To consume practically became patriotic in America. Luxury came to the masses. Everyone was an individualist enjoying the freedom, the power, of mobility. During the 1990s, marketing has targeted aging Baby Boomers with upscale light trucks designed to conquer the Serengeti on the way to the grocery store. As a result, gasoline consumption has soared over the 1970 and 1980 levels. The car is an expression of desire and wish fulfillment—consumer power in the form of a four-wheeled fighter jet or a suburban safari tank.

At another level, the "scientific management" literature constitutes one of the cybernetic feedback-control surveillance paths for maintaining the industrial system that was less than 100 years old in 1900. Systems theory and organization studies such as industrial psychology and sociology are products of the modern mentality. Although some, in the interest of claiming apodictic power for their theoretical statements, claim that their analyses are of a "natural," "universal" process, such social organization is evident only since 1800, and

originated in Europe and its colonies. In fact, modern colonialism was a mani-
festation of systematic resource acquisition for industrial expansion. It constitutes a unique mode of conceiving of and communicating with nature, and a
new organization of economic relations.

The first use of systematic evaluation of performance, as feeding back to a
dissociated power center where decisions originate, was in the service of marketing. Walter Dill Scott is credited with applying Munsterburg's techniques to
help in the selection of advertising and sales staff in 1901. Later, in the 1920s,
the founder of behaviorialism, John B. Watson, quit the university to do reseach
for the J. Walter Thompson advertising agency in an effort to promote the
creation of the mass consumer. Munsterburg's work, along with Alfred Binet's
(1913) efforts to measure intelligence as an instrumental asset (following Lin-
naeus and Buffon), led to the first large-scale study of "performance." It should
be no surprise that this study was in the service of militarism, specifically World
War I. During 1917 and 1918, 1,726,966 men were tested for "job knowledge,"
job specifications were written, and officer rating forms were devised. The objectification of labor commenced with the great (arguably central) consequence
being the ideological power of automated judgement. This was a hegemonic
move that Karl Marx did not foresee.

Surveying, as automated measuring, depersonalized both those doing the testing and those being tested. "Don't take it personally" meant don't revolt or get
mad at *me*, the functionary, the bureaucrat that simply (blindly) administers the
rules and tests (thank God). Those who make decisions and policy are untouch-
able, always elsewhere. This automation of judgement facilitated the abandonment of responsibility/freedom. Bureaucrats gladly abandoned consciousness
("subjectivity") in exchange for immunization from critique. Workers, educated
in causal determinism, fatalistically accepted their scores as the voice of scientific authority. They either were or were not "gifted." What constitutes a "gift"
was, of course, presupposed by the ideology of mass production/consumption.

Eugenics and genetic engineering are extensions of the desire to make the
best type of worker/soldier. Eugenics, from plastic surgery to genetic engineering, is the ultimate feedback loop, whereby the self is self-engineered. This is
anything but "objective." Rather, such metaphysics of the will, to use Arthur
Schopenhauer's phrase, is an expression of the modern hypertrophic ego that is
desirous of everything and defends its rights as such (Gebser, 1985). Since
everything in the universe is really just dead stuff (*Hyle*), that is atoms in motion,
then the will has no moral obstacle to reconstituting any gob of atoms into any
form it so chooses. All atoms are essentially identical and interchangeable. This
is the magical basis of modern technological action. Once animism and spirit
were banished, the libidinal force of technical control was freed. Chromosomes
too, are lifeless "building blocks," available for manipulation at will. The sky's
the limit. In modernity, progress became permanent because there is no goal
except the endless acquisition of power. Progress is its own legitimation.

External forces, like "nature" and "god," have been supplanted with the dichotomous interests of "society" and "self." Fads and fashion, most of which are commercial phenomena, constitute the self, and self-image (imagination). The power of making the self in its own image is modern magic or imagic. First we dream it, then we make it, including fantastic things like Saturn V rockets, mammoth skyscrapers, intercontinental tunnels, and whole new species. We "make *up*" the "empirical world" as we go, and in accordance with our power interests.

The work of Fredrick Winslow Taylor (1911, 1996) and Frank (and Lillian) Gilbreth (1911, 1973) are the culmination of the Enlightenment tradition's application of systematic thinking to labor, starting with Louis XIV's minister Colbert. It must be noted that these so-called "pioneers" (meaning Taylor and the Gilbreths) where not interested in the "science of work," as Drucker put it, but in the science of managing the work of others. The key is control—system. Harry Braverman (1974: 90) put it this way: "Taylor raised the concept of control to an entirely new plane when he asserted as an absolute necessity for adequate management the dictation to the worker of the precise manner in which work is to be performed." To be sure, craftsmen had studied work techniques long before the managers of mass production. Indeed, their techniques were taken over as they lost control of the production process. After this separation of the mind from the hand occurred, then labor engineers began to assume that workers were both stupid and lazy (even "by nature"), simply because they were not enthusiastic about being managed and confined to explicit, redundant, and simple movements (see Taylor's [1996] description of "Schmidt," whom Taylor referred to as a docile beast of burden, a "strong-backed half-wit," while neglecting the facts that Schmidt could not speak English, and that he was sophisticated enough to build his own house in his "off" hours).

Management, or "direction," or "supervision" presupposes that workers lack vision, or understanding, that they need coordination. Workers became atoms of production, mere "personnel resources." Since their labor is purchased, their bodies and minds rented, they are alienated from themselves. It should be little wonder why Taylor, who became a foreman at the Midvale Steel Company, had a "baptism by fire" when workers struck. The conclusions Taylor drew from their resistance to his systems for "maximal efficiency" are paraphrased by Braverman (1974: 100, 101):

Workers who are controlled only by general orders and discipline are not adequately controlled, because they retain their grip on the actual process of labor. So long as they control the labor process itself, they will thwart efforts to realize to the full, the potential inherent in their labor power. To change this situation, control over the labor process must pass into the hands of management, not only in a formal sense but by the control and dictation of each step of the process, including its mode of performance. In pursuit of this end, no pains are too great, no efforts excessive, because the results will repay all efforts and expenses lavished on this demanding and costly endeavor.

Hence, the rise of labor as itself, an organized force, and the huge salaries and bonuses for chief executive officers during times of massive layoffs.

The entire process of taking over the control of production presumes a spatial metaphysic that enables the separation of the hand from the mind and "systematic observation." Scientific management begins with what Michel Foucault (1979) has called the "expert gaze." Such gaze is not "objective," for it is very interested and focuses on only certain aspects of the world while ignoring others. It is highly prejudiced and goal oriented. Rather, the expert gaze is objectifying. The labor engineers embodied systematic observation in the interest of production efficiency (greed). Greed is good, or at least presumed good. Greed is a necessary condition for this sort of observation. Greed means the maximization and hording of return on investment. As labor was bought and sold in its own market, workers were thus dissociated from their own bodies. They lost control over their own movements. Anecdotal movement equals "waste."

In the "information age," the mind is for sale, and workers have lost control over their own thoughts. In this way, education is "valuable" only insofar as it can be translated into skills, including modes of thinking, that can be exchanged for money. Jurgen Habermas (1971) has noted this trend, as humanities faculty are paid the least, and education no longer serves the purpose of an informed and critical citizenry, but instead, a vocational resource for corporate culture, a resource largely funded by the workers/students themselves through tuition and taxes. In short, public funds support private interests. Hence, the ancient idea that education serves the independence of mind and the critical abilities of citizens has been co-opted so that its *telos* is now vocational (Habermas, 1973). *Techne* has supplanted *praxis* as the triumph of will manifests itself as pragmatism truncated to material production. Only matter (qua behavior) "counts." Unfocused thinking manifests the sin of waste.

With the advent of the information economy, the brain drain can take place via the Internet. Hence, software is written and data processing is increasingly done via telemanufacturing, which accesses "off-shore" minds in India (in the case of several software manufacturers including Microsoft), Korea, Ireland, Taiwan, and elsewhere (Pathak, 1996). Subcontracting and "permanent" temporary and part-time labor relationships manifest a widening of the dissociative gap between management and production. The toll is on the worker and the families that need lifeworld stability. Such flexibility in relationships serves the desires of managerial optimization, which is another way of saying loyalty gets in the way of profits.

As the production process became collectivized and externally owned (which is driving global urbanization—a phenomenon never before seen by the human species), the craftsmen, who for centuries had developed their own techniques of production, relinquished those skills. Like the fragmentation of the sensorium, the dialectic of the enlightenment promoted ignorant and docile labor (Adorno and Horkheimer, 1972). The key was the implementation of a currency economy which brought workers' interests into a relationship of dependency on capital gains. Judgements about production were dissociated from the actual process. Production was thus objectified, purged of consciousness. The mind was located in the offices, while hands remained down on the shop floor. "People" could be "retooled," or replaced as necessary. "Necessity" means those actions taken in the interest of profit for absentee decision makers, owners, and stockholders. Today the dissociation is so great that when unemployment drops Wall Street is unhappy, and when Wall Street is booming, workers are being laid off by the thousands and their wages are stagnating. Though still bound through a dependency relationship to capital currency, the bond is being stressed. There are only a few ways to get money, and without money one can barely survive in the current capital-based system.

The modern hypervaluation of private rights, such as property, has left the public sector floundering. Because the public sector is public, which means that deliberations take the form of open debates, the inevitable value judgements politicians express are obvious and denigrated. The public sector comes to be seen as incompetent and prejudiced. Ironically, and despite the fact that deliberation in the private sector is hidden and surveillance of individuals is much greater in the private sector, "individualists" prefer to turn power over to deregulated (unchecked) private power. Private sector power poses a greater threat to privacy than the democratic public sector. Private power is much more intrusive into the lives of workers and consumers, whether it be by supervision of work or control of credit. The greatest data bases of personal information are privately owned, and as proprietary information, personal information is bought and sold without any criteria except private gain (profit).

Since vision and deliberative debate have been relegated to the status of subjective nonsense and rhetorical hucksterism, power is draining away from those institutions that redistribute wealth in the interest of community. Private sector has emerged as being "competent" and "objective." The "political" world of subjective interests and value debates has been identified with the public "sector." Modern fragmentation has legitimized the separation of private wealth from community responsibility. Thus, just as urbanization around the globe is exploding, private capital is no longer supporting infrastructures, so that cities are becoming "walking wounded."

Thus, labor-power was, and is, controlled. Humans came to be treated as objects, as machines. The gaze, or mode of communication, is one of engineering. Input/output, stimulus/response was, and remains, the credo of this materialistic metaphysic. Precision, as discussed in Chapter 3, equals subdivision. The more precise, the more microscopic, or perspectival the gaze, the more minute the control. The sharper the focus, the narrower the beam. In this example, precision reaches right down to the smallest movement of the body, or the slightest glance of the eye (as in retinal tracking in testing advertising), or the smallest lapse in concentration. Suspicions and guesses have been replaced by endless examination and measurement. We are constantly compared to each other and to the "mean person." Why? For control. Much uncritical social science is really market research. That is where the grant money is.

The modern world is synchronized by clocks (including "alarming" ones and redundant ones like "time-clocks") and life/career trajectories. Children go to summer computer and math camps where they learn to stay one jump ahead of their peers in the struggle to be most valuable to employers. Entire national populations are pitted against each other by the rules of the market system. Nations, regions, and municipalities bid against each other to attract jobs, undercutting the tax base necessary for the maintenance of community infrastructure, including environmental protection and education.

The greater efficiencies that industrialization promised were originally supposed to enable people to produce more, faster, thus leading to a society of leisure. This has not been the case. Instead, people are in perpetual training and are working more hours today than they were thirty years ago, indeed more than ever (Rifkin, 1987). Only during a short (by historical standards) period from about 1850 to 1930, in industrial America and Europe, did people work longer hours than today. In so-called "less developed" cultures, people work far fewer hours per day. The difference is mass consumption and the material metaphysic gone "virulent" (see Immanuel Levinas's 1987 analysis of the *commercium*, and Karl-Heinz Volkmann-Schluck, as recounted by his student Algis Mickunas 1978). The increase in efficiencies has led to huge (unprecedented) concentrations of wealth and power, not the utopian leisure society of plenty, foretold by futurists in previous decades.

Many, including Braverman (1974) have described the neurotic behavior of the father of modern scientific management, F. W. Taylor. Taylor used to sleep sitting up. He was absolutely obsessed with timing everything. Today's industrial society, with its frenetic pace, endless competitiveness, and abbreviated forms of interaction/communication (what Gebser [1985] has called "temporal anxiety") may be seen as increasingly neurotic. Actually, being neurotic has become normative. The extended family has fragmented down to the "nuclear" family, which is now increasingly split into "subatomic" families. Both "parents" work, less out of a dedication to feminist ideology than to pay the bills. Children sit for hours (especially in the "Little [and big] Dragon" economies of East Asia like Korea, Taiwan, and Japan) being drilled for entrance into the labor market. Tracking in educational institutions does not serve the creation of reflective citizens, but instead, high "quality" (meaning valuable) labor. Millions of children are "medicated" with methylphenidate ("Retalin") for the "diseases" of "hypertension" and "hyperactivity," because they cannot sit for hours in neat rows.

During the mid-1900s, the engineering couple of Frank and Lillian Gilbreth used to attach small light bulbs to workers' hands in order to film the pattern of the motion they made while doing a task. Another technique they invented was to construct a screen or backdrop behind a worker. The screen was usually black with a white grid drawn on it so that they could film and measure the worker's bodily movements. They would break down each motion in an effort to minimize the worker's movements. All this was done in the interest not of the worker, but of those who purchased the labor-power. Unitization, or piece-rate pay was instituted. Bonus pay amounted to paying a little extra for much more effort. Everything was unitized as "hourly" wage, piece counting, functions, operations, and motion engineering.

Since the 1970s, managers have advanced to the idea of "teams." What this means is that workers accustomed to specialization must now master more than one functional operation. Thus, modern companies are promoting more expertise and redundancy. When people in a team are able to "rotate," then dependency on one expert is eliminated. If a person leaves or is fired, others can immediately fill his or her position. Everyone has to know everything with the consequence that more and more workers are suffering "burn-out," and perpetual fatigue. They still do not control the production process. The team concept was imposed from above.

The two major scales that form the grid for this world is the clock face and the monetary unit. It behooves the profiteer to increase production, to move product as fast as possible because profit is actualized with each unit sold. Economies of scale come into play. The Gilbreths applied their techniques to their own family by putting bells on their children's toes. They had twelve children, and one of them, Frank B. Gilbreth, Jr., later wrote a book about his experience growing up in a tightly managed environment, entitled *Cheaper by the Dozen* (1949).

Today, surveillance, the systematic gaze, has become much more sophisticated so that data entry personnel are monitored by the machines they work on. Surveillance has become a permanent fixture of work, not just a special occasion as in the famed Hawthorne General Electric studies. Performance evaluations are done regularly in more and more jobs and dossiers are compiled. Feedback is also manifested as computer programs, for example, automatically count the number of keystrokes a typist makes per minute. Networked computer terminals even flash messages to workers that they are going slower than their colleagues. The word "monitor" seems more appropriate than ever. Closed circuit (systems) video cameras are increasingly being used to monitor the performance/behavior of workers and children. For instance, in Australia in 1995, the postal system began to install tracks around the ceilings of offices, along which video cameras run so that workers cannot hide behind shelves. The cameras are operated by remote control. They can track at variable speeds, zoom, and back up for a second look.

Our lives are increasingly "on disk" and instantaneously retrievable. Precision in evaluation is becoming more and more minute as it is undertaken more and more often. As noted, sometimes the evaluation is continuous.

The civilizational expression of the grid expresses an attitude, and a mode of interacting with the world and other people. It is essentially modern, first appearing in the cartography of Ptolemy and popularized by René Descartes. Coordination and fragmenting (or slicing) unitization are the fundamental modus of the modern lifeworld. Operant control is the goal. The modern world manifests what Arthur Schopenhauer called the metaphysics of the will. Even academic communication requires "referees."

We are on the grid. But the grid is not all bad, and it must be presupposed in order to be free, for freedom is always freedom from something. There are aspects of the grid and ordination that one can appreciate.

IDENTITY VERSUS IDENTICAL: HERACLITUS VERSUS PLATO

This book is an effort to integrally appreciate the binary opposition of modern/ postmodern hostilities. Like a conventional variable, the logic of ratio is presumed by binary opposition such that one is living on a line between two extremes and as one moves toward one extreme, one *must* move away from the other end with equal and opposite measure. According to modern linear-rational thinking, one must either be modern or postmodern, just as it is presupposed that one must be either individualistic or collectivistic.

In his seminal work *The Ever-Present Origin* (1985), Jean Gebser explains how modernity is characterized by extremism. On the one hand, modernity is recognizable by the phenomenon of mass conformity expressed in various ways such as the modern consumer society, mass reproduction, and systems of techno-totalitarianism such as Nazism and Communism, both of which promised to generate the "new man" and a single "rational order." On the other hand, modernism is also marked by ego-hypertrophy and extreme individualism proclaiming inalienable rights and the highest ideal being self-actualization.

This Aristotelian intolerance and mutual exclusion (dialectical systematics) need not be presumed, especially since the world does not present itself in such a simple way. We may hop off the definitive lines others draw in the sand, or appreciate both ends at once, or recognize more than just one alternative and become aware of a spherical field of multiple possibilities simultaneously.

Freedom from being identified as merely an operator is promoted in this book. Modernity is expressed by both modernism and so-called postmodernism. While each dollar bill is identical, having absolute parity in exchange, it would seem that, due to the uninformative nature of redundancy, a person would want only one. But of course, the world is consumed with amassing as much money as possible. Mass is articulated by quantity. It is bonded with the hypertrophic identity of absolute uniqueness. For moderns "the sameness" of coherence and consistency and conformity is valued. For "postmodern" moderns, nothing is the same, the world is decoherent, discontinuous, uncertain, inconsistent. For both extremes, life itself is at stake. Life is only worth living if it is systematic and predictable, or only if spontaneity and adventurous difference exists. One worships domesticity to the point of nihilistic redundancy, the other worships wilderness to the point of nihilistic isolation. Both are thoroughly perspectival.

This book suggests an aperspectival integration and appreciation of this deeper difference.

The differences between structural-functional systematization and "post"-modernism, and integral (a)waring (or integrum) is the topic of this book. Both "modernity" *and "postmodernity"* exist as modern schools articulated by oppositional and mutually excluding philosophemes. They oppose each other. They are arrayed against each other in a logical and systematic fashion, each presenting an epistemological perspective. This book suggests an integral (not assimilationist) appreciation of both as they manifest a shared system of communication that enables each perspective to combat the other, as well as a free systatic awareness that plays off the discursive system, or diadic exchange they operate. Instead of parry and thrust, parry and thrust, we might wander off the grid.

Ferdinand de Saussure led the charge for control in the form of lingualism, that is, linguistic reductionism or the idea that language is the privileged world-system. However, Saussure's neo-Hegelian penchant for synchronic structure did not even address historical time as well as Hegel (or Hegel's critic Soren Kierkegaard) had done some half a century earlier. Edmund Husserl too, initially had a dream of transcending time, but after his long exchange with Wilhelm Dilthey, and his investigation into internal time-consciousness, Husserl modified his phenomenology, setting the scene for Martin Heidegger's radical relativism (his temporalization of time). Friedrich Nietzsche and Henri Bergson also broached the topic of change in such a way that no ground of final criteria could be established. Ludwig Wittgenstein, as well as Bertrand Russell, Alfred North Whitehead, and of course Albert Einstein, also came to grapple with the problem of fluxing rules, conventionalism, and arbitrariness. The mathematical sciences handle flux epistemologically. They restrict themselves to permanent provisionalism and probability. They are always careful to never say always.

The notion of a "standard" language game, like "standard" English, came to symbolize a cultural conservatism that is ultimately ethnocentric, if not fascistic. In the modern world, instrumentality is the mode of awaring. Even language became a tool of will. Rudolf Carnap (1963: 938) expresses the modern attitude well: "In my view, a language, whether artificial or natural, is an instrument that may be replaced or modified according to our needs, like any other instrument." If we think in language then we can change our minds by changing the very instrument which formulates the mind. This leads to instrumental mind control. Everything, including the mind, becomes a mere instrument. But in the service of what? Instrumentalism becomes self-legitimating. Everything, including entire ecosystems and other humans, is reduced to use-value, means to goals that cannot be debated. Soul and/or spirit no longer exist. Values are denied existence so critique of instrumental values is marked "off-limits." If you don't play by our (language) rules you can't play at all. We are our structural functions. What are you? is answered with an occupation. If that is lost, then all is lost. This is the tautological force of totalitarian metaphysics; and therein lies the power of enforcing what are arbitrary yet conventionalized (normalized) scales, taxonomies, definitions, terminologies, and relationships. When modern mass systems stumble, the people seek sanctuary in "previous" identities like nationalism and racism. They seek meaning at all cost.

Metaphysics is politics. The entire world is defined as "material." If a power can convince its enemy that his entire cosmology and sense of reality is false, everything else collapses. The gods die (are totally redefined as "nonsensical superstition"); the place of the ancestors, the not-yet born, and the self, all disorient and dissolve. The night of nihilism descends and souls find themselves at the bottom of whisky bottles, drinking Lysol, or worse. This is what has happened to many indigenous peoples around the world. They have been "proven wrong" with the force of a sledgehammer. They have been proven false at the point of a sword, gun, informed argument, or accountant's pencil. Once convention becomes institutionalized, the inertia of social sanction kicks in. A new order becomes normative, factual, moral, exclusive (Real). Everything else is mere entertainment. The only reason to restrain ourselves is for our own self-interest and for the sake of entertainment. Save the whales because they are fun to look at. We preserve some "nature," as in mason jars, in parks where it can be properly managed for our tourist gaze. We should be prudent because such-and-such is a nonrenewable resource.

A struggle for apodictic knowledge against flux, including progress and revision, forms the essential point of combat. Pragmatism has been evoked to legitimize conformism and resistance to multiversality. Practicality, in the form of efficient communication in the interest of production, has found a home in the cultural debates around the United States and the world. Tolerance of difference is conditional. So long as production is not hampered by multiculturalism or multilingualism, such variations are tolerated. But, the marginal are advised that if they want to "get along," or "get ahead" within the system, they must adapt or conform. The consequence has been endless ethnic conflict.

The more fundamental problem with Saussurian and Heideggerian lingualism is that language changes too. In fact, conservatives often complain that Heidegger himself, and his followers, like Jacques Derrida, commit the sin of making up words and new ideas as they go. Their sin is to be original at the ontic level. But that is what all taxonomists and producers of culture, including systems of knowledge, do. Flux is confounding; it demands growth to "keep current" within the river of new ideas and styles. Such complication is why Saussure abandoned diachronic philology, for synchronic snapshots of "reality." Synchronicity, it is presumed, leads to security. But it also leads to redundancy (meaninglessness). The entire Western and Westernizing world is defined by its "entrainment" or mass conformity to a single clock face. The modern city is possible only because of the first mass medium, clock time. Today we wear them on our wrists and necks and synchronize every life function. Some even schedule sex and make "dates." Saussure epitomizes in the academy what Gebser calls "temporal anxiety."

Modernism consists of a flight from lackadaisical flux into ordination. Synchronic systems analyses, though purely artificial, promote control and are therefore valuable to instituting a single version of reality. Systems theory does not describe anything natural but is instead a purely modern mode of ordination, constructivism without the admission of pro-visionalism, because that would weaken systemic power. Never mind that those snapshots are of discrete and contingent states. The system deploys feedback self-surveillance to maintain order. It appeals to external and eternal forces like "natural law" to legitimize its dominion. Modern urban culture is a system. Social science is looking into a mirror.

Meanwhile, the truth of flux and variance is ignored (self-imposed ignorance) because it is inconvenient for social engineering. And yet ironically, engineering, that most positive and progressivistic of projects, seeks to change things, and that means that engineering must presuppose time. But this sort of "planned" change for a preestablished vision of what is "better," or what "ought to be," tries to deny its highly valued sense of the "right." What is right is inevitable, so time (and discussion) is short-circuited. One cannot break the eternal laws of nature. Ultimately, mechanistically, everything is the effect of previous causes all the way back to the Big Bang. But then why do things constantly change? Why is not life satisfied with forms such as algae, which has proven to be extremely "successful," "survivable"? Why continually diversify into what are often more complex failures? If survivability is the ultimate and undeniable law, then why evolution? The oceans are full of plankton and have been for a very, very long time. Why fix it if it ain't broke? Is success the "goal" or is it failure that is the goal?

While others have discussed "transformational rules" and deeper-than-deep structures and other spatializing metaphors, time has been labeled the great bugaboo that thwarts apodictic certainty (for "all time"). The right way is based on "natural," meaning eternal, laws beyond debate. Otherwise, the mantra of value-freedom and the nonexistence of values also preempts the possibility to debate the merits of a goal. Perhaps goals too are arbitrary and contingent. Teleology is in flux.

Modernism and so-called "post"-modernism exist as opposing aspects of modern contentious thinking. They express contempt for each other and few read both "sides."[1] Integrality suggests that despite (logical) incompatibility, both modern and postmodern literatures are interesting and valuable. They depend on each other for meaning/difference. They are identifiable as such only through comparative differentiation. Modernity is marked by a fear or insecurity articulated as an obsession with formalization, and synchronic fixation. Modern (Platonic) and so-called "postmodern" (Heraclitian) theory are stuck in formal positions combating each other. They trace each other's boundary conditions, mutually constituting the formal differences between their axiomatic claims about signification, temporality, referentiality, rationality, and knowledge.

This book presents another attitude or "way." Synairesis, which is neither modern nor "postmodern" (in the way Levinas, and later Jean-Francois Lyotard conceived of it), is discussed at length in chapters 4 and 5. It is a term invented by Gebser, who was a teacher of comparative civilizations and considered to be the greatest German-language cross-culturalist (phenomenologist) to yet write. He did the great bulk of his writing in German while he lived in Switzerland, India, France, and Spain. He wrote in several languages and styles from the late 1930s until the late 1960s. Synairesis is an (a)waring of the appreciable contributions modern perspectivism and radical pluralism (toward the *aporia* of absolute relativity) have made to our current world. Synairesis involves the realization that it is futile to attempt to "arrest" or ignore change in the interest of knowledge. Synairesis is an (a)waring of morphological fluxing, not as a criminal that threatens the very possibility of law and rule, but as that which enables their conception and duration.

As Nietzsche observed, the modern system of knowledge has killed the gods. We have demythologized ourselves. Mythic symbolism is far too ambiguous and inefficient for modern production. Materialism has become virulent. The world has become obsessed with epistemology (media and methods) and metaphysics (physicalism). We worship authors who announce the end of man, the end of history, the end of philosophy, the end of truth, the subject, context, meaning, sense, interpretation, the end of everything that is alive or changing. Value does not exist, yet our economies are obsessed with its convertability, transformativity, and growth. The medium, whether real estate, paper bills, gold, or electronic pulses is less the issue than "currency" of "exchange." "Nothing" is exchanged. "Value" is the in-between of exchange.

We despise metaphor because of its inefficient, complex ambiguity, and strive to replace it with one-to-one signalic codes, dead machine language. The militaristic industrial value of efficiency has produced systems of codes that are intolerant. Even though you misspeak, or have limited capacity to navigate the system due to education or illness or injury, as I watch you fail to make the words, I "know what you mean." But a computer cannot make such semantic leaps and relate a message to its context. The context, how a word is (mis)used, is how we acquire that most human of capacities, language. That is why it is much faster to learn a language within its own world than in a dissociated classroom isolated from its world.

Strangely, the modern world strives to eliminate context, to be, as Edward T. Hall (1976) has coined the phrase under different conditions, absolutely "low [in fact zero] context" in its mode of communication. The computer knows no ambiguity. The modern dream for a nonfigural language was best expressed by Russell and Whitehead's great effort, *Principia Mathematica* (1967). Under such conditions, either I hit the right key or I don't. Either I included the comma in the program or I did not. There is absolutely no intellect, no interpretation, no tolerance. Ignorance of the law is no excuse. One's "p's" and "q's" must be in order. The sergeant yells "fire," and that cannot mean go get the hose. Simplification serves one master, production. Performance, and therefore simplification, are hypervaluated. Plato disliked poets and valorized military leaders because he dreamed of a perfect system of frictionless functioning. Once perfection, like absolute success, is achieved, nothing changes. The assumption is that the best communication is that without any reflection, ambiguity, or "misunderstanding." Time is of the essence.

Utopia is another word for death. *Ou topos* means "no where." The stagnation of Imperial China is a good example. Though they invented the compass, paper, gunpowder, and many other things, they saw little use for them. It is impossible to improve on perfection. The universe was already filled with "Shen" (god or spirit). If one thing changed, all had to change. When clocks were introduced to China by European missionaries, they were displayed as nothing more than toys, clever gadgets. The idea that one might use them to revolutionize the world was not thinkable. There was no room for change. Atomistic Europeans took these same inventions and used them to radically change the entire world. Every dictator has a utopian vision, knows The Truth.

So-called "primitive" tools and crafts have been replaced by highly complicated machines that can do only one thing but very fast, with high redundancy (consistency), and automatically (without thinking). Building on the work of Patrick Geddes (1915), Lewis Mumford (1963) noted that the "eotechnical era" was a time of desire for more power, a time of preparation for technique. Unlike a machine, a tool, like a knife, can be used to do many different things such as carve, kill, play games, skin, cut, pry, and so on. It is eotechnology. It is flexible and can embody imagination and creative variety. But a locomotive or other self-animating machine like a clock is very narrow in its interpretation/function. Its horizon of potential is programmed into its very structure.

Modes of behavior correspond to this shift in the world. The craftsman who made violins had to know the appropriate type of tree, its age and grain, and so on. He had to know when to harvest it. He had to know the various ways to cut and cure the wood and the tools to shape it as well as the complex construction techniques necessary for producing the best timbre and tone. By contrast, the assembly-line worker needs to know little, but must be fast. Reflection is taken out of her hands. She does not design the product nor her role in its construction. She is not encouraged to think, to interpret, to "second-guess," because such intellectual activity only slows the production process, the accumulation of wealth which is realized with each unit moved. Anti-intellectualism is virulent. Only pragmatic (often meaning empirical/economic) application has value. Praise the Lord and pass the ammunition. There is only one right way. The modern military-industrial world strives for simplicity and monosemantics, in a word, regimentation.

According to modern perspectivism, there can be only one "best" way. But according to systatic (a)waring, each system has "good" and "bad" aspects. More than one can be best, depending on the criteria used for judgement. So, for instance, the modern Western world stresses individualism. Individualism is an essential part of democracy. But, individualism can also lead to alienation and loneliness. The modern suburb is neither urban nor village. It exists because it manifests independence expressed as spatial isolation and privatization. Suburban living tends to be very isolationist. One cannot walk to any communal activities. The automobile is the only and private link to the outside world. Entire streets are inhabited by people who rarely meet and talk with each other, in part due to the modern scheduling of activities. But it does afford privacy.

Village life, on the other hand, is very community oriented. People live and work together. Extended families remain viable. One can step out of one's abode into the immediate womb of the group. People are available most of the time. But, privacy is very limited. Everyone knows everyone else so that it is hard to be an individual ego. One cannot be a prophet in one's own village because they know everything about you. But in the suburbs every man and woman can be a king and queen. Delusion reigns supreme. Consumption is the measure of the person. The suburban takes pride in what he or she consumes, and less in what he or she produces. Money and jobs are mere functional equivalents. But in the village, one may be the bow maker or utensil maker. One's name may actually signify one's productive skill and duty. Everything has an identity. The suburbs are clean and neat, spacious and private. But convenience has a high price in terms of exploitation of the environment. The village is dirty and crowded, busy and closed. If we abandon the variable analytics of Aristotle, that is intolerant, then an apparently contradictory truth can emerge, which is that each system is "best" and "worst."

In the modern world, culture and nature have been separated into two separate realms. Likewise, languages have been bifurcated into "natural" and "artificial." Artificial languages are conceived with a purpose in mind. They are codes. Even wild "natural" languages are being streamlined in the interest of some transcending will and its ulterior goals. A famous example is Mao Tse-tung's decree to simplify Chinese script in order to enable a technological "leap forward." The 3,000-year-old script contained too many characters, and too many characters consisted of too many brush strokes. The language, it was judged, was too complicated and took too long to master. It came to be seen as an obstacle to rapid modernization. What of all the books written in the 3,000-year-old script? Irrelevant. Burn them. Culture itself is revolutionized. Dictators and law and order types tend to do this. Parsimony is highly valued, even in the production of knowledge and culture, and for the modern from Aristotle on, knowledge is power. Unitization enables manipulation. There are no more warriors, only general issue soldiers that are made to be interchangeable.

The modern world is a world of codes, laws, preestablished and systematic neural pathways. The modern seeks, in the interest of power and efficiency, to replace language with unambiguous codes. Systems of codes include self-monitoring feedback control to safeguard against change or figurality. The reckoning of probabilities, as by actuarials, is used to spread, avoid, and limit risk—to defeat probability. Nothing is left to chance. We are hardwired, programmed.

And yet, though we despise figural language/world, we cannot escape ambiguity. Our attempt to escape figurality tells us much about ourselves, our goals, and values. Richard Rorty (1979) claims that mimetic projects like science and philosophy are doomed to never be accurate mirrors of nature. Reflection is impossible. How does he know that they are inaccurate without himself having immaculate access to the Real by which to draw a comparison? Instead, nothing is more impenetrable than a mirror. The more we describe the truth, philosophically, scientifically, poetically, historically, mythologically, the more we are building "mirrors" of ourselves. As we investigate these literatures, as we peer into these mirrors, the how and what they say tell us more about ourselves than anything else. We see in them the interests, will, and capacities of the authors, of the human species. Only humans, so far as is known, create such mirrors. Rorty is wrong. The mirrors are neither accurate nor inaccurate. They cannot lie. He is correct that they do not reflect, but they are articulations and manifestations of us. What Peter says about Paul may or may not be an accurate description, but says very much about Peter. His interests, choices, capacities, will, are naked in the expression. Even his skill at deception is laid bare.

METAPHYSICS, ANYONE?

This is the postheroic age. "Today belongs to the mob," to "despotic" logic and the Alexandrian theoretical man that combats Dionysian art and wisdom and seeks to dissolve spontaneity and value. Dumb repetition (automation) is the most highly prized mode of behavior. Being consistent and programmatic (preprogrammed) is valued. Acting "like clockwork" is rewarded. Ambiguity and originality are suspect, and must be contested, supervised. The world is subsumed under "oversight."

What are the great issues of our day? Don't be disappointed. They are not of the latest fashion or fad. They've been around for some time, perhaps because they do not lend themselves to systematic absolution like mathematical puzzles, which is why we have child prodigies in systematic grammars like math and music but not in philosophy. A few of the perennial issues are: Freedom versus responsibility, determinism versus indeterminism, the status of axiomatics such as "human nature," probability versus causality, certainty versus interpretation, system versus chaos, isomorphism and the status of referentiality, the role of imagination in knowledge (imagic). What metacriteria are presupposed in setting the criteria for validity, reliability, and accuracy? Truth versus interpretation: What constitutes success in our searches and re-searches? Is it technological manipulation? What constitutes "normal," and "well-adjusted," and so forth?

Another issue that may be used as an example is the brain/mind or consciousness dichotomy. Physicists, neurophysiologists, philosophers, psychologists, theologians, have symposium after symposium about this issue. Phenomenologists like Gebser rarely, if ever, attend. This may seem strange since phenomenology, which is neither a philosophy nor a science (and certainly not a blind dogma), is comprised of volumes on consciousness. But because consciousness is always consciousness of something, their works tend to be about "something," rather than "pure" (empty) consciousness. Because phenomenologists refuse to do metaphysics, they are not interested in "locating where" consciousness is. Phenomenology is interested in direct experience, because that is "where" we live, and "direct" is the only kind known. Even awareness of "subconscious" feelings, hallucinations, illusions, falsities, fantasies, and so on, are directly given as such; as hallucinatory, doubtful, unclear, erroneous, fantastic.

Phenomenologists neither deny nor affirm the existence of the brain or pure empty consciousness (although such a "thing" would seem to be utterly unknowable). They are not existentialists, although some existentialists have borrowed aspects of the phenomenological method. Nor do phenomenologists quibble with the demonstrable correlation of chemical changes to perceptual ones, a correlation evident at least since the discovery of alcohol. Nor has it ever claimed that one should not study such biomechanical phenomena. But, phenomenologists defend the right to describe direct experience without resorting to reductionism (reducing something out-of-existence, to something completely different). They defend the right to work without any metaphysical imposition, which is often expressed by phrasing like "seeing is *really* neurological activity."

Phenomenologists do not seek a hypothetical reality "behind" perception. Arguments about various levels of reality and their prioritization, causal or otherwise, are bracketed by phenomenologists. Edmund Husserl, a mathematician and founder of phenomenology, refused to do metaphysics/existentialism. Does a thing like the geometric right triangle exist? What is the nature of its existence? Such questions are irrelevant to phenomenology. Phenomenologists are not interested in manipulating perceptions (promoting "correct perception"), which is the motive for doing mechanical reductionism. While one may point at a waveform on an electroencephalogram or a bit of tissue and announce that here (spatially) is love or hate or memory or the power of speech, I experience none of these phenomena. Instead I see a waveform and a bit of tissue, and I contemplate such interpretations of them.

A blind person can study the mechanics of seeing. She may even get a perfect score on an examination about the mechanics of sight. She may be able to explain the physical process without error and to the satisfaction of current knowledge. But she does not understand what it is to see. She may be able to give a perfect explanation of color as electromagnetic frequencies and absorption, but she doesn't understand color. Understanding and explanation are different. Explanation requires articulation. Understanding does not. And I believe that if I could offer either a textbook explanation of seeing or sight itself to her, she would choose seeing. The difference is profound. Arguments about the brain/mind dichotomy are, from the point of view of phenomenology, silly. If I have a stroke which impairs my thinking, I may very well wish the help of a mechanic. Why? Because it means something, it's "important" to me. Such phenomenologically based problems are the very motive for biomechanical research, not the other way around. If I have a motorcycle accident which results in a brain embolism and concordant blindness the success of the surgery is not measured by the physical removal of the blood clot, but whether or not my sight has been restored. It is unlikely that a surgeon would argue that the surgery was a success just because she removed the blood clot, even though the phenomenology has not changed. The blood clot is gone but I am still blind.

With the exception of nonmedical (nonapplied) research, brain mechanics is of interest only insofar as it has phenomenological (symptomatic) implications. With the newer scanning technologies, people have been accidentally discovered who, from birth, have very little (in terms of physical mass) functional brain tissue. Such cases were not discovered previously because there was no reason to investigate; there were no symptoms, no "reasons" or effects, to motivate the search for causes. They have "normal" lives. Reason begins with axioms, beliefs, or faith. Is there a one-to-one parity between cause and effect? Can one cause have many effects? Can many causes have many effects? Can many causes have but one effect? It seems so.

The brain has no feeling. Sometimes during brain surgery the patient is "awake," so that she can answer the doctor's queries, thereby directing the surgeon's probing. The surgeon is in effect doing phenomenology because that is the goal. When the doctor probes and asks "What is happening now," the answer may be, "I smell the bread my late mother used to bake when I was a child," or "my toes are tingling."

Why do such surgery? Precisely to alter the experience, to "correct" it, or to save a life. The brain and experience are correlated but there is no need to equate them metaphysically. In fact, the surgeon must ask the questions or otherwise be "shooting in the dark." No matter how precise and detailed description of brain activity may become, it will never be the same as direct experience. We may watch brain activity "live" on video screens and map it mathematically and generate holographic images of it, but none of these gets any "closer" to consciousness. The map is ontologically different from the grass, bugs, trees, and rivers it models. The experience of the physical world is not a physical thing, it is experience of. . . . The nexus of interest, or the focus of the problem that motivates research and mapping, is precisely the phenomenological quality of life. This, along with sheer curiosity about the organ itself, is what motivates the study of the biomechanics of the brain. If we had no thoughts, the brain would be of little more interest to us than the appendix. It is important because of its correlation with thought and awareness/consciousness.

INESCAPABLE INTERPRETATION

The preeminent Princeton anthropologist Clifford Geertz (1973) asks, what is the difference between a wink and a blink? Levinas (1987) says, we know the difference through recognition. I recognize myself in the Other. I do not mistake agony or bliss on the countenance of the Other. Even if I don't "know the language,'' I still recognize pain in the scream of the Other, even a rabbit or dog. We are the same but different. I have blinked and I have winked and I know the difference. Flirting and harassing too are very different. How do we know? Because we have been the target of both. We inhabit a common world and conversation.

Different cultures present different rationalities in the sense that they posit different presumptions, different axioms about life and death, time and space, good and evil. But these presumptions change according to will and context. In one case I may be playing, in another I may be teasing. We can recognize and consider these differences because we share the conversational field. What may seem reasonable given one set of axioms may seem immoral or ridiculous given a different set of axioms. The ''reasonableness'' of behavior can only be determined if one knows the presuppositions the person harbors. But even then, the mode of ''reasoning'' ''from premises'' may not be linear. There may be no linear ''beginning'' or teleological ''ending.'' I may start out playing but end up teasing. And the difference may be indeterminate or inconsistent. I may be doing both at once. The Other may be my companion and/or victim. I may be teasing even though I meant to play.

When one is confronted with conflicting beliefs, norms, mores, behaviors, then judgement becomes foregrounded. If there must be a strict hierarchy, then one must ask what metacriteria should be used to determine which morality is best, which behavior most appropriate, which culture most ''natural,'' ''holy,'' or ''reasonable.'' But then, this begs the question of how one chooses the metacriteria, and the meta-metacriteria, *ad infinitum*. Even history fails as the ground of judgement because history is written always ''after the fact,'' so that the selection of which facts are ''important'' depends on what ''counts'' as acceptable ''reasons,'' ''excuses,'' or criteria. Also, the choice, or privileging of one (''version'' of) history over another indicates current interests as much as past realities.

Who's to say abortion is wrong in China? What ground, or metacriteria for granting criterial authority is to be privileged? Does it simply come down to might makes right? The inertia of custom and tradition rules? The victors write history? Money talks? Who writes the history of morality and the morality of history? When asked his reaction about his divorce and first family, Congressman Newt Gingrich said that it was all right because he is responsible and able to pay for the lifestyle of his two daughters. So divorce is not okay for poor people, but it is for well-to-do people? Are family values really reducible to economics? Does hypocrisy matter? When once confronted by a student about the obvious dissimilarity between his writings and his behavior, the great moral philosopher Max Scheler responded that a road sign that indicates the direction or distance to a city need not go there to be correct.

There are social scientists who claim to be disinterested in what constitutes human nature and other axiomatic premises. However, what is revealed in their modes of investigation are their interests and capacities. They uncritically presume human qualities such as responsive action, praxis, and judgement. When they claim to be antiphilosophical, they are proclaiming a philosophical position variously called "pragmatism," "utilitarianism," or sometimes "hedonism." In the case of Talcott Parsons, he blamed his "troubles" in handling philosophical issues when discussing them with Alfred Schutz on "the fact that by cultural heritage I am a Calvinist" (Parsons, in a letter to Voegelin, August 18, 1941, quoted in Rehorick and Buxton, 1986: 13).

When social scientists claim to be antimetaphyiscal, this often means that they espouse an absurd school of thought called empiricism, which is a metaphysical philosophy that denies its own existence. They act as though they know the essential difference between their subject matter and other regional ontologies. A social or humanistic scientist seems to know that she is not a physical, or general life scientist like a zoologist. Social scientists presuppose what is essentially different between a human and a rock or chimpanzee. But the qualitative differences that mark their regions of investigation remain unspecified. So they are not even sure what it means to be a human or social scientist, because they cannot define "human," or "society" or "culture."

Therefore, they become entangled in variety and cannot, phenomenologically speaking, discern essential qualities that allow them to identify their subject matter of investigation, and methods most appropriate to it. George Homans (1984) recounts, for instance, how Parsons regularly misused terms like "theory" and "deduction." Consequently, the social sciences follow the physical sciences, borrowing their theories and methods, concepts that have been developed to fit completely different categories of phenomena. The consequence is that social scientists rarely solve social problems. Wars and poverty continue, violence and injustice remain. The dream of the Saint Simonians, to engineer Utopia, to help alleviate suffering, remains unfulfilled. The physical sciences and engineering isolate problems and solve them. They build skyscrapers and suspension bridges that do not fall down. They do what the will calls for. We want something completely new and never before seen, a 100-story skyscraper. Engineers go back to their drawing boards and make it so. The same is the case for men on the moon and dammed rivers. But social problems seem intractable.

Is this because social scientists are stupid or lazy, or do not have the power Auguste Comte called for when he envisioned a new "priesthood" of positivists? Perhaps an objective observation may help. Reflecting on the wholesale borrowing and importation of the Newtonian model of behavior into the service of explaining human motion in space, Stephen Hawking has noted that "We cannot even solve exactly for the motion of three bodies in Newton's theory of gravity, and the difficulty increases with the number of bodies and the complexity of the theory . . . we have, as yet, had little success in predicting human behavior from mathematical equations!" (Hawking, 1988: 168). Social science lacks a set of equations like Maxwell's mathematical explanation of electromagnetism or Planck's equations for quantum states. At best we apply basic statistics in a generalized fashion to data of dubious quality, such as surveys of undergraduate college students. We proclaim human constants, "cultural universals" which Geertz (1973: 38) calls the *consensus gentium* (a consensus of all mankind) of "banal generalities," and A. L. Kroeber (1953: 516) has called "fake universals" like "religion," "property," "shelter," "marriage," or "trade."

The constants that social sciences have "uncovered," seem self-evident. Thus, Geertz and others claim that it is the variety of human expression that is interesting. But yet we dream of "invariant points of reference" (Talcott Parsons, quoted by Geertz, 1973: 41). And despite the variety, we believe that we are talking about essentially "human" behavior. But some, like Foucault, suggest that the category "human" is of no use. It is either too broad or too narrow to mean much. Hence, social science is adrift. It seeks "stratigraphic" grounding elsewhere in biology, brain chemistry, or genetics. It struggles to identify sequential priority. For instance, did the marvelously versatile human hand evolve because it needed to make tools and manipulate the environment, or has the environment become a resource base because the hand can manipulate it. Integrally speaking, prioritization reveals more about the researcher than the hand. For phenomenologists it is the imagination that makes all the difference between humans and everything else. "Reading" ink on paper, the stars, or the hand positions of the Buddha depends on imagination. The "invariant points of reference" vary.

DECOHERENCE

While conservatives insist that the world is already known to be logical, coherent, continuous, predictable, once again nothing less than physics challenges these assumptions. In the May 1996 issue of *Science*, C. Monroe et al. published the results of a fascinatingly creative experiment which generated, for the first time, a "Schrodinger cat-like" state of matter. According to Schrodinger's uncertainty principle, one should be able to create conditions that are utterly unpredictable. For example, one could put a cat in a box along with one radioactive isotope. The box is fitted with a mechanism that will release a deadly poison the instant the unstable particle decays, thus releasing energy that a Geiger counter can detect. The problem is that the probability that the particle will decay within a certain time-frame is impossible to predict. Therefore, it is impossible at any given time to know if the cat is alive or dead.

Because all that can be known is what is perceived, and since one cannot look in the box, the cat remains in a superpositional state, "smeared" between two or more distinct values like alive and dead. Its mortality is "in principle" (which is the ironic twist) indeterminable. The cat is in a perpetual state of uncertainty. One cannot look "behind" the particle to see when it will really decay. There is no "behind" to direct perception. Prediction is pure metaphysical speculation (a concern for the existential status of hypothetical future states). And therefore, to the extent that perception is always perspectival, it is always ambiguously "smeared" (interpretation).

In the Monroe et al. experiment, a "superposition state" of an atom was generated. The researchers trapped a $^9B^+$ ion and then laser-cooled it to the zero-point energy state. They then prepared it in a superposition of spatially separated coherent harmonic oscillator states. "This" state(s) was created by application of a sequence of laser pulses, which "entangled" "internal" (electronic) and "external" (notional) states of the ion. Monroe et al. verified a "Schrodinger cat superposition" by detecting quantum interference between localized wave packets. What this means is that they experimentally provided insight into the "fuzzy boundary" between classical and quantum descriptions of the world. Via controlled studies of quantum measurement and quantum decoherence, they generated a peek at the indefinite boundary between "two worlds," or two descriptions (physics). This too is, as Werner Heisenberg and others understood, hermeneutically indeterminate. There is a fuzzy boundary between the two descriptions and/or also between description and interpretation, between dualistic translation and interpretation. Either we are confused about our simulation of the world, or about the decoherent quality of *the* (external) world. But in the end, all we have are our descriptions of perceptions. The difference between the description and the described is indeterminate, as is the difference between the perception and the perceived. Since phenomenologists do not concern themselves with metaphysics and go with direct experience, they remain relatively coherent or unconfused.

According to Immanuel Kant (1929), perception renders phenomena (not used in the same sense as Husserl). But, according to Kant, phenomena are essentially different from the noumenal thing-in-itself "out there." In short, perception is not the same as the perceived. Similarly, Francis Bacon argued that he somehow knew that he could never know. In *Novum organum*, he discussed four barriers to knowledge. They are: the "Idols of the Marketplace," the "Idols of the Cave," the "Idols of the Tribe," and the "Idols of the Theater." The idols of the tribe include the inherent limitations of being human (human nature) such as excessive emotionalism, obsessions, and narrow-minded, prejudicial thinking. The idols of the cave include individual limitations such as intellectual capacity and education. The idols of the theater include self-perpetuating dogmas that present imaginary (meaning false) worlds like stage plays. The final set of idols are those of the marketplace and they are the most troublesome source of falsehood. Idols of the marketplace constitute misuse of language including poor definition and imprecise categories.

According to Bacon (1937: 71), "Everyone (besides the errors common to human nature in general) has a cave or den of his own, which refracts and discolours the light of nature; owing either to his own proper and peculiar nature; or to his education and conversation . . . or to the authority of those whom he esteems and admires." For Bacon, the idols constituted tangential barriers (limited perspectives) to the entrance into "the kingdom of heaven." Like Descartes,

Hegel, Einstein, Kepler, and Hawking, knowledge, for Bacon, equals experience of God. But we are doomed because perception is always perspectival, always distorted. This is so due to poor eyesight, less-than-perfect intellect, less-than-perfect knowledge, seeing through jargon and prejudices, and so on.

But the question remains. How did Bacon know that such distortions exist? "Distortion" is the difference between pure apodictic knowing and mortal perception. Since one cannot escape one's own embodied mortality, then one has no recourse to The Truth, and therefore distortion cannot be discerned. Method is, of course, supposed to be our savior. It is supposed to transcend time, fix relationships as measures, be objective, and make things comparable. But method too, is selected on criteria of truth already presumed. The appropriateness and power of a method presumes a notion of comparison between its version of reality and reality itself. At best, method is a medium that enables controlled, coherent communication between people. Method enables replication and verification. But yet, there have been times when the *consensus gentium* (truth by consensus—or common sense) has been wrong. Times and truths change. Methods are constantly changing, presumably getting "better." But how do we know they are "getting better" (closer to mimetic perfection) without already knowing The Truth prior to methodical control and manipulation? Bacon seems to be saying that he knows God and knows that what he sees or imagines God to be is not him. This is like the prohibition some religions have against portrayals of divinity. What artist would be so arrogant as to claim to be able to capture the image of God? So too, what methodologist would be so arrogant as to say that his method is fallible and only renders approximations? How could he know, unless he is also claiming to already know The Truth?

Neither Descartes nor Bacon ever explained how perception can be designated as "limited" or "distorted," or "false" unless one allows for the possibility of pure immaculate access to Reality so that one could then compare the Real with the mere perception of it, thereby exposing perception as lacking. In short, we are told that the only source of knowledge is perspectivally limited, but if this is true, how would we ever know? If all experience is indeterminate "interpretation," then how does interpretation have any meaning? In a word, if we (1) accept the fallibility of direct (personal) sense perception, and (2) claim that sense perception is the only access to Reality we have, then (3) we can neither claim to know that we know, nor that we do not know. Words like "approximation," "distortion," "fallibility," "interpretation," "perspective," and so on, all presume a dualistic metaphysic that separates the unknowable referent from the knowable reflection of "it." Such fragmentation makes knowledge an impossibility. The result of such illogic in the midst of logical positivists has been the growth of existentialism and deconstruction. The oxymoron of absolute relativity is the postmodern condition. All that is left is might and rhetoric. This is the ultimate level of indeterminism that Nietzsche explored. Nietzsche's hermeneutic analyses influenced the German academy including its postmodern quantum metaphysicians.

If Bacon is correct, that all experience is perspectival and subject to the various idols, then how does he know? Does he have some gift the rest of us do not? If all truth is class-based, then how did Marx escape his own situatedness to tell us this? From what high mountain do these experts descend to give the rest of us valley dwellers the bad news of being condemned to living false lives and suffering false consciousness? Are they examples of Plato's hero returned to the shadow world of our subterranean existence to save us? Do they represent the "light ages"? Nietzsche suspected that they, too, were cave dwellers and not salvific divinities. He questioned their transcendental powers which enabled them to escape from their own truths. If they speak the truth of perspectivism, then this truth, too, must be limited and distorted. That is the cost of coherence, continuity, perfect system. As Kierkegaard noted of Hegel's grand system (and long before cyberneticists like Norbert Wiener [1948: 161, 162] figured out the dilemma), it is unfit for human habitation.

Nietzsche never claimed to be able to "turn his own corner," or lift himself by his epistemological bootstraps. And so, he left us in the lurch of being human, all too human, but at least "awake." Perhaps either/orism needs to be abandoned for superpositionality. We must go beyond truth and falsity, beyond good and evil. Life is not a simple binary construct. We can describe and critique systems precisely because we can "get outside of them" and be free thinkers. This is possible via systatic, aperspectival (a)waring. We must bracket our metaphysical allegiances and explore the differences between systems, to see their identities through their differences. Identity depends not on binary opposition, but on multifarious differences. For instance, there can be no "whites" in America, without "colored." Whites depend on "nonwhites" for their identity. To exterminate the nonwhites is to exterminate the white self.

Ironically, the necessary conditions for prediction are consistency, continuity, coherence. In short, context including history. It is ironic, because those who believe most in the ability to predict also tend to find history and context a waste of time. In this sense (as with the denial of the subject, and meaning) positivistic empiricists and deconstructionists agree on the "end of history," as a meta-narrative, as the privileged story that enables explanation. Yet they believe in their own history, in literature reviews and programmatic replication. Predictability presumes coherence and continuity, so that anyone who believes in predictability must presume history and other forms of context.

But yet, the world seems discontinuous and indeterminate, mutational. Even induction begins with my direct, personal experience. Kant claimed, like Bacon and Descartes, that the world is dualistic, but he could not prove it. Realizing the quagmire this entails, Kant offered the realm of categorical intuition and logic to safeguard the possibility of knowledge. So, too, did Husserl. Truth cannot be derived from contingent and fallible observation. No matter the sample size, multiplying error never leads to truth.

The problem for all of these dualists is that they suffer from what Paul Ricoeur (1981) has called the "hermeneutics of suspicion," or what Umberto Eco (Eco et al., 1992: 54) has called the vocation of the "followers of the veil" (*Adepti del Valame*). They suspect, but cannot prove, that there is something "out there" and that it is ontologically different. They believe that our senses are a screen. Screens reveal (like "monitors") as well as conceal. According to modern materialism, my senses are my only access to the real, and, at the same time, the source of fallacy. "The world" is not known, but only interpretable. But what the difference is remains unstated.

The difference between a wink, a fake wink, a pretend wink, depends. The problem is the "on." Depends "on" seems to defy final explanation. Context? Intent? Will? Stimulus responsiveness? Interpretation? The Other? Maybe all of them. There does not seem to be a foundation, a final and firm ground. Before one can generate an instrument to "measure" the differences, one must first understand the phenomenon. For instance, the telescope has been developed to investigate distant objects. The microscope is not appropriate to the nature of stars. One does not use a telescope to measure cholesterol. The instrument must conform to the nature of the phenomenon. The necessary conditions for an empirical thing to exist have been specified by Kant and Isaac Newton. Dilthey dreamed of being the "Newton of the human sciences," but seems to have fallen short. His hermeneutics and historicism of the moral sciences has had great heuristic value such that it has promoted rather than resolved endless speculation about human behavior.

In the physical sciences, the sequential priority of instrument to phenomenon studied goes to the phenomenon. But in operational definition, all things, regardless of their essential differences, are presupposed *a priori* to be measurable. In fact, knowledge is truncated and equated with measurement which is based on purely arbitrary scales. What is a thing? It is the sum total of all its measures. An operational definition includes the way to measure the thing. Survey instruments, and some experiments, create the phenomenon. They are less "about" than productive of the thing studied (see Chapter 5 on "race"). In social sciences, too often investigators apply to everything the one or two tools they have borrowed, without asking themselves the phenomenological question (which physicists do), what are the necessary conditions for this thing to exist? If you don't ask this, then you do not know the object and therefore cannot be sure how to accurately model it. But in natural scientific experiments, the researcher has the advantage of creating the phenomenon. In order to be able to create a thing, one must first understand its essential properties. Natural, experimental science has this powerful (manipulative) advantage over the social sciences. Because of those empirically nonexistent phenomena "values," social scientists are not "allowed" to create wars or violence or criminals just for the sake of knowledge.

This is an example of the hermeneutic circle. Natural science makes the circle of phenomena they work on. Social scientists attempt to describe it (the hermeneutic circle of culture) "from the inside," because they, too, are cultural beings. To look for, and describe, a work of art, one must first know what art is, but one cannot know what art is until one has experienced it. The same is true of deviance, conflict, violence, abnormality, obscenity, and so on. An example is the conflict over what constitutes "violence" on television. Deconstructionists might suggest that violence is whatever the viewer, including the researcher, says it is (by definition). Perhaps this is correct and therefore there is no phenomenon separate from perception. The survey simply records reactions regardless of any "objective" reality. As social standards change, so, too, does reality which is, of course, the essence of the social constructivist theory. Community standards prevail, including for academic communities.

But to be able to even ask if such and such is a case of violent content presumes a shared hermeneutic horizon, a shared sense of the word "violence," and even a shared sense that this question about violence is appropriate and meaningfully interesting. To ask if this is a case of "violence" is to use the word "violence" at the eidetic (transcendental) level. But all of language is eidetic. For instance, I say "look at the car," otherwise I have neither the time nor the energy to describe each "car" as a unique object. We speak and think categorically because it makes communication possible. Without presuming the eidetic level of communicative competence, all communication, including research, would be so totally arbitrary and specific (empirical) as to be meaningless. I would have to use different words for each car. As Ludwig Wittgenstein (1974) has pointed out, a necessary condition for a language to exist is at least two people.

What are the necessary conditions for a method to render mimetically "accurate" descriptions? The problem here is that on the one hand, we are told that we must use a method to "get at" the phenomenon. But on the other, we are asked to choose the best one before trying them all out. So how can one determine, comparatively speaking, which method is "better," without somehow knowing in advance, *and free of methodological imposition*, the nature of the phenomenon? What really happens in the social sciences is that researchers tend to use the tools they were taught. What else can human, all too human, researchers do? The question is, is it possible to not be perspectival, to not be a historical being, to not be a "person of my times and circumstances"? Dilthey would say no, Husserl yes, and Nietzsche would say that it remains indeterminate. To say, "ah that's more like it," presupposes knowledge of what an accurate picture should be.

RELATIVE RELATIVISM

Today, we revel in our own suicide. Today the subject is obliterated, meaning is a fantasy, value unreal. Our teleology is truncated. What is the goal or point of our massive systems? Can we even debate the value of a goal? Such questions are deemed irrelevant philosophizing. Instead, only the mechanics of short-term *telos* is valid. The ought is abandoned for endless surveying of the is, which we make. "Why" is displaced by "how." Life is easier that way, more practical. Our audience wants results. Theory is reduced to self-evident and explanatory data.

Hermeneutics includes scholars like Heidegger and Derrida who do seriously ponder the indeterminacy of meaning, but also scholars like Rudolf Bultmann, Emilio Betti, Rene Wellek, William Wimsatt, Wilhelm Dilthey, E. K. Hirsch, Friedrich Schleiermacher, and Jurgen Habermas, who insist that the author's intention is available in his work and that a reality is available for critique. Granted, many contemporary hermeneuticians have moved toward the behavioristic abandonment of meaning and intentionality. But yet, we do read each other's writings and believe that we understand them, at least enough to respond, to form schools of thought and programmatic positions. We hold not books, but authors responsible.

Phenomenologists believe that there are essential differences between deconstructionists and positivists so that each term has meaning. Postmodernism, too, is essentially different from modernity, precisely in its erasure of boundaries like inside/outside and classical/modern in art and architecture. Postmodernism is deconstructive but this is just one hermeneutic tactic. Deconstruction seeks to bring the marginal interpretation into central focus. For instance, what if we saw the world through the eyes of an impoverished child, or the homeless? In this way, a voice rarely heard, rarely written, is empowered by scholars like Robert Coles (1967, 1992). As different perspectives are expressed, the empirical world is suddenly manifold and complex. It is enriched, rather than reduced to a single code.

Though this book was written before Alan Sokal's hoax against the journal *Social Text*, much of what this book says is actually in agreement with Sokal's intent. It tends to turn a jaundiced eye toward those who proclaim that there is no truth and that's the truth; those who rightly equate socialization and education with indoctrination and then get upset about it. After all, if a person can spend four years in a university and leave utterly unchanged, she should demand her money back. Clearly, even deconstructionists attempt to change the very way their students think, making them more independent, critical, and empathic.

This book presents a relative relativism. It suggests many truths, rather than many nontruths, something conservatives like Sokal don't like. In Chapter 1, the kynical, cheeky approach to truth-saying is introduced. However, the difference between kynical and cynical is important. Cynicism, as Andreas Huyssen (1987: xx) notes in the "Foreword" to Peter Sloterdijk's book *Critique of Cynical Reason*, "depends on the logic of hostility" that is expressed as objectifying and satirical laughter. Thus, I would say that Sokal is a cynic, while this book attempts to be kynical. Huyssen wonders what such laughter actually does to the people being laughed at. Kynical play is not the same as cynical and arrogant deception with intent to demolish someone. The logic of hostility is bracketed by the kynic. Also in Chapter 1, I confess my faith in the existence of the external world, but in the wide-awake sense that I cannot prove this faith anymore than anyone can prove the nonexistence of gods. I believe that the moons Galileo discovered around Jupiter existed before he discovered them and exist independent of his telescope and our observations. But neither I nor anyone else can prove this. On the other hand, I often question the ontological status of phenomena that seem dependent for their existence on the instruments developed to measure them, on operational definition. Psychological illnesses seem to come and go with each new revision of the DSM (*Diagnostic and Statistical Manual of Mental Disorders*, published by the American Psychiatric Association [DSM 1, 2, 3, 4]). Like crime, IQ seems to be an issue of definition. But, in Chapter 5, I present a history of oppression in America that is hard to interpret out of existence, or to interpret as being anything but unjust, cruel, and hypocritical (for the Christian whites).

Nearly all information comes with an appeal to trust. I take a science class and most of it is testimony about events I will never personally experience, including experiments and discoveries that constitute the history of science, its foundation of presumed facts, the presumably replicable ground of what Thomas Kuhn (1962) calls ''normal science.''

I acknowledge the ever-present dimension of trust and interpretation. The human world is filled with meaning. What things mean is important to people. The Wailing Wall in Jerusalem is empirically just a pile of old stone blocks, but yet millions of people around the world, especially Jews, are willing to die defending it, just as others are fixated on destroying it. Why? Such questions about human behavior cannot be adequately addressed without acknowledging interpretation, meaning, history, emotion, context. I can stand on a street corner in Shanghai and absorb all sorts of stimuli. To me they mean confusion, uncertainty, untranslatable sights and sounds. I do not share the hermeneutic horizon the millions of others around me do. I do not know their language or culture. Therefore, my behavior and their behavior are different.

In order to explain (not merely record and correlate) human behavior, meaning cannot be ignored. For positivists, meaning is a myth because it defies measurement, while physical movement lends itself easily to observation. For postmodern deconstructionists, meaning is not important because it is always indeterminate. This book stands in the shadow of Nietzsche, Husserl, and Gebser. It stands in defense of meaning and against the forces of nihilism that champion value-free knowledge on one hand, and the impossibility of it on the other. This book resists the hypervaluation of monosemantic systematization, the defiguralization of language. This book praises unsystematic thinking and ambiguity. Is there truth herein? That is up to the reader to decide.

I have found far too many scholars who have very, very strong opinions about things they have never read such as Nietzsche, Husserl, Heidegger, Derrida, Kristeva, and others. This is a total lack of intellectual integrity. The truth is that these scholars had very deep disagreements with each other. I hope this book is not so unfair.[2]

NOTES

1. Scholars and comedians alike are serious to the point of hostility. Even his play is vicious, as in Alan D. Sokal's hoax perpetrated on the journal *Social Text* in the May 1996 issue. His deception and "gloating revelation" (Fish, 1996: 37) took advantage of the ignorance and humility with which social scientists and pluralistic humanities teachers approach physical sciences. Trust was shattered and suspicion, paranoia, and a call for heightened vigilance is the consequence. If one wanted to, one could with enough effort do such a thing to almost any journal. What Sokal, in his crusade against "postmodern literary theory," seems to misunderstand is that unlike physical scientists like himself, those in the humanities and social sciences are not so sure of The Truth, and its alleged logicality. Human history, including the use of scientific discoveries, tends to call into question the status of "Man the rational animal." Of course, not all physical scientists are like Sokal, as is made evident in this book. The danger is of course, that not so well-informed spectators may conclude that Sokal represents all physical scientists and that his hoax has, in one fell swoop, demolished 2,000 years of hermeneutics, Nietzsche scholarship, and honest reflection on the problem of relativity. For instance, in his column cheering on Sokal's attack against "leftist," "progressive" academicians, George Will (May 30, 1996: 6) claims that hermeneutics posits that "the meaning of all communication is radically indeterminate," that intentionality is irrelevant. Actually, it is non-phenomenological positivists (and I put it this way because Edmund Husserl was correct when he proclaimed himself to be the last and most radical antimetaphysical positivist) who doubt the ability to know intention, and therefore disregard it as indeterminate and irrelevant, preferring description of brute behavior patterns. This, of course, disturbs conservatives like George Will who lionized Sokal in his newspaper column saying that Sokal "has perpetrated a hilarious hoax that reveals the gaudy silliness of some academics." According to Will, Sokal's parody "proves that any nonsense, however prolix and preposterous, can win academic approval if it includes 'progressive' murmurings about feminism and the baneful effects of 'the Western intellectual outlook' "(Will, 1996: 6). While this book takes to task both constructivists and deconstructivists, it does not mix politics with scholarship like some silly journalists. Instead, it insists, as the conservative drum beat in support of Sokal demonstrates, that metaphysics is politics. Who controls the definition of reality, who defines what is the appropriate way to describe reality, has power. Conservatives have always claimed that there is only one reality and they know what it is. That is why totalitarians burn books.

2. For instance, there are more than a few who have read the popular *Will to Power* without seemingly being aware that it was compiled from fragments by Nietzsche's sister after he had fallen into dysfunctional madness. This work does not present his intention (see comments by Walter Kaufmann, the definitive translator of Nietzsche into English, 1980). This "book" was used by the Nazis to justify some of their irresponsible actions. If anything, Nietzsche was no Nazi. He strenuously distrusted people of all political persuasions who were so confident in their own reality as to be willing to force others to conform. Likewise, many people have proclaimed to me that Nietzsche was a nihilist. This is completely wrong. Nietzsche observed the twilight of the idols, and fought systems that were bleeding the world of its meaning. He believed that humans are not satisfied with simply improving the efficiency of production, that what they really crave is meaning, beauty, and other phenomena hard to put under the microscope.

REFERENCES

Ackerman, D. (1990) *A Natural History of the Senses*. New York: Random House.

Adorno, T. W., and M. Horkheimer. (1972) *Dialectic of Enlightenment*. New York: Herder and Herder.

Bacon, F. (1937) *Essays, Advancement of Learning, New Atlantis and Other Pieces*. Garden City, NY: Doubleday, Doran & Company.

Binet, A. (1913) *A Method of Measuring the Intelligence of Young Children*. Lincoln, IL: The Courier Company.

Braverman, H. (1974) *Labor and Monopoly Capital*. New York: Monthly Review Press.

Carnap, R. (1963) *Philosophy of Rudolf Carnap*, edited by P. Schilpp. La Salle, IL: Open Court.

Chuang Tzu. (1974) *Inner Chapters*. New York: Vintage.

Coles, R. (1967). *Children of Crisis*. Boston: Little, Brown.

———. (1992) *Their Eyes Meeting the World: The Drawings and Paintings of Children*. Boston: Houghton Mifflin

Drucker, P. (1942) *The Future of Industrial Man: A Conservative Approach*. New York: John Day Company.

Eco, U., R. Rorty, and J. Culler. (1992) *Interpretation and Overinterpretation*. Cambridge, England: Cambridge University Press.

Fish, S. (1996) " 'Morphogenic Field' Day.'' *Newsweek*, June 3, p. 37.

Foucault, M. (1979) *Discipline and Punish: The Birth of the Prison*. New York: Vintage.

Gebser, J. (German 1949; English 1985) *The Ever-Present Origin*. Athens: Ohio University Press.

Geddes, P. (1911) *Evolution*. New York: Holt and Company.

Geertz, C. (1973) *The Interpretation of Cultures*. New York: Basic Books.

Gilbreth, F., and L. Gilbreth. (1911) *Motion Study: A Method for Increasing the Efficiency of the Workman*. New York: D. Van Nostrand.

———. (1973) *Primer of Scientific Management*. Easton, PA: Hire.

Gilbreth, F., Jr. (1948) *Cheaper by the Dozen*. New York: T. Y. Crowell.

Habermas, J. (1971) *Knowledge and Human Interest*. Boston: Beacon.

———. (1973) *Theory and Practice*. Boston: Beacon.

Hall, E. T. (1976) *Beyond Culture*. New York: Doubleday.

Hawking, S. (1988) *A Brief History of Time*. New York: Bantam Books.

Homans, G. (1984) *Coming to My Senses: The Autobiography of a Sociologist*. New Brunswick, NJ: Transaction Books.

Husserl, E. (1962) *Ideas: General Introduction to Pure Phenomenology*. New York: Collier.

Huyssen, A. (1987) "Foreword: The Return of Diogenes as Postmodern Intellectual." In *Critique of Cynical Reason*, by P. Sloterdijk. Minneapolis: University of Minnesota Press (pp. ix–xxxix).

Kant, I. (1929) *Critique of Pure Reason*. New York: St. Martin's Press.

Kaufmann, W. (1980) *Discovering the Mind, Volume Two: Nietzsche, Heidegger, and Buber*. New York: McGraw-Hill.

Kroeber, A. L., ed. (1953) *Anthropology Today*. Chicago: University of Chicago Press.

Kuhn, T. (1962) *The Structure of Scientific Revolutions*. Chicago: University of Chicago Press.

Levinas, E. (1987) *Time and the Other: And Additional Essays*. Pittsburgh: Duquesne University Press.

Mickunas, A. (1978) personal conversation.

Monroe, C., D. Meekhof, B. King, and D. Wineland. (1996) "A 'Schrodinger Cat' Superposition State of an Atom." *Science* 272 (May 24): 1131–1133.

Mumford, L. (1963) *Techniques and Civilization*. New York: Harcourt, Brace and World.

Munsterburg, H. (1913) *Psychological and Industrial Efficiency*. New York: Houghton Mifflin.

Pathak, A. (1996) graduate student term paper, University of Oklahoma.

Pribram, K. (1971). *Languages of the Brain: Experimental Paradoxes and Principles in Neuropsychology*. Englewood Cliffs, NJ: Prentice-Hall.

Rehorick, D., and W. Buxton. (1986) "Recasting the Parsons-Schutz Dialogue: The Hidden Participation of Eric Voegelin." Paper presented at the International Society for the Sociology of Knowledge, New Delhi.

Ricoeur, P. (1981) *Hermeneutics and the Social Sciences*. Cambridge, England: Cambridge University Press.

Rifkin, J. (1987) *Time Wars*. New York: Henry Holt and Company.

Rorty, R. (1979) *Philosophy and the Mirror of Nature*. Princeton, NJ: Princeton University Press.

Russell, B., and A. N. Whitehead. (1967) *Principia Mathematica*. Cambridge, England: Cambridge University Press.

Sloterdijk, P. (1987) *Critique of Cynical Reason*. Minneapolis: University of Minnesota Press.

Taylor, F. (1911, reprint 1996) *The Principles of Scientific Management*. Dusseldorf: Wirstschaft und Finanzen.

Wiener, N. (1948) *Cybernetics: Or, Control and Communication in the Animal and the Machine*. New York: John Wiley.

Will, G. (1996) "Communication and Science." *The Norman Oklahoma Transcript*, no. 323, p. 6.

Wittgenstein, L. (1974) *Philosophical Grammar*. Oxford, England: Basil Blackwell.

1

Getting Out of Line

No cynicism can outdo life.

—Anton Chekov

MONO-TON-OUS WORLD: MON-ASSTIC TRUTH

This book expresses an attitude which Olof Gigon (1959), and later Heinrich Niehues-Probsting (1979) and Peter Sloterdijk (1987) have called the "kynical impulse." "Kynical" is an alternative spelling of "cynical." Kynical is a conceptualization of the cheeky, positive side of cynicism *embodied* by Diogenes of Sinope. Diogenes, whom Plato (in recognizing his undeniable genius) called the "mad Socrates," was the philosopher who lived in a tub, who invented the gay science, worked his truths through physiognomically eloquent gestures, pantomimes, wordplays, farts, and laughter, rather than formal texts. He was famous for "getting out of line," a sin for serious "typographic" linear "perspectival" humans (McLuhan, 1962; Gebser, 1985).

What Diogenes laughed at was the "high society" of truthsayers, the logicians, theologists, metaphysicians (including natural philosophers or "empiricists" and materialists), moralists, and ideologues. He snickered at how they eagerly built fortifications of arguments on axioms he would not "give," but instead would prod them to earn, and not permanently, but as a loan. He played with those who, in all seriousness, established facts and causal "chains," once and for all, the hyperreality of the eye and line, and the "virtual" golden mean (which has become the last and only "value" that explains the less real and faded "actual"). Diogenes noted their hypocrisy when they conveniently excluded themselves from their otherwise universal principles. He wondered out loud at such people who claim to be "gifted" with "super-vision," who are privy to various absolutisms which they self-importantly parade, enabling them-selves to define the Real, to define the rest of us mass of sweaty ignorance; our "race," our "opinions," our "intellects," our "characters," our "selves," our "place," our "worth," our "past, present, and future." With their various re-alisms, predictions, and frames (such as Ptolemy's grid geometry, Roger Ba-con's and Alhazen's (Ibn-al-Haitam) works on optics, Jan Van Eyck, Leon Battista Alberti, and Filippo Brunelleschi's perspective), they seek to delimit our dreams and to capture our essence on two dimensions, to control from a distance.

But in the Athens of Diogenes, creativity was rampant, and he (like Socrates) could *talk* with truthsayers in public, and temper their epistemic force, keeping alternatives alive, the future open and undomesticated. Commentary was not limited just to talk. Conversation about the most serious of topics was play. The rules of forensic and deliberative speech had not yet been written. At its height, the city-state had a population of less than 180,000, yet it managed to support a thriving community of warriors, slaves, artists, statesmen, athletes, thinkers, traders (at least until the invasion of Attica by the Peloponnesians and the great plague of 430 B.C. which decimated the population, reducing Athens to a village of about 25,000, the population around which it hovered until German and English archaeologists and romantics rekindled interest in its vision).

Today, the noose of systematic truth is tighter than in the days of Socrates and Diogenes. Today, the system has formalized/industrialized into a structure of binary logic known as double-entry accounting. The dualistic ratio-imperative is so sedimented that many, like Sloterdijk, wonder if satire is possible anymore. In the postmodern world, power is anonymous. Institutions, like the "corpora-tion," have public images and mighty voices that lack bodies to put with them, to hold accountable. There is literally "no body" to talk to. Consciousness and intention have been displaced by stimulus/response, and with that causal unit has gone responsibility. We vote for video images we've seen while watching a dead box of flickering lights for hours every day. This is the screen world. Like all screens, something is concealed but we cannot know for sure. We are taught to believe only what we can see. We are visiocentric (Kramer, 1993). And so, the anonymous image managers produce the virtual truth.

I am confidently told who and what I am by experts. Hofstede and Bond (1984) tell me that I am "individualistic," *as opposed to* "collectivistic." Par-sons (1951), with his pattern variables, tells me that I am either "ascription" oriented, or "achievement" oriented, "instrumental" or "expressive"; I am either a means-type person, or an ends-type person. Each pole must be mutually excluding. All of analytic social science presumes a mode of thinking that is a necessary condition for such articulations of me and my interactions. They pre-sume a spatial metaphysic which enables them to draw lines with dualistically opposing ends, and Aristotelian, two-valued logic which defines a world with no middle, no maybe.

This is the imperative of ratio, the excluded middle which Newton formalized. For instance, it is assumed that as I (a data point on the line) move toward absolute individualism, I *must* also move away from absolute collectivism, and with the same but inverse rate and distance (force). This is a necessary condition for control and prediction of me. But, as postmodern logicians like Hans Reichenbach (1944) and Carl Weizsacker (1975–1977), and "plain folk" have observed, this invisible law of ratio does not hold. Depending on the context, whether I am with family, or friends, or enemies, or strangers, whether I am in this or that mood, and so on, I can be either collectivistic or individualist, or even both at once or neither. They are not necessarily oppositional or dualistically separated; nor are they exclusively linked by the linear imperative of two-valued logic. Maybe I want to jump off the line of variance, to express a different dimension, to resist the imperative of "must," that I must be either this or that.

Even if a variable is more rigorously conceived than these (as should be), as simply "A, not A," still the nature of the relationship is found to be flexible such as "maybe A," or "A and not A simultaneously." The linearly conceived temporal dimension that a thing cannot be and not be, both at once, is over-determined by the lifeworld. Simultaneity and complementary have displaced exclusive, two-valued perspectival thinking, which is presumed by modern systematics.

In this, the twentieth century, truth has been fragmented still further into "regional ontologies" (truths) such that historiography renders the true causes, physics renders the true causes, sociology renders the true causes, psychology, chemistry, and so forth; all claim to be able to reduce each other to the true ground of the real (Husserl, 1962). When you "get right down to it," everything is really quantum states, everything is really brain chemistry, everything is really social construction, everything is really motion in space, everything is really narration (language-games), everything is really power, or capital, and so on and so forth. "Everything" is a great inverted pyramid leading back to the prime mover or indivisible singularity. We are confronted with many mutually excluding and absolutist truths. The disciples of each paradigm insist with all earnestness to be able to explain the others, to reduce them totally—really. But according to the high priest of a rational universe, Stephen Hawking (1988: 172), "Laplace's determinism was incomplete in two ways. It did not say how the laws should be chosen and it did not specify the initial configuration of the universe. These were left to God." Well, I'm glad that settles it.

Diogenes denounced the idealistic alienation of truth from the body at the moment it occurred. But he was unique because he wrote the alter ego of knowledge. "Others," notably women and minorities, have not written, but have turned a jaundiced eye toward the total systems, flashed an obscene hand sign at those who claim to simulate, to organize, to understand, and to undercut the weak and feeble-minded. The subjects of study bodily resist the models and theories of themselves that claim the definitive priority over them, that claim to be more real than their smelly flesh can stand still for. The system remains while the jobs and people "pass on." The system "downsizes," the system is the sum total of dictatorial, even natural, rules like market forces and genetics. The system profits when the workers do not, and vice versa. The system has become so dissociated from the hands that create it that when the government released startlingly low unemployment figures (good news for workers), Wall Street took its third biggest drop in value in history (March 8, 1996). Wall Street and Main Street are metaphors for what Theodor W. Adorno and Max Horkheimer (1972) called the "dialectic of Enlightenment," the schism between mind and body, management of the system and physical labor, the executive suite and the shop floor. The abstraction of the truth from the body is naturalized. It's no one's fault that blacks are genetically inferior and therefore fail in the system. The system explains them without having ever walked in their grimey, contingent shoes. It does not need to, because the simulation is more powerful than what it simulates. The simulation is transcendental. People come and go but the plan that arranges their coming and going is permanent. It can be run in fast-forward to see the future and judge it/them (their future) and manipulate it/them (Baudrillard, 1983). In predicting the future, it is made via "self-fulfilling prophecy." But "making" implies responsibility, something the makers do not want, so it is naturalized, it is "out of their hands." Ideology, all isms, is a "naturally" occurring process. It is self-legitimating. But there seem to be many pyramids, many natures, many gods.

The truthsayers are thus "gifted." They are uniquely (perspectivally) positioned atop *the* pyramid or cone of life, with the panorama of all at their feet. The truthsayers have the power of "super-vision" and "over-sight." The most important information is beyond the horizon of the rest. The ignorant are kept that way. They are allowed access on a "need to know" basis only. And the truthsayers define "need." Access involves competition. Only the strong get to see the secret and sacred records, and getting to see is the source of their strength. The holders of the truth, those who do the "allowing" of access are the master gatekeepers, indeed the designers of the gates. For instance, Newt Gingrich preaches "power to the people," "local autonomy," while creating the largest political action committee (money-laundering scheme) in history to bring "soft money" into localities from a national center to influence elections. It is all "legal" just so long as the money is not connected to names, just advocating "issues" and ideological "positions" (which in perspectival modernity are equal to video candidates). The money belongs to no one, and is linked to no one. This is the underground of postmodern politics, the disembodied, amoral voice of power. "Substance" has vanished. Only rules remain. Value is the amorphous in-between of exchange; no exchange, no value.

But the truthsayers are suspected. As when the Marxist shouts at/defines the "poor deluded workers" (as such) that they are all alienated from themselves, the workers poke fun at the would-be savior, kynically shaking their heads at his spitting, apodictic fury, wondering if everyone in "paradise" is so serious about "historical imperatives," and why they should bother to talk about destiny at all if it is "inevitable" anyway (with "iron necessity" to quote Marx, 1967:

8). The rhetoric of truthsaying works by convincing people to create the future, because it is expertly prophesied, predicted, and as such, inevitable anyway. This is the power of metaphysics, from magic to science. Why argue with Reality?

But from the beginning, the unwashed masses seem to recognize that the truthsayers are hypocritical and unjust; that they are not so "gifted," and may need a bath, too. It is hard to be a prophet in one's home town because everyone there knew the prophet before (s)he was an image of perfection. The hypocrisy shows when a gap appears in the screen that hides the wizard at the controls. The hypocrisy shows at the ever-present moment when the possibly deluded or hypercynical truthsayers absolve themselves from their own systems. They "know better," like Karl Marx claiming that all other truths are merely the ideological manifestations of contingent class consciousness, except this claim itself, except Marx himself, who somehow escaped both his own truth and his class, to ascend to absolute, immaculate perception. Likewise, Michel Foucault (1972) claims that all other truths are limited to their episteme except this, his truth, which is transepistemic. Social scientists claim that the world is by nature socially contingent, except this truth itself, which transcends itself, its own social positionality. Materialists too reduce everything to nonsentient stuff except their own thoughtful proclamations about dead matter. Historians claim that history determines everything except their own objective history writing. History writing is somehow not affected by history. Freud's cigar is just a cigar, but for the rest of us ignoramuses. . . .

Bertrand Russell and Alfred North Whitehead (1967) discovered that a set cannot be, yet (to be fair) must be a member of itself (the set of all sets). For instance, all Athenians are liars. I am Athenian. If I am telling the truth, I am lying. And if I am lying, I am telling the truth. After years of seeking an airtight either/or absolutism, Russell came to speak in terms of "systematic ambiguity." Set theory harbors a fundamental antinomy such that set theory must be inconsistent in order to be consistent. It must cheat to win. This is the problem of the "special status," or self-exclusion, of the postulate of "constructibility" from the axiom system of set theory itself, in order to prove the consistency of the continuum hypothesis in set theory. From Bernard Bolzano to Kurt Godel, including Georg Cantor, Cesare Burali-Forti, Ernst Zermelo, Paul Bernays, John von Neumann, and the group of French mathematicians who collectively publish under the pseudonym of Nicholas Bourbaki, all have demonstrated the awkward situation in which mathematics, in its entirety, finds itself. There exists no set that contains all ordinals, all cardinals, or all alephs. There is no social scientist who can speak of collectivism and/or individualism except from a perspective that is either collectivistic or individualistic, unless (s)he is "right in the middle," the perfect balance, the personification of the "golden mean," so that (s)he is neither and both, divinely objective, pure and untouched.

Those who self-proclaim such profound and exclusive supervision insist in all seriousness that reflective dialogue cease on their command because the truth

is already known (at least by them, which is all that ''matters''), so reflection/
thinking is impractical, ''unproductive.'' We must get on with the business of
truthsaying! (with making the world), and only according to their ''disinterested'' (balanced) lights. Against the truthsayers stand a few, ''embarrassing''
treatises that just won't politely shut up (disappear), works like *Candide* and
Zarathustra. Works that just refuse to tell *the* truth. But they are hardly new
voices in this conversation for the sake of conversation.

Sloterdijk points out that right at the beginning of the history of European
truthsaying, laughter rose up to meet its abstracting, self-serious bombast. Laertius tells the tale of Thales, the protophilosopher and father of Ionian systematic
thought, who was ''the first in the series of men who personify Western *ratio*''
(Sloterdijk, 1987: 534). As he was on his way to study the heavens, he fell into
a ditch. The old servant woman who was accompanying him said, ''You can't
even see, Thales, what lies before your feet, and you fancy that you know what
is in the heavens'' (Laertius, 1925). This mockery inaugurates a parallel, largely
invisible, unrecorded dimension of history, namely, the history of the ''subla-
tion'' of truthsaying. According to Friedrich Nietzsche (1974), the kynical, un-
tutored voice is life, refusing to be subjugated and finalized. It is not
anti-intellectualism so much as a refusal to be seen as a lower form of life, as
''decentered,'' ''unbalanced,'' ''deranged,'' begging for guidance.

Kynicism is not cynical acquiescence and resentment in the face of master
narratives, but a vital acknowledgment of the connection between perception,
movement, and understanding, an agile, worldly-wise intelligence that is suspect
of The Truth (the whole and nothing but). The kynic dares to ''fool around''
with the serious discourse of death (the termination of talk). Instead of the voice
of truth at center stage demanding that the dissident voices in the peanut gallery
be silenced, the kynical impulse, which is the protean vitality of change, makes
the stage relevant, but on its own terms, as the butt of jokes. The system has
defects and defectors, escape artists from the convent of the conventional world.
They keep talking as the gavel pounds. They are ''out-of-order.''

The power to resolve, to end discussion, to be original, which means to write
the first and last word at once (the *alpha* and *omega* of divine universalism), is
the power to grant legitimate voice to a specific body of knowledge or person
and silence ''the rest'' by explaining them into mute resource base. One might
well argue that the ''real power'' is in those who do the granting of voice. This
is not wrong, but it assumes a duality that is not necessary. Francois Lyotard
(1984) has argued that in the narrative process of defining what is real (knowledge), the very act of narration is self-legitimating. The storyteller is ''legitimated by the simple fact that they do what they do'' (Lyotard, 1984: 23). As
author(ity) they define what is said and *done*.

The ''research game'' of scientific discourse might seem to offer a refuge
from self-legitimating megalomaniacs. And, in fact, the subjection of truth
claims to dialectical interrogation by others leads to consensual validation. Objectivity is thus intersubjective agreement. Solipsism is defeated, right? But, in

the wake of modern mass movements of destruction, such as the Nazi Holocaust, the consensus theory of truth has become suspect. In fact, it has been since the trials of Anaxagoras and Socrates for "impiety." When reflecting on Jurgen Habermas's (1992) argument with Nicolas Luhmann (1982), Lyotard (1984: 66) writes:

Diskurs is his [Habermas's] ultimate weapon against the theory of the stable system. The cause is good, but the argument is not. Consensus has become an outmoded and suspect value. But justice as a value is neither outmoded nor suspect. We must thus arrive at an idea and practice of justice that is not linked to that of consensus.

Consensus is the end of dialogue and the beginning of power/action.

THE CONVENT AND CHASTITY OF TRUTH

On one hand, all truthsayers claim to be neutral channelers, disinterested vessels that receive The Truth. But on the other hand, they rarely reject the accolades of the "followers" they cultivate; followers who want so much to believe. When truthsayers stoop to the consensus theory of truth, then convention is enforced with great intensity. However, truthsayers prefer to be seen as mediums that truth happens to, sometimes even against their wills. Being the unconscious victim of truth actually enhances the truthsayers' status. They are chosen, not choosers. Their objective innocence and purity is enhanced because The Truth forces itself upon them. They are surprised by their own research results, so it must be true. In this chaste view, the best, most disinterested truthsayers, from the Bible to John Locke, are really pristine lumps of malleable clay. They are literally mindless. Purity is admired as in "pure" science and "pure" mathematics. Truthsayers are different from the rest of us, specially "touched," "naturally (or supernaturally) gifted," "clean," as in the sanitation of controlled experiments. The battle for the least conscious awareness of what one is doing rages. The most naive win.

But we mere mortals suspect that the truthsayers (including scientists and other modern experts) are wrong when they claim that (unlike the narrative production of truth) no social bond is necessary for their truth to live and breathe, that truth has no perspective, that it is transcendental and pure of the pollution of contingency (time). Kynics suspect that hermeneutics *is* presumed, for a scientific community must share a language in order to be able to debate and agree, to "network"; what the physicist Fred Hoyle (1992: 61) condescendingly calls "scenarios." We suspect that the truthsayer is really one of us, that we share a sordid history and human odor sedimented in the language and "flesh of the world" (Merleau-Ponty, 1964); and that language is *not* a scientific product. That, as Hans-Georg Gadamer (1975) has argued, language and the world are always-already, that they do not belong to us. We belong to them as we do them. The world and prescientific language are necessary conditions for all communal activities, *including* science, to exist. And, like all sign systems, language is arbitrary. Magic, including religions, takes care of this problem by equating language with divine and mystical generative power itself—direct, concrete intent. The Book, The Word, The World are all equal. But over the aeons, and through the hermeneutic debates about cultural and linguistic translation, interpretation, relativism, and relevance, we lowly types secretly begin to wonder, does God change His mind? Can He create a rock that He could not lift? Augustine assures us that this is an ignorant (and nearly heretical) question, because God is not in time, so He cannot change His mind. I guess that that is why damnation is eternal (which somehow also must include the past and present, so that when I did the sins in the past, which justify my damnation, I did them while already in hell). The truth eludes stoops like me.

But, modern truthsayers strongly insist that neither intent nor meaning is real. So, can I wallpaper my living room with their computer-generated truths? Politically speaking, "only" at a price. So don't take seriously their so serious claims of the arbitrariness of signs, of the fallacy of intentionality, their disinterestedness, or the meaninglessness of meaning. Their meanings and intentions are sacrosanct.

More specifically, as Nietzsche, Edmund Husserl (1962), and (the late) Ludwig Wittgenstein noted, what is necessary for science (or any other communal activity) is a shared lifeworld and "language-game" with conventional rules and criteria (Wittgenstein, 1958: 5). This world, this game "simply is the case," it exists so long as we are interested in playing it. The metacriteria of which language-game is "best" is rooted in human *desire*. They depend on what we want the game to do to and for us. Otherwise, the language-game itself has no "good or bad." Like culture, it simply is the case. It is life for its own sake, self-validating and mutable. If we change the rules, the game ceases to exist, for the game is nothing but the sum of rules; new rules, new game. Without a master game, a metanarrative, one cannot say that one game is "better" than the others, only that one is more interesting, desirable, pleasing, serving than the invisible alternatives that are ever-present as potential.

So, a necessary condition for the existence of scientific truth is communication (hermeneutics), which is neither a product of science nor uniformly consistent. This basis for science seems pretty shaky. Science, having learned from other failed systems like magic and myth, avoids this by proudly, bravely insisting that it only speaks the language of probability, that *only* probability exists. In its zeal for being only probably correct, science goes overboard to the point of being absolutely sure that it is only probably correct; and that degrees thereof are calculated using mathematical logic that is absolutely certain about being accidental.

We are certain that we only know 68.75 percent of the truth. Really. Zero and one hundred are assumed so that we can calculate how much of the truth we know. Frustration sets in because the kynic will not allow the false innocence to slip by unchallenged, the trick of rhetoric to go unnoticed. The truthsayer asks us to "give" him or her the premises. Once "given," then the machine of systematic thinking can take it (the truth) from there. Automation commences. But the kynic senses that what is being asked for is her silence, her complicity to muzzle herself, her mindless devotion. For, once the premises are given, then the only talk allowed is preordained, prefabricated, predetermined, predictable. The kynic is automatically defined an "outlier." A not-so-"standard" deviation, that should, for the sake of parsimony and utility, be cut off like the two tails of the "natural" bell curve. Dissident speech is at best "tolerated," until it is cut off, when it is time to "progress," to move on to the next conquest.

Narrative knowledge too, presumes community. Narrative knowledge formation is, however, condemned by science for being barbaric and primitive. And yet,

Scientific knowledge cannot know and make known that it is the true knowledge without resorting to the other, narrative, kind of knowledge, which from its point of view is no knowledge at all. Without such recourse it would be in the position of presupposing its own validity and would be stooping to what it condemns: begging the question, proceeding on prejudice. (Lyotard, 1984: 29)

This is precisely what motivated Husserl's entire project of phenomenology. That is, his realization that either science, too, is self-legitimating (is validated by its own internal processes) and therefore no better than narrative discourse, or relies on a transcendental ground ("first philosophy") of indubitable principles such as the Cartesian *cogito ergo sum*, which is more fundamental, essential, and therefore privileged than science, which science, of course, rejects. Since science is not a naturally occurring phenomenon (Bacon did not discover the scientific method lying in a forest), and since scientific claims are contingent upon additional information, Husserl believed that phenomenology would save science from the absurdity of relativism by grounding it. But he "failed." But since nothing is absolute, he absolutely could not fail absolutely. Furthermore, empirical science is not an empirical thing, it is a philosophy, a metaphysic that guides a certain style of investigation. It explains what the empirical is. So empirical science cannot validate itself by its own criteria. In fact, it violates its own criteria of existence. This, among other absurdities, indicates that science is merely a cultural artifact, a mode of discourse, defining, categorizing, arranging, organizing, inventing, communicating. It too is human, all too human. Rather than transcending space/time, the invention of science can be localized in space/time, next to the rest of us. Relativity theory absurdly claims that "everything" is relative except itself.

FROM THE MONASTERY TO THE UTILITY ROOM

Science, like philosophy and religion, is about nothing less than The Truth. As an institution, its power is derived from defining what is and is not real.

Since that is out-of-reach, however, cultures, including scientific discourse, are self-legitimizing. Thus, science is never "concluded." The Truth keeps getting truer. Progress and science are synonymous. Absolute truth perpetually recedes into what Husserl (1970) called infinite or "transfinite" horizons. To avoid this, science plays another power game, that of utility. Consequently, a variety of language-games are utilized in the pragmatic interests of power. If it "works" it's true. Or according to consumer culture's "pecuniary truth," if it sells it's true (Henry, 1963). The false is lazy.

Truthsayers attempt to inoculate their version of reality from interrogation by claiming a holistic status for it. Only *nothing* (real) can be outside of the system. Reality is natural, objective, independent of subjective interests, and since only nothing can be outside of reality, that's why the subject defines herself and her lifeworld out of existence. He is "disinterested." Science, like religion, claims to be of spontaneous generation, like the old theory that flies spring from rotting meat.

This is so for religion, philosophy, and science. In this way they are all totalitarian master narratives. During speeches, Adolf Hitler used to grab the flag of the Third Reich and loudly proclaim that it had been "ripped from nothing." Like building a boat while at sea, truthsayers arbitrarily launch their projects, but once underway, everyone must get onboard, or face the sharks of chaos. "It's not my fault you're going to hell. It simply is the case. Read the scales of blind justice yourself." The inevitable wheels of the cosmic machine turn without consciousness, automatically, objectively, causally. Thus, a reality becomes The Reality (Baudrillard, 1983; Foucault, 1980). Science may protest that it does not belong in this sordid company of "dark ageism," that it is fundamentally superior, insisting absolutely that it has no intent, no meaning, that it is only and *always* (permanently) provisional. In that case it becomes that which it hates most, rhetoric. Which is exactly what Aristotle (who invented empiricism and probability theory) said. The enthymeme is the mode of artic-ulation for rhetoric, and the syllogism the mode of philosophy. René Descartes (1941) made the same argument, thus launching the modern project of science.

This author prefers to call "truth" a civilizational expression. It is not "about," but it is, like art, artifacts, marching, battling, loving, constructing, maintaining, destructing, birthing, and dying. This is why William Carlos Wil-liams declined to stay in Paris (where truth presumably was) with literati elite like Hemingway, Stein, et al., and returned to New Jersey to help women give birth. He believed that truth is not an abstraction or dissociated formalism. The "about" of modern referentiality is only one truth. This realization is articulated by Jean Gebser's (1985: 309) notion of "verition." Truth is embodied, not disembodied. The truth of the human world simply is. It need not be rendered, as if it is "somewhere else" ("hidden") as according to the ancient doctrine of "hermetic semiosis" manifested by the "followers of the veil" (*Adepti del Velame*) (Eco, Rorty, and Culler, 1992: 45, 54).

But it is also important to laugh at the self. When this happens, what then is laughing? This would take us to a totally non-Western world, that must be left to other times and places.

HONEST? CON-FESSIONS

Before the officials came to take Galileo Galilei away to the inquisition, he knew they were coming. In preparation for their arrival, he set up his telescope to view the most wonderful spectacle in the night sky, the moon. He had hoped that once they saw for themselves the mountains and spherical surface, they might be willing to take a look at the moons of Jupiter, which proved that not everything in the universe revolves around the Earth; one of his heretical claims.

My belief, my faith in the abductive clues available, is that the moons around Jupiter existed long before Galileo or his telescope; that they have an independent existence with complete disregard for Galileo, or his telescope's existential status. In strictest honesty, neither I nor anyone else can prove this. It is a faith. As the communication scholar George Campbell (1823) and the Hungarian chemist Michael Polanyi (1958) have rightly argued, even natural science is a thoroughly communicative phenomenon, based on "tacit knowledge" that can not be explicitly stated, but is absorbed through practice (doing), trust, and tradition (hermeneutic horizon). Both modes of "knowing" are rhetorical and pragmatic in nature (of "reputable use"). I have never, myself, empirically witnessed most of what I was told in my science classes, but still I believe in those things.

This trust is not utterly blind, however. Trust is the result of a very powerful rhetorical device, demonstration. Not so much the natural sciences, but their engineering derivatives, have demonstrated many times in the past that, by employing Newtonian mechanics for instance, they can in fact solve problems by making things that never before existed, like bridges and airplanes that work. By contrast, the social sciences have failed miserably to solve any of the problems that called them into being, like violence, alienation, bigotry, suicide, poverty, injustice, insanity, and so on. And when social science is taken seriously and widely practiced, as with intelligence testing, it raises as many problems as it solves. Social science is discredited, for instance, by the specter of psychology in the courtroom, where even the sanity of a defendant cannot be clearly established by "experts." This is because these "problems," these concepts are just that, theoretical concepts (justice, poverty, sanity), discursive entities, and as such, they are relative.

When it comes to human behavior, manuals on parenting, tenure decisions, penal "corrections," and a myriad of other instances when people honestly try their best to be "objective," subjectivity is rampant. After all, we are subjects, not objects. Because natural science deals with not-conscious things (like molecules, gases, and bits of tissue), these objects have no interest in what is being done to them. In the natural sciences, the objects of study are, for the most part, *believed* to be naturally occurring and totally disinterested in the scientists who study them (scientists who are themselves very interested). In pharmaccutical laboratories (for instance) even "dumb" subject animals quickly learn that when the researcher appoaches it means something, and expectation alters their chemistry, confounding quality control. Subjects have interests, moons do not.

The social scientific use of the operational definition, and other instruments, is much more problematic than mere observation. Operationalization is a definition which presumes *a priori* that a "thing" *is* a measurement. An operational definition includes the means of measuring the entity. The physical sciences restrict themselves, according to the Kantian schema, to things which have extension and are therefore measurable. Also, in natural science things are almost always discovered by accident or merely "given." Like Galileo's swinging church lanterns, most of the objects of natural science predate science. Science constituted a new way of looking at them. Still, most objects of science are discovered by accident, like background radiation. Science is a source of "news." Once discovered, then the scientists do phenomenology (although most wouldn't call it that even though Einstein and his hero Ernst Mach, Werner Heisenberg, and many others explicitly have) in order to determine more fully the "essential nature" of the entity they wish to investigate.

Physics differs from phenomenology in that it is concerned to establish laws. Phenomenology only establishes the possibilities. Thus, phenomenology would be the grammar of the description of those facts on which physics builds its theories. To explain is more than to describe; but every explanation contains a description. (Wittgenstein, 1975: 51)

Wittgenstein abandons this special language of phenomenology, what he once called "primary language," and instead comes to speak of languages that "serve purposes." Language speaks for itself, and nothing else (Wittgenstein, 1974).

The instruments natural scientists develop (over time) must conform to the essential properties of the object of study. An optical telescope is useless for observing blood pressure or radio waves.

Operationalization, in the social sciences, however, too often works in the opposite direction. In the social sciences, far too often, an entity exists as a measurement, and only as a measurement. It has none of the Kantian *a priori* properties that mark it as an empirical thing (duration in time and extension in space). Many social-scientific entities exist "by definition," or as statistical entities "discovered" as correlations between measures. Reliability is assured by insisting that others use the *very same* technique, which is possible because operationalization is an ideational process generating pure mathematical entities, thereby assuring replicability. This is convenient but not satisfying of strict natural scientific standards. Natural scientists do not use the identical instrument. Their instruments are empirical not ideal, so they cannot be "the same." Not only Galileo's telescope reveals the moons of Jupiter.

The trick of the social scientist is to "know better," to expose the unconsciousness of the rest, to say, "yes it seems obvious but what you did not realize about yourself is. . . ." This is the hermeneutics of the veil mentioned above. The truth about me, I cannot see. It is sublimated, and repressed. It takes technique in the hands of the truthsayer to divine me, to reveal the true me to me. And once done, once exposed to myself, am I still myself, or have I been cured of my self-delusion, changed into someone else? Do I now stand "corrected," "reeducated," "de-deluded?" Am I the "new man?" If "I" am now properly well-adjusted, what did "I" adjust to? And what if there is something like height, or skin color that escapes my newly acquired self-monitoring and self-adjusting? Do I grow a "double-consciousness"? (Adell, 1994; Gilroy, 1993).

While under house arrest for life, the unrepentant Copernican Galileo did present a double-consciousness. He wrote his famous *Dialogue Concerning the Two Chief World Systems* (1632) in such a way as to get around the church censors. In the fragmented mind, does one self despise the other? Is self-hatred the fruit of social engineering? I must change because I am incorrect, but while my behavior can be modified by stimulus manipulation, "I" must work to change my "heart's" desires, values, wants, and beliefs. This is self-denial, which is seeing one's self through the critical eyes of the authorities. Making their eyes mine, their voice my voice, seeing everything from their perspective, thinking "their way." But what if their perspective is one that despises me? I become the conundrum of a set of all possible sets, that cannot contain itself.

Not only Galileo looked at the moon. Not only he described it, and marvelled at it long before it was measured. He brought a new way of looking at it, a new "attitude," which yielded a "new moon." But, other versions persist and, via integration, give each other meaning. A scientific way of seeing presumes a nonscientific one. Without one, the other does not exist, as such. There is no central perspective for compelling critique, but instead a multiplicity of perspectives that no single "grand view" can subsume. In 1928, Walter Benjamin put it this way:

Fools, who complain about the demise of critique. For its time has long since run out. Critique is a matter of proper distance. It is at home in a world where perspectives and prospects are important and where it was still possible to assume a point of view. In the meantime, things have become much too close for comfort for human society. "Disinterestedness," the "unbiased perspective," have become lies, if not the completely naive expression of plain incompetence. (Benjamin, 1969: 11)

Since Aristotle, hermeneutics (the first great general study of communication after the analysis of persuasion specifically) has maintained that "mediation" always involves interpretation. Maps do not look at all like the terrain. One must learn to read them. Measurement is a kind of interpretation. Both Bacon (1942) and Aristotle (1991) understood that measurement is a cultural product, an activity, a human behavior, a way to translate things into a shared language and thereby promote agreement (reliability). Measurement does not exist independent of humans. It is not a naturally occurring phenomenon. Measurement is a technology, a tool. One does measuring, and produces measurements. Measurements are messages. Many communication scholars (Foucault, 1972; Husserl, 1977; Gurwitsch, 1974; Derrida, 1977) have investigated the process of operationalization, the discursive formation of "scientific" messages, and the construction of a scientific simulacrum (mathematical copy of reality) (Baudrillard, 1983). This reflexive analysis tends to outrage the true believers in operationalism, who dogmatically resist having their self-privileged, ontological position investigated just like they themselves investigate others, such as the agenda-setting construction of reality by journalists. Naive operationalists refuse the mantel of mere mortal. "How dare you study me, like I study everyone else!" Because the objects of social science are cultural entities, without spatial extension, the validity of such operational reckoning is probably narrowly restricted to the ingenuity of the researcher, his or her cultural knowledge, and the place and time for which the entity was devised. Such limitations are no one's "fault." It is the nature of the subject matter, human motive, as compared with molecular causation.

Even if we do discover a complete unified theory, it would not mean that we would be able to predict events in general, for two reasons. The first is the limitation [of] the uncertainty principle. . . . There is nothing we can do to get around that. In practice, however, this first limitation is *less restrictive* [emphasis added] than the second one. It arises from the fact that we could not solve the equations of the theory exactly, except in very simple situations. We cannot even solve exactly for the motion of three bodies in Newton's theory of gravity, and the difficulty increases with the number of bodies and the complexity of the theory . . . we have, as yet, had little success in predicting human behavior from mathematical equations! (Hawking, 1988: 168)

DEFINING

Change suggests that social science is arbitrary and contingent, dependent upon interpersonal agreement (convention) for its epistemic strength. Social science is "improving," "progressing." Some editors of social science journals demonstrate a powerful prejudice against citing "old" research because it is "out-of-date," no longer relevant or generalizable to today's reality. They may be correct. The Micronesians that Margaret Mead made famous are now gone— modernized. Her descriptions may be very accurate, but are no longer applicable to anyone. I believe that it is possible that one genius can be correct while practically everyone else is wrong. But I know that this one-person truth is impossible to know.

And yet, I also believe that much conventional (popular "mainstream") social science is too much a product of discursive construction, the "herd." For instance, "race" is such a discursive construction. Differences in color are not. Ironically, while race has become rather irrelevant in the physical sciences, it remains an important parameter in social science. So long as many people share the discourse of "race" and play this language-game (including social scientists), it is a real product. As such it is not independent from human action. The consequences of racism take on reified lives of their own, like immigration quotas, racial correlational thinking, and segregation. Unless one ascribes to the metaphysics of lingualism, which I do not, phenotypes exist independently of discursive formation, but "race" does not. Young children can and do recognize people who look "different," but they do not generalize to the ideational level of "race." They are very empirical. They have not yet been trained (internalized an ideology) to think in terms of mathematical entities like "variables," or political stereotypes like "enemy." Association is not an empirical thing.

REFERENCES

Adell, S. (1994) *Double-Consciousness/Double Bind*. Urbana: University of Illinois Press.

Adorno, T. W., and M. Horkheimer. (1972) *Dialectic of Enlightenment*. New York: Herder and Herder.

Aristotle. (1991) *Art of Rhetoric*. London: Harvard University Press.

Bacon, F. (1942) *New Atlantis*. New York: Classics Club, W. J. Black.

Baudrillard, J. (1983) *Simulations*. New York: Semiotext(e).

Benjamin, W. (1969) *Illuminations*. New York: Schocken Books.

Campbell, G. (1823) *The Philosophy of Rhetoric*. Boston: Charles Ewer.

Derrida, J. (1977) *Edmund Husserl's Origin of Geometry: An Introduction*. Stony Brook, NY: Nicholas Hays.

Descartes, R. (1941) *A Discourse on Method*. London: J. M. Dent and Sons.

Eco, U., R. Rorty, and J. Culler. (1992) *Interpretation and Overinterpretation*. Cambridge, England: Cambridge University Press.

Foucault, M. (1972) *The Archaeology of Knowledge and the Discourse on Language*. New York: Pantheon Books.

———. (1980) *Power/Knowledge*. New York: Pantheon Books.

Gadamer, H. G. (1975) *Truth and Method*. New York: Seabury Press.

Gebser, J. (1985) *The Ever-Present Origin*. Athens: Ohio University Press.

Gigon, O. (1959) *Grundproblem der antiken Philosophie*. Bern: Francke.

Gilroy, P. (1993) *The Black Atlantic: Modernity and Double Consciousness*. Cambridge, MA: Harvard University Press.

Gurwitsch, A. (1974) *Phenomenology and the Theory of Science*. Evanston, IL: Northwestern University Press.

Habermas, J. (1992) *Postmodern Thinking*. Cambridge, MA: MIT Press.

Hawking, S. (1988) *A Brief History of Time*. New York: Bantam Books.

Henry, J. (1963) *Culture Against Man*. New York: Random House.

Hofstede, G., and M. Bond. (1984) "Hofstede's Culture Dimensions." *Journal of Cross-Cultural Psychology* 15, no. 4: 417–433.

Hoyle, F. (1992) Essay in *Stephen Hawking's "A Brief History of Time": A Reader's Companion*, edited by S. Hawking. New York: Bantam.

Husserl, E. (1962) *Ideas*. New York: Collier Books.

———. (1970) *The Crisis of European Sciences and Transcendental Phenomenology*. Evanston, IL: Northwestern University Press.

————. (1977) *The Origin of Geometry*. New York: Nicholas Hays.

Kramer, E. M. (1993) ''The Origin of Television as Civilizational Expression.'' In *Semiotics 1990: Sources in Semiotics, Vol XI*, edited by J. Deely et al. Lanham, MD: University Press of America (pp. 28–37).

Laertius. (1925) *Lives and Opinions of Eminent Philosophers*. New York: G. P. Putnam's Sons.

Luhmann, N. (1982) *The Differentiation of Society*. New York: Columbia University Press.

Lyotard, F. (1984) *The Postmodern Condition*. Minneapolis: University of Minnesota Press.

Marx, K. (1967) *Das Kapital, Vol. 1*. New York: International Publishers.

McLuhan, M. (1962) *The Gutenberg Galaxy: The Making of Typographic Man*. Toronto: University of Toronto Press.

Merleau-Ponty, M. (1964) *The Primacy of Perception*. Evanston, IL: Northwestern University Press.

Niehues-Probsting, H. (1979) *Der Kynismus des Diogenes und der Begriff des Zynismus*. Munich: W. Fink.

Nietzsche, F. (1974) *The Gay Science*. New York: Vintage.

Parsons, T. (1951) *The Social System*. Glencoe, IL: Free Press.

Polanyi, M. (1958) *Personal Knowledge: Towards a Post-Critical Philosophy*. Chicago: University of Chicago Press.

Reichenbach, H. (1944) *Philosophic Foundation of Quantum Mechanics*. Berkeley: University of California Press.

Russell, B., and A. N. Whitehead. (1967) *Principia Mathematica*. Cambridge, England: Cambridge University Press.

Sloterdijk, P. (1987) *Critique of Cynical Reason*. Minneapolis: University of Minnesota Press.

Weizsacker, C. F. (1975–77) *Quantum Theory and the Structures of Time and Space*. Munich: C. Hanser.

Wittgenstein, L. (1958) *Philosophical Investigations*. Oxford, England: Basil Blackwell.

————. (1974) *Philosophical Grammar*. Oxford, England: Basil Blackwell.

————. (1975) *Philosophical Remarks*. Oxford, England: Basil Blackwell.

2

Comparative Validities: Styles of Expression

> Those who claim to have all of the solutions are part of the problem.
> —George Carlin

PRELIMINARY REMARKS

The modern world is essentially marked by the arrogance of materialistic metaphysicians. But it is not uniquely privileged as the only vain and narrow-minded age. Each age has its glory and foolishness, its delusions and productions. Each age believes it is The Light Age. Each age has doubt. Each people believe they are the "chosen ones." Each life is a struggle that swings from agony to ecstasy, boredom to invention. Humans, all too human, busy themselves with great and mundane concerns, preparations for life and afterlife, diversions from nothing, because all that is is diversionary. In the modern world of spatialism (linearity), happiness is a pursuit and progress a constant. Ceaseless mobility leads away from the sense of habitat and into a world of continual obsolescence and boredom because, when we dedicate ourselves to things, then we are dedicated to a world that is always growing old. In such a linear world, loss and longing becomes the constant state of being. The impossible trick in the modern world is to continue to want something after you've already got it. The solution offered, that is, to just get more, more things, status, power, does not escape the materialistic conundrum. Quantity cannot address quality. Likewise, unperspectival spiritualism cannot address material needs. An integral way that avoids the duality of quantity/quality is necessary.

In the modern world, only extension and surface exist. For instance, race is the color and shape of the surface of the flesh (phenotype). It is rationalized by explicit (unambiguous, operationalized, categorical) definition as in modern social scientific, legal, and genetic discourses. Ironically, for social "scientists," who pride themselves as being just like their "harder" scientific brothers, geneticists no longer recognize race as a meaningful category. Geneticists, like quantum physicists, recognize that nothing is "hard" and fast anymore.

Increasingly, humans can make themselves in accord with their own imaginations. We now grow human ears on the backs of mice, and mix mice with rabbits. Unlike most, if not all other forms of life on Earth, humans do not passively adapt to the environment but instead, they adapt the environment to their own interests, wants, and needs. Interests, wants, needs, and capacities constitute the very shape of the human world.

When gross counting is the interest, however, then one must be categorized as in a census (or other formal procedure) in order to make policy decisions and to allocate resources in an organized fashion. This is the purview of the social scientist. This is the domain of the interest of analytics and measurement. A necessary condition for measurement is a spatialized (visiocentric) mode of thought. For most visiocentric (what is visible is what is real) moderns, race is simply (without reflection) physical feature. Of course, the phrase "physical feature" is already extremely complex since these words are category statements which themselves are not physical entities. This is why David Hume (1973) was correct to note that the metaphysic of "empiricism" is absurd. It defines itself (a metaphysical philosophy) as meaninglessly nonexistent.

For the modern, race is an arbitrary sign. Hence, for analysis of the modern notion of race only (although no such pure state exists), the analysis of "visible surfaces" (also category statements, *not* "empirical" ones) is appropriate. However, the arbitrariness of the sign is superseded by continual efforts to correlate color with other measures like income, and IQ, and to emotionally associate color with ethical and aesthetic valuations. "Race" is a super-category. Measurement, as a process, presumes the ideational nature of transcendentalism. To measure and to compare involves the arrogant application of one scale (a single and arbitrarily devised standard) for different things. Comparison is a transcendental process pursued in the interest of evaluation and control/standardization.

But in order to appresentiate magical, mythical, and perspectival (modern) styles of racing, for instance, systasis is necessary (see Chapter 5). Synairesis (recognition of the integral nature of these different worlds) is an awareness that all human creations are expressions of consciousness/world. Artifacts manifest human styles, including valuations/priorities. All fragmenting ordinations of time and space (regardless of civilization or culture) presume a nonoriginary origin that is neither spatial nor temporal; a nondistinction which all distinctions presume; hence, the title of Jean Gebser's (1949) magnum opus, *Ursprung und Gegenwort* (*The Ever-Present Origin*, 1985). World presents multiple cosmologies and invisible but vital potential.

Synairetic awareness is a recognition that the so-called ineffectual "past" designations (magic and myth, for instance) are not extinct, but are present as influential structures of awareness. Hence, the recognition of "ancient" Platonism in the robe of modern Galilean-style science (explicated later in this chapter). Because synairesis does not pledge its allegiance to any exclusive metaphysic like materialism, it can appreciate how we see through, for instance, ruins.

For example, ruins are ruins of something which is both absent and present. We see the invisible through the visible. We readily "see" through the crumbling and sun-bleached stones of a pre-Columbian pyramid or the Acropolis, the whole articulation of an attitude, or cosmic orientation. We can reconstruct them on computer screens and on the ground by extending broken lines and curves into empty space. We can and do ask questions of these artifacts, these expressions of need, desire, want, capability, belief, fear, and so forth. Similarly, one can look at the Hubble space telescope and ask, what is it? It is titanium, plastic, glass. It is an instrument, a vehicle, a machine. But it is also an expressed wish, desire, need. Instruments embody a power-drive to "see into the dark" beyond the eyes.

Although the world of the Sphinx and the world of the space telescope are different worlds, they share human expressivity itself with us. And they answer, presenting their cosmologies, themselves. They are not only about something, they establish and manifest values. They are *manifest* desire, wish, capability, need. They *establish* these human ambitions and fears. But these worlds change before our eyes. They are meaningful, even fascinating *because they change, because they are alien*, different from us.[1]

Magic

Likewise, one can systatically attend to race. "Race" presents layers of articulation that can be "seen through" synairetically (see Chapter 7). Magically, race (and very often class) is expressed as blood/semen-based identity, these being the universal magical fluids presumed to ground "breeds," Christian communion, and vampirism, only to mention a few forms of transformational phenomena. Blood holds the very identity of the person or animal, so that when consumed its characteristics, its essence, is passed to the one who drinks it. This belief led from the practice of bleeding to intravenous medication and transfusional treatments. It also grounds the peculiar fear surrounding HIV. Birth and death are associated with blood as are the extension of self and ownership of children determined by sexual "propriety."

Just as the consuming of the blood and flesh of another human or animal is believed to transfer essential qualities to the consumer, this same magical transformation often occurs when a modern human, reduced to the label "consumer," consumes a product. People are proud, and identify with what they consume and produce. "Racial cleansing" ("ethnic" often being misused in its stead) almost always includes rape as well as murder.

Myth

Race is also expressed mythologically as ethnic tradition. For instance, the royal family of England, beginning with Alfred the Great, claims to trace its existence to the Saxon and Danish god Odin, on the one hand, and Antenor, cousin to Priam of Troy, on the other. However, much of the pomp and ritual of English royalty is actually less than two hundred years old. Yet it is presented as being timelessly ancient, and therefore sacred (Hobsbawm and Ranger, 1983). The imaginal aspect of story telling indicates the mythic aspect of traditionalism. That too, has been commodified as a major tourist attraction and source of tabloid gossip.

Taking one's own pictures, and buying souvenirs, enables one to form a personal attachment to a place or event, to alter one's identity as being "part of history." Visiocentric modern humans present such objects as proof of being; being associated with whatever it is that one deems important enough to record for the sake of some posterior. For the modern, biography is the essence of self. For instance, I may clone an exact duplicate of my physical "self," but what constitutes "me" remains as an inhabitant of this body. The "me" that cannot be duplicated, which is always different and never "the same," is memory. The modern emphasis on self is mythically expressed as a relationship between biography and historic tradition. We collect and re-collect bits of stuff to prove to others, and perhaps ourselves, our place in history, our being. Being in modernity is dependent upon memographic traces such as birth certificates and other official markers, home movies, diaries, and other recordings. To the modern mind, if one is not recorded, one never was. The phenomenon of knick-knacks proliferated with the curious invention of museum space where permanence is promoted, where things of the world are carefully reserved and arranged for the sake of display.

Tradition, that repository of fact and justification, that definer of self, of things and selves already done and finished; as sure a ground as any and obviously worthy of defense to the death, is actually fickle. Tradition is loyal to affections, public relations, and personal needs. While it pretends to be the master (narrative) it serves the capricious needs of many masters. History is no more "concrete" than ancient Egyptian ruins. It, too, can be seen systatically as transparent and shifting. History is written by (a) the literate, and/or (b) the winners. It is a peculiar desire (will-power-drive) to control the memories of the future. Like sacred temples, history attempts but fails to fix the permanent constant.

Histories, like other artifacts, manifest interests, needs, and capacities. So-called "great" historic figures are *selected* and recouped from oblivion to act as totems of a *current* wish. They become fetishes of worldviews and repositories of values. For example, the Renaissance thinkers who acted as midwives to Aristotle's second coming chose him from among many other historic figures. Why? Why did Martin Heidegger select a different pivotal figure, Heraclitus, from which he derived a vastly different history of the West? For many behaviorists, history, truth, "daybreak," begins with Carl Rogers. For many post-modernists it is Friedrich Nietzsche whom they use as the prime legitimator in the phraseology of "according to. . . ." Aristotle did not choose or determine his followers. They chose him. From the mythic mode of being, history determines the present, but systatically, history is both determining and determined. And the either/orism of which comes first is indeterminate. Histories manifest the interests of those who write them. The real power lies in the agenda setters, those who select and canonize. But the causes of their prejudices seem to be ideological/historical. One cause causes the other, and vice versa. Temporal "priority" is erased.

As Aristotle was raised to a nearly divine status, so Plato's star set. The pagan emphasis on the self and experience-based knowledge, promoted by Aristotle, legitimized the hedonism of the emergent class of wealthy but (and ironically) nonaristocratic traders in Renaissance Italy. Likewise, Ptolemy's grid system for topography had remained a curiosity of little consequence in Greece until this same class of Italians perceived in it the potential for global navigation and vastly expanded trade (wealth). When scholars berate us to "know history," we must ask "which one?" (see Chapter 6 about Afro-American history). When they tell us, they are telling us very much about their own interests and ambitions. An era that writes histories of war and patriarchal power tells us less about the past than about the ambitions, dreams, prejudices, and wishes of the present. As feminist histories and histories of "everyday life" become more popular, a shift in interest is evinced. A similar shift occurred when, to the shock of the client audience, artists like Rembrandt and the French Impressionists stopped painting flattering portraits of the bourgeoisie and began painting "mundane" people and spaces. The same is true of theoretical, methodological, and ideological "positions." The method one chooses, for instance, betrays what one wants to "get at," to *establish*, to make evident, to "honor" with learned attention. There is no dance without the dancer, and there is no experiment without the experimenter. Incantations like "value-freedom," "detachment," "systematic thinking," and "objectivity" are pathetic maxims.

Mental-Rationality

Perspectivally, race is expressed as a legal-rational status, eugenically, statistically, and as a systematically arranged (strict) grammar of genetic codification. The color of one's skin can identify one, symbolize some other quality, or be seen as purely arbitrary. But even the arbitrary has meaning. To be arbitrary is not the same as being meaningless or senseless. All civilizations have their respective "validities" and "limitations," but this polyversal recognition is available only by the (a)waring (or "seeing through" or transparency) of identities constituted by a variety of world "structures" (or "logics" or "grammars"). Each has its own "way."

MAGIC CONSCIOUSNESS

According to Gebser (1985), at any place, "historical period," or moment when magic consciousness predominates, it manifests a world that is univalent whereby a one-dimensional unity is expressed as global identity. The magic world is characterized by equal validity and significance without differentiation. It is a world of being, rather than having. This nondifferentiated world is expressed by the identity (not exchange as such) of *pars pro parte* (a part for a part), *totum pro toto* (all for all), *totum pro parte* (the whole for the part), and *pars pro toto* (a part for the whole) (1985: 50). The magic world is "prior to" (consciousness of) space or time perceived as discrete quanta.

Magic people are not individuated, but rather "share" (are of) the same blood and semen. They may see themselves all as children of a single source as in premodern Japan (*ie* as compared with *kazoku*) (Ikeda, 1992). The magic world is one of unity, which is evinced by pictorial representations of an emergent awareness of "enmeshment" in the whole. Tapestry-like patterns and geometric-ritualistic interlacing characterize expressions of magical holism (see Gebser's extensive investigation of such patterns in ancient "art," 1985: 49–63).

It is in this sense that modern systems theory expresses a rational veneer or veneration of logical explanation, such as when Anatol Rapoport (1968) introduces systems theory by defining system as a "unique whole" with patterns of interdependence. Further rationalization is expressed by attempts to "systematize" the whole, meaning to establish causal hierarchy among the parts, thus giving each a unique function or identity within the biologized (organic) organization (structure).

Gebser has determined that "There is a word group correlating among others the words 'make,' 'mechanism,' 'machine,' and 'might,' which all share a common Indo-European root *mag(h)-*" (Gebser, 1985: 46). According to Gebser, "magic," which is a Greek derivative from Persian origin, connotes man-the-maker now rationalistically articulated through material magic—technology.

The metaphysics of modernity has even been further reduced (in the name of precision) by means of the so-called linguistic turn.[2] In the modern world, reductionistic misconceptions argued by neo-Heideggerians, conversation analysts, and variable analysts alike, are understandable as failures to articulate the magic of the world, including the magic of making sense and making conversation without a line of reasoning. Linguistics and fragmenting analytics (i.e., phonemes and semes, turn-taking, and bits and bytes) are to communication what atoms and molecules are to the physical world. Lingualism reduces the world to being either writerly or readerly, phonocentric or logocentric, and so forth.

The ever-present archaic is prelinguistic. One can describe a caress poetically, chemically, legally, physiologically, and so on. For instance, a caress is "really" an outside force that stimulates (is transduced by) neuroreceptors in the cutaneous and subcutaneous levels of the skin. Bioelectricity runs on a carrier wave up to the brain where it is transduced once again into a different level of neurophysiological energy. This reified and haptified effort to express what a caress is remains fundamentally, ontologically, different from the caress itself. The caress is prelinguistic, or in nonlinear terms, simply not linguistic. To call it language, or a sign or a symbol, is also to presume an entire terminology and system of designation which are different from the experience of being caressed.

The effort to reduce everything to language is not new with Heidegger but was so conceived by ancients such as Isocrates, who claimed that thinking is in words, and the medieval tradition of sacral text so influential on European biblical scholars, hermeneutics generally, and the Anglo-American tradition of psycho-linguistics initiated by Edward Sapir (1949) and Benjamin Whorf (1956). The identity of experience and thought with words betrays a magical tendency in such theories of communication. Magical words are necessary for things to change. The chant and incantation must be said for the magic to happen. Potential is released through the initiation of vibration that can be felt with the whole body. Wave and medium are the same. The vibration is both inside and out; everywhere. It is acausal. It is always there though sometimes too low to hear. The horns of Tibetan lamas, the bells and fish knockers of Buddhists, the bells of cathedrals, and the call to pray from minarets; all of these disturb the cosmic silence announcing human being. A bell with no clapper is the original state presupposed by the empty, disinterested universe; thus can be interpreted the Hindu hierarchy of self-actualization (stolen by Abraham Maslow, 1968) and Hegel's divine reflection. God is infinitely lonely, so we sing our praises, which means that he sings to himself.

Roland Barthes (1967) tried to articulate the idea of the magic of the world by inflating signification to the point of a "universal semantic." While these efforts are more encompassing, the failure of the linguistic turn to adequately articulate the felt need to overcome dissociation, and the inflation of reading to be all experience, or conversely to reduce all of the world to text, is a symptom of conceptualization itself. Can we think of language only in words? Is there preinterpretive experience? For the semiotician, with her limited and dissociating conception of experience, language itself becomes an aporia such that since everything is a case of language, then the category language is meaningless because there is nothing "outside" of it to which it can have diacritical relations. The bell has no hammer, or as Ludwig Wittgenstein (1971) claimed, the cosmos can be met with either silence or statements. Thus, if everything is language, nothing is language. To say that "x" is a case of language becomes impossible because everything is language. The semantic rule of binary opposition is violated by those who live by that rule, which dissolves the concept of rule.

But Edmund Husserl's (1962) contention that experience is fundamentally experience (of) meaning (if we bracket some"thing"), and Barthes's argument that everything can be a sign remain compelling despite their failures to articulate this condition of, as Maurice Merleau-Ponty (1962) put it, being condemned to meaning. In another way, Paul Watzlawick, Janet Beavin, and Don Jackson (1967) have said that we cannot not communicate, which presumes that

meaning is communicating which involves a spatial conceptualization of transference. If we bracket the spatial presumption, again what is being said is that
we cannot escape significance. While the homeless person lies sleeping on the
sidewalk, although there be no intent to communicate, he is communicating to
the passersby. So, too, is the sunset and the ''song'' bird. This is the magic of
the world.

As Gebser (1985) has noted, other traditions such as the Hindu, Taoist, and
ancient Persian, claim that the world is power (Gk. *dunamis*). In his work *The
World as Will and Representation*, Arthur Schopenhauer (1966) also struggled
to articulate this understanding. So, too, did the earliest articulators of the Judaeo-Christian tradition. Aristotle put it most simply, ''power is the ability to
be and to make be.'' But the binary question of to be or not becomes less clear.
Expression is disruption, distinction, change. Vibrations go forth articulating
space and time. But a Buddhist bell does not stop ringing. It fades slowly. It is
always and never attenuating. You cannot tell when you can no longer hear it.
Despite the sense that it is ''clear as a bell,'' its sound lingers on the edge of
being, which has no edge. Sound is mingled with memory and imagination.
Distinctions dissolve.

Animation

Oration is inspiration and conspiration. The breath, the most fundamental
expression of life, is aspiration. Oration is an attempt to breath life into words,
to make them live, and to inspire the audience; to animate them. Animism is
the essentially magical dimension of all life. The involuntary grunt, the cry, the
chant, the song, the poem, the converse of dialog which is the struggle to conversion, all are fundamental expressions of life. To express is an effort to pronounce and announce. It may be to warn, to react, to express, or to present the
self as an individual, a group member, or as a nondistinct aspect of ''us.'' The
phrase ''let me make myself perfectly clear'' is a statement about the self and
its expression via demarcation (conceptualization).

Sigmund Freud (1918: 101) has correctly argued that animism ''makes it
possible to comprehend the totality of the world from one point, as a continuity.'' But this is not a logical contiguity (identity). He was correct to point out
that animistic magic presents the world as an ''entirety'' (Freud, 1918: 101).
However, Freud, like Wilhelm Wundt (1926), Wilhelm Schmidt (1939), Salo-
mon Reinach (1939), Edward Burnett Tylor (1958), and James George Frazer
(1910), betrays a dualistic rationalization, mistaking magic for ''theory'' that is
''independent of bodies.'' Other Cartesian analytic explanations describe magic
as being ''strategic'' (Reinach), ''externalized spirit'' (Wundt), and ''connectedness'' (Tylor). Magic is prespiritualistic. Animism is pure behavior, and all
deeds, as unitary acts (resulting from union), are predominantly magic (Gebser,
1985: 191). For instance, even Sir Francis Bacon in *Natural History* suggested

putting a salve on the weapon that caused the wound in order to hasten the healing process.

In *The Magic Art*, Frazer mistakenly applied the Cartesian mind/body dualism to magic. He explained magic as "imitation," and the "omnipotence of thought" whereby the magic person fails to understand that control over thoughts is not equal to control over things. But it is the will to wish fulfillment that changes the face of the earth. Imitation presupposes a spatial (perspectival) mode of thinking that enables difference. But animism is nonspatial. Michael Landmann (1974: 27) explains:

One field anthropologist reports a conversation he had with a native whose race regarded the otter as their totem animal. An otter just then happened to be crossing a nearby river. The man said; "Look, how beautifully I am swimming across the river!" To all objections that he had only meant that this animal was his protective spirit, that a special stream of energy linked him with it, . . . the native insisted firmly that he himself was really the otter.

The punctiformal nature of identity and unity is the essential nature of animism. This is why we marvel at automated machines, moving pictures, and virtual reality. This is why many exhibit intense emotions when watching "their" team or gang. The use of words like "my" country, "our" team, and wearing the colors of one's group is an expression of possession. Membership is possessive. One for all and all for one.

The *animus* power of making things happen involves the powers of unification and identification. Every point is transposable with every other point (Pilotta, 1992: 99). Magic world is manifested as the power of interchangeability without regard to linear space-time. The localizable and interested (directional) personal ego is not evident.

Although Benedetto Croce (1960), Giambattista Vico (1974), and George Hegel (1953) rejected the irrational in favor of a history arranged in one sequence, the desire to re-collect memories into histories, things into museum space, and organize experience into taxonomies, manifests a "reasonableness" which is dependent upon a goal-oriented mode of being. History is the attribution of sense to senselessness, direction to the directionless. To make a history is to express a desire, to infuse deeds with magic. "This common and widespread form of historiography is dominated primarily by the masculine point of view of power; even where it inquires as to 'strengths' or 'forces' it reifies the non-substantial factors" (Gebser, 1985: 191).

The *Numinosum*

In 1745, the Pietist Count Zinzendorf discussed the force behind divine right and history as the *numinosum*. Nearly two hundred years later, Rudolf Otto plagiarized Zinzendorf in his discussion of the "*sensus numinis*." The word *numinosum* is derived from *numinous* (Latin *numen*), "divine power or rule." It is an articulation of the prerationality and irrationality of vital experience (the "pious shiver"). In the past, that which defied reason or causal explanation as "completely other" presumed the participation of the *numinosum* in history. Even today, large-number theory applied by "actuarials" in marketing and insurance ultimately concedes to "acts of God." The great cosmic principle of "standard distribution" happens by itself, as if by magic. The belief that one can explain "with impunity" all historical phenomena in terms of ideology, social structure, economy, and so on, is evidence of magic consciousness (Gebser, 1985: 193). Forces, causal, distributive, and otherwise, are said to be "applied for advantage," "managed," "transmitted," and "obtained." Logic and "system" have their own "epistemic power" and airtight imperatives or "nomothetic force." Behaviors, including proper thinking, are governed by transcendental laws. Such animistic "mechanisms" and properties agree with how the Melanesians described *Mana* to R. H. Codrington (1841) in the early 1800s.

Spelling and Vitality

Similarly, as Winifred Noth (1995) has reminded us, writing is concerned with proper spelling. The spell is fundamental to scripture. To spell is to perform, to repeat the script properly. The dissociative process of conceptual distinction makes difference, makes sense. But distinction happens at the cost of archaic unity. If this is correct, then archaic unity is *logically* meaningless, speechless, but vital through and through. Magic evinces a vital, not causal/material nexus. And yet, if behaviorism is applicable to any mode of consciousness it is the archaic, because the archaic is a seamless flesh. The archaic is touch. But it is not so simple. The will of the world, the magic of lifeworld, cannot be demarcated so easily. The very diversity of life itself is already a prehuman condition for difference/meaning/will.

If it is the case, as Husserl (1962) argues, that the world/experience is meaning, and as Barthes (1967) argues, that the universe is semantic, and as Watzlawick, Beavin, and Jackson (1967) argue, the world communicates, then we must try to understand Friedrich Nietzsche's description of life itself.

At the beginning of *Thus Spoke Zarathustra*, Zarathustra is moved (out of sympathy) to leave his mountain top retreat, his dissociated place of transcendence, and to go down to the human beings in the valley, to "go under," to rescind into life and paradoxically teach the transcendental truth. Soon he finds this to be impossible. Since the people in the valley are not listening, are not willing to die, he leaves. This is a journey of affirmation. He discovers that transcendence is no different from immanence, that there is no such thing as a law or rule that is never embodied. The Buddhists would argue that the journey is long but it goes nowhere because in the final realization, one could not be lost from life's impulses even if one does falsely believe that he or she has transcended them; left them "below," or "behind": elsewhere and elsewhen.

Christ goes into the desert of nondistinction like the mariner who is happiest alone in the "middle of nowhere," and the wolf that trots "across" the boundless steppes. The wanderer has no map, no flow chart or calendar; no cause to kill and die for. Patterns, which are reified perspectives, loose their grip on the imagination. Similar realizations are expressed in the affirmative articulations of Hinduism. Likewise, Joseph Campbell (Campbell and Moyers, 1988: 187) calls the realization of life experience "libido over credo," the life impulse which is rooted in the magic organ, the heart.

In the West, out of the Thracian mountains and forests came a prepagan bliss. Orpheus, the voice of the woods, raised his flute without purpose. His playing (like the sirens' call) leads to abandon and enchantment. Orpheus is the precursor to Pan and Dionysus, and the descendant of untold generations of playful characters associated with the wild, prehistorical nontime, as Chuang Tza put it, when "true" men slept "dreamlessly": the time before patriarchal dissociation, before we fell out of tune and out of harmony and fell into time as into a trap of parametric boundary conditions, haptified systems and patterns. Music is the voice of the soul. Even the dissociated church organization bends to the reality of life through music and passion. Here we find the Dionysian magic of wine/blood. When Siegfried slew the dragon (the dissociated self) he tasted its blood, and heard the song of nature. All great mythological/magical figures including Heracles, Jonah, and St. George must descend into the dark, labyrinthine chaos of the vital nexus to fight the beast and return reborn to the community with the knowledge of life. While the monsters of the mythical world were, like the minotaur, half man/half beast, the monsters of the modern world are half man/half machine.

In the West, harmonics and their mathematical ratios are discovered only after the spontaneous playing of Orpheus is lost. The demarcation between the civilian and the blood-lust becomes clarified, as if it were always so but not seen. Other cultures, however, have remained "uncultured," "uncivilized," and rescendant in the flesh of the world. Later, much later, would come musical notation, and later still, time signature to fixate even the beat, to separate it from the feelings of each performance. The beat is separated from the heart. Sound will eventually be equated with number, frequency, and music digitized. To some ears there is yet a difference between the digital "master" and the analog slave.

Travelers, explorers, scientists are amazed that in the Galapagos Islands, the animals will come and sit in one's lap and perch on one's shoulders. This is not because they have been tamed, or have no so-called survival instinct, but because they are still wild. We no longer share the same watering hole.

Automation and System

Gebser's entire effort is to show a progressive alienation, and widening gap of dissociation from the magic icon, to the mythic ambivalent symbol, which is yet emotionally charged but which stands in for something else, to the perspectival sign which is totally arbitrary and stands only for itself. Art becomes more and more abstract until it is for its own sake. We have passed from an emphasis on identity to one of referentiality and now to "detached" disinterest. Relic becomes art, and art loses its sacrality to commodity reason. Accounts and equations must be balanced. The golden mean and central tendency are the sacred values of the new mass society. Even deviance is standardized. Finally, value exists only by exchange across an arid vacuum. As George Homans (1958) has argued, communication is reduced to informatics, exchange. The formula for all behavior/communication is "Profit = Reward — Cost." The cybernetic feedback loop version of stimulus/response, that made Norbert Wiener (1961), Peter Monge (1977), and Gregory Bateson (1951) academic superstars, closes the system into static self-surveillance. The emphasis is on feedback in the interest of self-maintenance (equilibrium). Care and feeding of the self proliferates from books of etiquette to manuals for organizational management and self-help.

The great leap forward beyond Claude Shannon and Warren Weaver's (1949) Aristotelian concept of life is essentially a reduction of humanity to an arrow feeding back on itself. Thus, communication theory is elevated to the glorious status of absolute fascism. These theorists seem utterly oblivious of Kierkegaard's critique of Hegel's divine prison and the Socratic suspicion of unauthentic authority. Thus Ludwig von Bertalanffy (1968) and Klaus Krippendorf (1975) exalt the global thermostatic model of a cosmic egg with a titanium shell. Arthur Koestler, in his work *The Ghost in the Machine* (1967), not only demonstrated his understanding of the hierarchical nature of systems, with his explanation of the "Janus effect," but, more importantly, his work *Darkness at Noon* (1941) points out the danger of a dehumanized, disenchanted world system. Koestler, like George Orwell and H. G. Wells, recognized the terror of totalitarian movements masquerading as instruments of deliverance (absolution). The individual is subsumed under the general tendency of the mass calculus. Things run on principle, automatically—without life/consciousness.

In the perspectival condition of alienation, egology dominates the world. In his attempt to accurately describe the modern world, Gottfried Wilhelm Leibniz (1951) conceived of a monad "without windows"; Jeremy Bentham (Bentham and Ogden, 1977) conceived of a system of social control based on spatial isolation and surveillance (super-vision) where the guards, too, are watched. This is a world where the touch of the flesh (even in punishment) is displaced by incarceration, "grounding," "time-out," and other modes of enforced loneliness. This is a world where modes of production, distribution, and consumption are fragmented, where technologies serve to isolate us from each other so that the AT&T motto "reach out and touch someone" demonstrates the impossibility to be satirical in the late-modern world.

Modernity is when/where the virtual challenges the actual for life. Likewise, economists argue that nations should cut public sector spending in order to invest in private sector initiatives, as if public funds do not find their way into private lives. This world gives birth to Nietzsche's call for friendship, Marx's call for humane meaningful production, Husserl's appeal for meaning, and the entire thematization of communication. Even statistical variable analysts are obsessed with a deformed and wretched child of modernity, quantitative significance. But what Nietzsche is saying, along with the Zen master and the shaman, is that the journey is long but you are already there. Incarceration works because we still need each other. Administrative reason is obsessed with the average, which presumes surveillance (data gathering), manipulation, and coercion of the Other (rewards and punishment); the insistence of the logic of cause/effect; the imperative of consequences. All of these emerged when and where they did because the dissociative tendency had reached a critical point. Existentialism, crises of identity, the fragmentation of life, all manifest the sense that a change is needed. They herald the aperspectival sense that the world is magic and magic is making connections, making sense, making friends and enemies. The world cannot not be meaningful.

Magic sympathy/affectivity is without separation, direction, or duration (Batille, 1955). For instance, spirit beings are here (indeed everywhere), not segregated to a distant mountain top or even more remote astral plain. Nor are they "exteriorized" spirit, a phenomenon conceivable only in the dualistic world of Wundt (1926) and Marshal McLuhan (1964). They are also immortal, and as such, without temporal dimension. Hexes and curses can affect those "far away," even beyond death. Magic knows no barriers. The power of language as incantation is still evinced by the use of the word "spell." We still "pronounce" major changes in identity such as marital status, and "Christen" things like super high-tech nuclear submarines. Oath taking still exists, as well as initiation rituals.

In the predominantly magic world, the perspectival competition between soul and matter is not evident. Machine technology is the animation of matter. A machine, unlike a tool, is autonomous (automatic). It runs "by itself."

Magic communication is sympathetic, in the most basic sense of the term, so that neither space nor time are gaps (obstacles) to knowledge. Neither doubt nor hesitation emerge until mythic polarity occurs. In the magic world, modern method is not necessary in order to bridge a gap between a subject and an object, or to "get at" some hidden or absent truth. With mythic polarity comes ambivalence which is articulated as allegory, metaphor, and the need for "messengers" like Hermes, oracles, and prophets ("channeler" is a modern acceptation) to "interpret" messages. The modern scientist transforms "raw" data into knowledge, in the process creating an organized image of experience. Imago and imagination are fundamental aspects of the mythic mode of being. They are the goal of science too, that is, to generate a clear and consistent picture or imitation of wild "natural" reality "out there."

In the mythic world, communication, as such, and understanding become issues. Interpretation is an ambivalent process which is not restricted to either "data transmission" or translation. Modern mental rational criticism articulates a further widening of the dissociative gap between "reader" and "text." Sympathy and mythic empathy are displaced by tests of logical consistency.

By contrast, magic people cannot "be wrong" or "lie" in the sense of conception and deception that individuals perpetrate in mythical and modern worlds (Burke, 1950). Being wrong, or having inaccurate or distorted perceptions, presumes a distance between the original and its imitation as in mimetic knowledge; a distance between individuated knower and the known, which is not evident in magic awareness. For instance, if rain fails to happen after the rainmaking ritual has been performed, the individual performer is branded neither charlatan nor incompetent. The magic simply failed to exist. In a world of nonindividuals, "responsibility" is communally felt. Perhaps the birth of a two-headed lamb is directly connected (identical) with the lack of rain. According to Gebser (1985: 49) in the magic world all things are "interweaved," and "merged."

Everything is symbiotically significant. Validity and reliability, which presume individualistic suspicion and abstraction, are not problematic. Symbiotic interpenetration precludes any sense that communication is a problem. There is, in short, a wholly different process of semiosis from the binary logic that marks the perspectival world. The magic world is without reflection or causal determination. In a spaceless and timeless world, "relationships" are not invested with causal direction or concern (investigated). Nor is the toggle of intentionality/accident an issue. Interpretation, as a process of clarifying "hidden" or "distant" significations, does not exist as such. The shaman does not render an "interpretation," which connotes contingency and distance, but pure reality because his or her pronouncement makes it so. There is no "about." Neither meaning nor reason(s) are presumed. Nihilism is a perspectival preoccupation. Without self-objectification suicide is impossible. Sacrifice is very meaningful and affects even those not "directly" (physically) involved.

For instance, the magic dimension of race is expressed by an at-one-ment. Identity is not dissociated as in property. One does not "have," or "belong to" a race, but is (without question). To be "racial" presumes contingency and the categorical abstraction. This enables one to talk about all races as "racial" variance. For magic people, it is not a "random accident" that one was born this or that way. Such an extremely abstract perspective, to imagine that one could be anything other than what one is, is very modern. To see the world as random variables is very ethnocentric.

The Million Man March (October 16, 1995) in Washington, D.C., was a combination of mythic and magic ritual. The need for a reaffirmation of racial identity indicates a sense of loss, an emerging dissociation from self. A gathering can only happen after a fragmentation. But it was deficient magic because once achieved, critical consciousness cannot be "forgotten" or permanently suspended. For the modern, the enchantment is only momentary. The spell wears off. Like most religio-magical experiences in the modern West, it was a momentary upsurge of pathos. From the "disinterested," "arbitrary" perspective of modern rationality (meritocrate and blindly competitive), the march was a pathetic call for oneness and might (ordination), even in militaristic dress. It was a momentary resistance to modern dissociation, alienation. But it articulated more layers in need of archaeology.

At the same time, the organization of the march manifested a strict perspectivism along two parameters, maleness and blackness, which was an attempt to marginalize nonblacks and females, to present a "sea of black men." These barriers were rhetorical because the organizers welcomed an indiscriminate and massive television audience, but not as participants. This invitation to watch but not participate helped to reinforce the difference between in- and out-group identities. Identity, in the modern perspectival sense, is always dependent on difference. Aristotelian binary logic is the logic of modernity.

This march for atonement and self-clarification included a very modern dimension. The compulsion to "find one's self" is a modern malady. This plan enhanced centralization as manifested by the structure of modern mass communication (millions focused on a single source). Numbers were the issue. The cult of personality (hypertrophic individualism) was served most. Though perhaps momentarily inspired, the mass audience in the Mall was cynically (perspectivally) used as a prop to enhance the stature and power of the speakers, all of whom regularly give public addresses, but cannot by themselves draw national media attention. This is modern celebrity as opposed to mythic heroism, which is characterized by self-effacement. The emotional mythology of "heritage" and mental-rational ideology (the modern logic of "idea" which several esteemed scholars including Daniel Bell, Edward Shils, and Seymour Martin Lipset misconstrued as the domain of passion) were simultaneously effective.

Wherever there is diversity there exists a heightened awareness of race. Blond hair is an event in China because it is unique. People who have never seen difference may not even be aware of themselves, of their hair or skin as having a color or texture. Because of fundamental, qualitative differences across cultures, the application of unidimensional variables, like "race," is quite ethnocentric.

For instance, "power distance" (which is "the extent to which the less powerful members of institutions and organizations accept that power is distributed unequally" [Hofstede and Bond, 1984: 419]) exists in both Chinese and Japanese cultures, but in fundamentally different ways so that they are comparable but not reducible to a single dimension or way of conceptualizing power. They do not merely vary along a single axis or concept. Instead, "power distance" is qualitatively different for each culture. Despite the fact that the idea is expressed as a "distance," the difference is qualitative. Both modes of communicating exhibit deference and respect for superiors, but in very different ways, and for different motives.

The difference in motive does not show up in a single sampling of visible, interpersonal interaction at the moment of superordinate/subordinate communication, but "across," "in," and "through" different times and places. If the

Chinese person perceives that showing respect for the superior is not going to pragmatically pay off somehow in the future, that respectful behavior is likely to cease, while the Japanese subordinate may act respectful not for personal gain, but because it is expected. Consequently, the Japanese is not functioning from the same interpersonal logic. The Japanese subordinate is likely to continue to show respect. For a time the two modes of behavior may appear identical, but the interpersonal politics is very different. It is like the difference between a wink and a blink, or flirting and harassing. Discernment presumes context.

Physical differences are not taught. Even children can recognize phenotypic difference. But, emotional associations and expectations are learned. What race means is a cultural, meaning communicative, phenomenon (Cassirer, 1944; Geertz, 1973).

Magical ascription is not perceived as "ascription" by those who live it. Identity is not "identity" either, because such *concepts* are spatial (with critical distance available) and, as such, available for reflection and quarry. Magic peoples never have "identity crises" or lack "self-esteem." There is no self, as in the sense of modern individualism, to lose. Magic wanes in the presence of others who do not identify or are not identical with that world. Thus, the chronicle of Frey Bernardino de Sahagun, based on Aztec accounts, and written eight years after Cortez's conquest of Mexico, described how the vastly outnumbered Conquistadors were immune to the most powerful magical weapons of the Aztec sorcerers. Being invalidated, the magical-mythic world of the Mexicans completely collapsed.

The worst thing one people can do to another is to forcibly deny their metaphysical assumptions, because then all orientation is lost. Modern China (after Confucianism and Maoism have been discredited) and modern Japan (after the invalidation of the divine order) seem to be suffering from extreme alienation and the threat of nihilism (Bestor, 1989; Rauch, 1992; Reingold, 1992). The same is true of the post-Soviet condition throughout Eastern Europe (Kramer, 1993). When modern centralized systems fail, it is not unusual for mythical consciousness to reemerge. This also happened as the Roman Empire disintegrated. Ego-hypertrophy had become deficient and magic and myth revitalized (became efficient) marking a period moderns call the "Dark Ages." The "Dark Ages" manifested a turning away from spatiality inward to the soul. The open pagan temple and secular architecture were displaced by the Romanesque church which constituted a cave-like enclosure, a return to the womb (of the church as sanctuary), as in Notre Dame.

Magic can be light or dark, white or black. Ages are said to be "dark" and "enlightened." Peoples are said to be primitive and complex, barbaric and civilized, developed and underdeveloped. But it depends on who is making the assessment. Such distinctions presume the ability or tendency to think in such terms and in such a binary way. People living in the so-called "medieval dark ages" did not identify themselves this way. A difference in the way human beings, history, and the cosmos are conceived is necessary for such distinctions to be made, and reified. Distinctions, such as these, are made in order to exercise the power of definition. Metaphysics and power are identical. Those who control the definition of reality have the ultimate power. The most fundamental distinctions are magical ones that conjure up the liminal border between something and nothing, order and chaos.

Summation of Magic Qualities

The magic world is predominantly a world of identification where the modern individual does not yet exist, or to put it another way, there is no evidence that magic humans have direct awareness of individuality in the same sense that moderns do. They exist within the security of the clan. However, insofar as evidence exists of magical expression (artifacts), this indicates rudimentary will, direction, purpose. In short, communication develops which is in the form of idolatry, whereby the image is identical with the meaning. The statue or talisman does not "symbolize" a god or mystical power, but *is* the god and power. As dissociation occurs, a "gap" opens. From magic to mythic, and finally perspectival articulation, the form of communication shifts from the idol, to the mythic symbol (which is ambivalent about its identity with the thing for which it stands), to the modern sign, which stands for nothing but itself as pure arbitration.

The magic world heralds the first stirrings of an emergent sense of alienation (species identity) from, and anxiety toward, "forces" that perspectival humanity has labeled "natural" and "supernatural." Magical atunement is vital to survival in a world of mysterious powers that interpenetrate everything including the tribal "we" or anonymous "one" (not "I") (Gebser, 1985: 3–7). The magical group has a symbiotic mergence with the world.

MYTHIC CONSCIOUSNESS

By comparison, the mythic world is ambivalent, expressed by androgyny, for example, and an erosion of absolute (fatalistic) "trust." Ambition and free will are muted, but evident by implication. Nascent reflection (not the critical mode manifested as philosophy and science) and the search for causes or "reasons" are evident in the mythic world, although mythic "causation" is not unidirectional. A good example is the principle of Karma, whereby phenomena appear separate but are sympathetically connected. The mythic world is a world of emergent, two-dimensional polarity, not perspectival (oppositional) duality. What exists in the mythic world is psyche, not ego or mind. According to Gebser (1985: 71), mythic polarity is characterized by "an abiding accompaniment to every consciousness emergence." Every experience is accompanied by its polar bivalence. The quest is the fundamental motif.

Mythic language reveals the mode of communicating that world. Several linguists such as Terebessy (1944), Abel (1884), and Freud (1943) have demonstrated the ambivalent sense of the mythic "*Urworte*" or "primal word." Often in mythic language a word can be used for both polar complements, thus indicating the ambivalence of the unity of mythic cyclicity. This ambivalence is evinced by words that express what later comes to be separate, even antithetical, connotations. For instance, Latin *altus* meant both "high" and "low." *Sacer* meant "sacred" and "cursed." Another example is *Totus* which meant "all" or "whole," and simultaneously, "nothing" (later transformed into German *tot* meaning "dead").[3]

In mythic language, for every active part there is a passive polar complement that is unspoken, silent, invisible, yet present as absence (Jung, 1956; Eliade, 1963). Sky implies earth, male-female, birth-death, and so on. Magic nondifferentiation gives way to polar identity. The mythic human is directly aware of various cycles that orient everything, creating cosmic and (its polar complement) particular sense. Cycles of birth and death, solar, stellar, and lunar cycles, the seasons, day and night, and so forth, dominate the mythic world.

While mythic polarity enables a validity of ambivalence, modern duality enables contradiction (perspective). For instance, a death in the village, especially a "bad" death, may have repercussions for births to occur in the next lunar cycle. In the mythic world such complementarities are poles of a singular aspect that is rendered completely separate and unrelated by the perspectival structure (Geertz, 1973). Seen through perspectival eyes, mythic symbols are unclear, and prone to multiple interpretations. When perspectival eyes (which are interested in purity and clarity) set out to "resolve" mythic messages, myth may be reduced to digital, even binary, structures. Myths are seen to be in need of diagrammatic organization. Claude Levi-Strauss's "science of mythology" is a perfect example of a modern reading that rejects the validity of the mythologeme (Levi-Strauss, 1969).

Under such a (mis)reading, the mythologeme must be transmutated into the philosopheme in order to make sense. The arrogance of science manifests one of modernity's greatest ethnocentrisms. It is presumed that (a) science "brings order" (as if none already existed), and (b) scientific order is not a cultural artifact, but an accurate mirror of "natural" order so that (c) scientific order is not only good but actually inevitable. Its mode of observing is presumed to have universal validity. Imagine that a person from "Amazonia" (wherever that is) knocks on your door one day, invites himself in (in traditional garb), and stays for a year making "notes" of everything: what's in your refrigerator, how you handle family disputes, your sexual and courtship behavior; he sits and watches you watch television, and then on another day takes his leave. You may not even understand where he was from or where exactly he is going or why he came in the first place. This is "natural," this is "rational"? It is creatively arational. The mimetic veracity ethnomethodological "descriptions" (as compared with inventions) claim seems to be in doubt. Being more "naturalistic" may be just another delusion of modern referential method.

In the mythic world, ambivalence, rather than perspectival contradiction, is the hallmark of polarity. Due to the polar relatedness of all things in the mythic world, harmony is valued over competitiveness. Individual ambition may be seen as illness or evil, rather than a virtue. The ambivalence of the mythic world is expressed in the first "(a)warings" of communication as such. For example:

The corresponding verb for *mythos* is *mytheomai*, meaning "to discourse, talk, speak"; its root, *mu-*, means "to sound." But another verb of the same root, *myein*—ambivalent because of the substitution of a short "u"—means "to close," specifically to close the eyes, the mouth, the wounds. From this root we have Sanskrit *mukas* (with long vowel), meaning "mute, silent," and Latin *mutus* with the same meaning. It recurs in Greek in the words *mystes*, "the consecrated," and *mysterion*, *mysterium*, and later during the Christian era, gave the characteristic stamp to the concept of mysticism: speechless contemplation with closed eyes, that is, eyes turned inward. (Gebser, 1985: 65)

While myth is related to mouth, it combines the polar aspects of both speech and silence, emphasizing the necessity for interpretation of the "hidden," or silent meanings. Hence, the importance of oracles, channelers, and interpreters (metacommunicators) even for the gods. Needs are expressed by such symbolic entities as Hermes and the Muses. Mythic distance is not spatial, but emotional and semantic. The mythic world heralds the first emergent separation of the protoego from the group as the polar implication of Other. This is the age of heros and villains. But the duality of stimulus (text) response (reader) is not evident as a problem, nor is the crisis of "external" criticism. However, with the first experience of communication as such, a gap between what is said and what is meant or done, trickery and deceit emerge. Communication studies begins with sophistry.

The potential for misunderstanding gives birth to the first separation from, and subsequent reflections on, communication as a semi-autonomous process. This emergent awareness, or reflexive distance, enabled the classical Greeks, and ancient Jews before them, to think of communication as a separate act, and potential art (and problem). While incantation is identical with events, mimesis presumes a difference which enables distortion and lying. Form and content are finally sundered in the perspectival world of Plato (one of the first moderns). The critical reflective mode of being gave birth to two genres of spatialized and opposing modes of communicating: the philosophical syllogism and the rhetorical enthymeme. Each form of talk has the same linear structure. The difference is that the syllogism is an enthymeme that yields 100 percent "probability," because it starts with infallible premises. The formal structure was very different from magical incantation.

While both rhetorical and philosophical discourses presume a distance for analysis and disputation *about* a state of affairs, incantation brings affairs into being and is one with them. While magic speech presents no separation, myth has symbolic distance, metaphor, and allegory. With this nascent separation of human from environment, pedagogy also begins, which is to teach (talk) *about*, as different from calling into being through the very utterance of magical sounds and acts. As inclusive magic ritual disintegrated, Greek drama heralded the semi-separation of the audience from the performer. Participation became an issue of demarcation. The invention of the semi-autonomous chorus not only paralleled the birth of Platonic concerns about truth and method (hence the lens shape of the amphitheater to focus the attention of the many on the one), but also exhibited a need to make further explanation/interpretation (commentary). The theater also defined passivity from activity.

Socrates was part of the mythic Greek world. According to Gebser (1985: 57–65), the words "myth," "mythos," "muse," and "mouth" all share the same root term *"mu,"* and are also related to the concept of "mass." Mythic consciousness is manifested by orality. Socrates was a member of a world that was predominantly oral and, as such, writing did not hold the importance for him that it did for his followers. One can trace the mutation from mythic to perspectival consciousness from oral Socrates, to Plato's ambivalence about writing/speech manifested in written *dialogues*, to the singular perspectivism of Aristotle's monological analytic texts. For Socrates, writing and computation lacked style, which was regarded as an essential aspect of character (generally, and specifically in the theater). By contrast, while myth deals with the phenomenon of the soul (psyche), whose organ is the heart, including its chronemic aspect (beats), perspectival consciousness is expressed by reason, space, the mind, and the line (vision).

Another example of mythic dedication to the soul is found in the mummification of ancient Egyptian elites. During mummification, the body of the person was preserved as well as possible so that the person's *"ka,"* or spiritual guide, would recognize her/him after death.[4] To this end, no effort was spared in the attempt to preserve everything with but one exception, the brain. The most important parts, the internal organs, were removed and mummified separately, and placed in individual limestone vases. These organs included the intestines, the liver, and, of course, the heart, which was considered to contain the essence of the deceased. A magic aspect was also evident as incantations were recited during each operation in the mummification process. Also, because the hiero-glyphics were idolic, and not dissociated (as arbitrary marks separated from meaning or referent) such as symbolic or signalic articulation, images of animals were often either not completed on purpose, or presented in segments, for fear that otherwise they would literally jump off the surface and run away.

According to the *Egyptian Book of the Dead*, which was recited over the "mouth opening ceremony" of the deceased (like the *Tibetan Book of the Dead*), it was the heart that would be weighed on a scale by the god Anubis, opposite a feather. Before the "two-and-forty" gods of the judgement hall, the jackal form of Anubis would adjust the balance while Thoth, the god of wisdom, dutifully recorded the result. Deeds (expressed emotion, wants, and desires), and not abstracted thoughts, constituted the criteria of judgement. On the way to the judgement hall, the dead had to pass through twenty-eight gates, each guarded by a deity. The recitation which enables the passage must be word-perfect. To this day we read "passages." Long before J. L. Austin (1975), words were considered deeds that make things happen. It was not until unperspectival myth was dis-placed by perspectivism that words became dissociated from action (reduced to human bodies in motion), and as such, became arbitrary, invalid, inconsequential, meaningless.

Throughout antiquity, and the medieval epoch, the heart remained supremely important. This is demonstrated by physical evidence of head injuries and rudimentary surgery which indicate that it was understood by ancient peoples that the brain was the seat of reason. In the process of Egyptian mummification, the brain was considered so trivial that it was thrown away. This is in contrast with the removal and storage of Broca's (the man who first "mapped" the brain) and Einstein's brains, both of which have been stored.

Selective preservation clearly indicates the valuation of different aspects of the human world. The soul, the seat of emotions and passion, was believed by the Egyptians, as with virtually all mythic cultures categorically, to be far more vital than disinterested reason. This attitude is evinced across several civilizations including the Aztecs, who virtually removed the hearts from their sacrifices, not the brains. The efficient guillotine was invented only in the spiritual ecology of "Enlightenment" France. The Egyptians invented a phonetic form of recording but discarded it in favor of their hieroglyphics. Perhaps they were rejecting the sense of separation from the world that abstraction entails.

In current political machinations, religio-mythic fundamentalists are more concerned about the "character" of candidates than their intellectual prowess or organizational competence. Many prefer an inspirational leader to a precise manager. Being an actor, and having worked in an industry that survives on its ability to conjure mythic emotionalism was the strength of Ronald Reagan and the essence of his "Teflon" (especially humor). He understood that most people prefer to follow an agreeable fellow, rather than be managed, an insight George Bush and Michael Dukakis utterly failed to grasp. Mythic people prefer inspiration over insight. Myth is still very vital in the contemporary West. Political theatrics are saturated with it, as exemplified by presidential candidate and U.S. Senate leader Bob Dole's response to President Clinton's 1996 State of the Union address. Dole evoked the magical and mythical symbol of blood, "of our forbears, which courses through our veins," to conjure passion for himself/ message (which are magically identical).

Although Socrates was a member of an oral world, he was revolutionary precisely because his penchant for a dualistic, dia-logical mode of seeking truth revealed a nascent mutation from a mythic to a perspectival world. However, his attitude was disruptive of the clan. His student Plato also expressed this fundamental shift toward linear reasoning and relentless critique. Plato's writing articulated a world in transition, for while he wrote a philosophy, it remained in the form of a dialogue. He also attacked the bards of the soul, the poets, for being a threat to a rational order. Plato's philosophical writing expressed both a mythic dedication to orality and emotional rhetoric at the same time that it manifested a linear structure and strong prejudice in favor of reason.

Aristotle's philosophical effort manifested the shift to a perspectival "mentality" as such. Aristotle not only wrote his philosophy, but expressed an obsession with categorical logic as the very medium of knowledge itself, a conviction the medievals rejected in favor of Plato's mysticism. Aristotle's style was the message. He was monologically analytic, not dialogical. Demonstration via agreement was displaced by transcendent, logical consistency. Aristotle wrote the first analytic, or "objective" analysis of rhetoric. The fundamental prerequisite for an analytic hermeneutic, a separation between subject and object, was completed by Aristotle, who should be called the first modern.

In ancient Greece, the transition from a predominantly mythic to a predominantly perspectival world is evinced in the theater. The very architecture of the amphitheater formed a lens that focused attention on a single space (the stage). In modern concert halls, the soft fabrics of clothing and the absorbing bodies of audience members must be taken into account during the process of tuning the acoustics of the overall instrument (the house chamber). The parabolic shape of the ancient Greek seating arrangement is pure modernism. It is indicative of modern ego-hypertrophy (celebrity), accentuation of a single perspective, and mass passivity/consumption.

Likewise, the autonomous narrator had special transcending knowledge of states of affairs that was enlightening for the audience. But tragically (or comically), the actors in the drama could not hear this "objective" knowledge. The actors were on the way to becoming objectified. The narrator was the ultimate audience member, with the privileged perspective that transcended and encompassed all the relationships of the drama without being touched by them. The narrator thus divined the future pathetic outcome of blind behavior patterns. The narrator was the repository of permanence, of principle, while the drama was in flux and often transgressed natural and moral law, and hence the inevitable consequences. The actors fell into comedic or tragic conclusions that might have been otherwise if only they could have seen and foreseen like the narrator's pure (and often righteous) vision. Their scope was personal and narrow compared with the narrator's relatively disinterested (unemotional) master perspective.

Today, a mixture (integrum) of attitudes is evident in the avalanche of letters that soap opera *characters* receive from loyal (magically and mythically dominated) viewers that attempt to inform and warn them of impending consequences that the characters cannot foresee. Such special knowledge of relationships which those in the drama do not fully grasp (are blind to) both engages and distances the audience. The audience magically identifies with the characters.

The classical dramatic narrator articulated a new *position* (perspective) that was interested, but yet outside the dramatic frame. This formal and dissociated (dispassionately "pure") observer would later develop into the protoscientist in Aristotelian monologue. While theater created the audience/stage dichotomy, it also transformed human life into pure spectacle. This dissociated spectacle articulated the rudimentary relationship necessary for discursive analysis (informed comment or explanation) and would be developed by Cicero and Quintilian, and constitute the foundation of perspectival pedagogy and investigation. The path of actors (theatrical or social) is "dissed" or challenged by an opposing perspective which demands dis-course. The narrator embodies "oversight" and "supervision."

The dramatic narrator assumed the rhetorical and hermeneutical posture of a disinterested protoscientist who merely spoke an unambiguous and singular truth, no matter how tragic it might be. The complex process of interpretation fragmented and truncated to one-to-one translation (pure referentiality or presentation of "the same"). This would later influence homiletics as well. Neither clergy nor scientists offer subjective interpretations, but rather claim to speak The Truth. They evoke the tradition of "references" and "citations" to avoid responsibility, to be "objective," and to legitimize their version of reality. They narrate the drama of a uni- rather than a polyverse. Divine inspiration is a breath that enables total disinterest. Like automatic writing, mediating the truth is beyond one's personal interest. One becomes a tool, a receptacle, so that Martin Luther called Mary (mother of Jesus) a "divine whore."

For the modern, only one version can prevail. But if pretenders arise, conflict commences as each perspective attempts to "demythologize" (meaning to expose as a falsehood) each other perspective. For the modern, reason is the chosen tool (or weapon) for demythologizing and debunking or revealing delusions, the epistemic status to which all rivals must be reduced (as in Jurgen Habermas's [1984] critical rationality). Stition mercilessly undercuts superstition. Reason deflates all faith to mere contingency, but keeps its own.

Summation of Mythical Qualities

The mythic world is predominantly a world of symbolic polarities and emotional "tension" that does not manifest a strong directional "intention" (Gebser, 1985: 61–73). Nascent spatiality characterizes the mythic world which exhibits an ambivalent sense of direction and individual will. The bivalent mythical world is fundamentally different from the trivalent perspectival world that stresses individual mental power and competition. Guilt and responsibility characterize the mythic world. By contrast, the perspectival modern individual is an arbitrary medium for a functional force (as Michel Foucault [1970] claims that language speaks man, not man language). Mythic cyclical time is a dynamic constituent of the mythic world. By contrast, the perspectival individual is an arbitrary medium for a functional force. Mythic time acts as an ambivalent divider of qualitative differences, not a quantitative fragmenter.

While the magical world is univalent, and the mythical ambivalent, the perspectival is trivalent. Depth and distance emerge with perspectivity. With depth-space comes isolation. Space is that which is in between discrete things.

Objective observation and incessant reductionisms or ideologies (definition, meaning subdivision) become thinkable. This is why Thomas Sowell (1994) is correct to insist that slavery is not the consequence of ideology. Subjugation of the weak by the strong, even when overlaid with a veneer of efficient rationality (as in Nazi Germany or Soviet collectivism), expresses a mythic and magical preoccupation with power.

NOTES

1. Synairesis recognizes the validity of alienation or *ostrennie* (Russian for "estrangement"); an artistic process of making the familiar strange or different via comparison so that it can be seen again.

2. In the modern world, "communication," and informatics (information systems) as such, have become ubiquitous. Whenever there is a problem, communication, meaning listening and talking (dialoging), is the solution. Communication is both the problem and the solution to itself. It is the tautological discipline of modernity, the solution through the hierarchical structure of discourse and metadiscourse. The necessary condition for this new awareness has been dissociation. Communication is a product of the dissociating and categorical imagination of the perspectival mind generally, and more specifically, the social scientific attitude. Communication, as a separate activity/idea, is conceived as an ontology.

3. What is dead in a totalitarian or fundamentalistic world is change, so that just when human will achieves the apex of its power, change ceases and *status quo* prevails. This is the logical conclusion of all reductionisms including the ideology of systematic self-monitoring and self-correction. It is an overdetermined obsession with the self or what Gebser (1985) called hypertrophic perspectivity (Nietzsche, 1974; Ricoeur, 1965; Sloterdijk, 1987; Krippendorf, 1975). Thus, the strength and horror of modernity is organization. The perpetual "interest" of the self-monitoring system is to defeat difference. It constitutes absolute intolerance.

4. The fragmentation of spiritual and material metaphysical dimensions does not occur until Aristotle, and even with him it is not as complete as post-Renaissance modernity perceives and conceives the split.

REFERENCES

Abel, K. (1884) *Gegensinn der Urworte*. Leipzig: Friedrich Heitz.
Austin, J. L. (1962) *How to Do Things With Words*. Cambridge, MA: Harvard University Press.
Barthes, R. (1967) *Elements of Semiology*. New York: Hill & Wang.
Bateson, G. (1951) "Information and Codification." In *Communication and the Social Matrix of Psyhchiatry*, with Jurgen Ruesch. New York: Norton (pp. 168–211).
Batille, G. (1955) *The Birth of Art: Prehistoric Painting*. Lausanne, France: Skira.
Bentham, J., and C. Ogden. (1977) *Bentham's Theory of Fictions*. New York: AMS Press.
Bestor, T. C. (1989) *Neighborhood Tokyo*. Stanford, CA: Stanford University Press.
Burke, K. (1950) *A Rhetoric of Motives*. Cleveland: World.
Campbell, J., and B. Moyers. (1988) *The Power of Myth*. New York: Doubleday.

Cassirer, E. (1944) *An Essay on Man*. New Haven, CT: Yale University Press.

Codrington, R. (1841) Letter to F. Max Muller, quoted in G. van der Leeux, *Phanomenologie der Religion*. Tubingen: Mohr, 1933.

Croce, B. (1960) *History: Its Theory and Practice*. New York: Russell & Russell.

Eliade, M. (1963) *Myth and Reality*. New York: Harper and Row.

Foucault, M. (1970) *The Order of Things*. New York: Pantheon.

Frazer, J. (1910) *Totemism and Exogamy: A Treatise on Certain Early Forms of Superstition and Society*. London: Macmillan.

Freud, S. (1918) *Totem and Taboo*. New York: Vintage.

———. (1943) *Gesammelte Werke chronologisch geordnet*. London: Imago.

Gebser, J. (1985) *The Ever-Present Origin*. Athens: Ohio University Press.

Geertz, C. (1973) *The Interpretation of Cultures*. New York: Basic Books.

Habermas, J. (1984) *The Theory of Communicative Action, Vol. 1: Reason and the Rationalization of Society*. Boston: Beacon Press.

Hegel, G. (1953) *Reason in History: A General Introduction to the Philosophy of History*. New York: Liberal Arts Press.

Hobsbawm, E. J., and T. O. Ranger. (1983) *The Invention of Tradition*. New York: Cambridge University Press.

Hofstede, G., and M. Bond. (1984) "Hofstede's Culture Dimensions." *Journal of Cross-Cultural Psychology* 15: 417–433.

Homans, G. (1958) "Social Behavior as Exchange." *The American Journal of Sociology* 63, no. 6: 597–606.

Hume, D. (1973) *A Treatise Concerning Human Understanding*. London: Oxford University Press.

Husserl, E. (1962) *Ideas*. New York: Collier.

Ikeda, R. (1992) *Ie to Kazoku: A Shift in the Communication Pattern of the Japanese Family*. Master's Thesis for the University of Oklahoma.

Jung, C. G. (1956) *Symbols of Transformation*. Princeton, NJ: Princeton University Press.

Koestler, A. (1941) *Darkness at Noon*. New York: Bantam.

———. (1967) *The Ghost in the Machine*. New York: Macmillan.

Kramer, E. (1993) "Investigative Journalism in Bulgaria: A Postponed Renaissance." In *Creating a Free Press in Eastern Europe*, edited by A. Hester and K. White. Athens: University of Georgia, The James M. Cox, Jr., Center for International Mass Communication Training & Research, The Henry W. Grady College of Journalism and Mass Communication, University of Georgia (pp. 111–159).

Krippendorf, K. (1975) "Information Theory." In *Communication and Behavior*, edited by G. Hanneman and W. McEwen. Reading, MA: Addison-Wesley (pp. 351–389).

Landmann, M. (1974) *Philosophical Anthropology*. Philadelphia: Westminister.

Leibniz, G. (1951) *The Monadology and Other Philosophical Writings*. London: Oxford University Press.

Levi-Strauss, C. (1969) *The Raw and the Cooked*. Chicago: University of Chicago Press.

Maslow, A. (1968) *Toward a Psychology of Being*. New York: Van Nostrand.

McLuhan, M. (1964) *Understanding Media: The Extensions of Man*. New York: Mentor Books.

Merleau-Ponty, M. (1962) *Phenomenology of Perception*. London: Routledge & Kegan Paul.

Monge, P. (1977) "The Systems Perspective as a Theoretical Basis for the Study of Human Communication." *Communication Quarterly* 2, no. 1: 19–29.

Nietzsche, F. (1974) *The Gay Science*. New York: Vintage.

Noth, W. (1995) *Handbook of Semiotics*. Bloomington: Indiana University Press.

Pilotta, J. (1992) "Media Power Working Over the Body: An Application of Gebser to Popular Culture." In *Consciousness and Culture: An Introduction to the Thought of Jean Gebser*, edited by E. Kramer. Westport, CT: Greenwood Press (pp. 79–102).

Rapoport, A. (1968) "Foreword." In *Modern Systems Research for the Behavioral Scientist*, edited by W. Buckley. Chicago: Aldine (pp. xiii–xxv).

Rauch, J. (1992) *The Outnation: A Search for the Soul of Japan*. New York: Little, Brown and Company.

Reinach, S. (1939) *Orpheus: A History of Religions*. New York: Liveright.

Reingold, E. M. (1992) *Chrysanthemums and Thorns: The Untold Story of Modern Japan*. New York: St. Martin's Press.

Ricoeur, P. (1965) *History and Truth*. Evanston, IL: Northwestern University Press.

Sapir, E. (1949) *Selected Writings*. Berkeley: University of California Press.

Schmidt, W. (1939) *Primitive Revelation*. London: Herder.

Schopenhauer, A. (1966) *The World as Will and Representation, Vols. 1 and 2*. New York: Dover Press.

Shannon, C., and W. Weaver. (1949) *The Mathematical Theory of Communication*. Urbana: University of Illinois Press.

Sloterdijk, P. (1987) *Critique of Cynical Reason*. Minneapolis: University of Minnesota Press.

Sowell, T. (1994) *Race and Culture*. New York: Basic Books.

Terebessy, K. (1944) *Zum Problem der Ambivalenz in der Sprachentwicklung*. Trnava, Germany: Urbanek.

Tylor, E. (1958) *Primitive Culture*. New York: Harper.

Vico, G. (1974) *Opere giuridiche: il diritto universale*. Ferenze, Italy: Sansoni.

von Bertalanffy, L. (1968) *General Systems Theory: Foundations, Development, Applications*. New York: Braziller.

Watzlawick, P., J. Beavin, and D. Jackson. (1967) *Pragmatics of Human Communication: A Study in Interactional Patterns, Pathologies, and Paradoxes*. New York: Norton.

Whorf, B. L. (1956) *Language Thought and Reality*. Cambridge, MA: MIT Press.

Wiener, N. (1961) *Cybernetics or Control and Communication in the Animal and the Machine*. Cambridge, MA: MIT Press.

Wittgenstein, L. (1971) *Prototractatus*. London: Routledge & Kegan Paul.

Wundt, W. (1926) *Wilhelm Wundts Werk: ein Verzeichnis seiner samtlichen Schriften*. Leipzig: B. G. Teubner.

3

The Ancient Birth of Modernity

PERSPECTIVE AND PATRIARCHY

Modernity, which is fairly synonymous with "Western," prides itself on de-mythologizing the world, as though rationalization does not presume a mytho-logical dimension. To "demythologize" the world is tantamount to "deculturizing" a human being (Chomsky, 1972; Geertz, 1973; Morris, 1967, 1969; Pribram, 1971; Gudykunst and Kim, 1992). Short of a frontal lobotomy, neither is possible. Furthermore, both ancient Greek and Judeao-Christian my-thologemes manifest the essential properties of modernity.

What is myth? Myth is neither invalid, unreliable, nor extinct. It is a form of communication. Each civilization is articulated most fundamentally by myth. The question for myth is not the degree of referential (empirical) agreement it has with some reality "out there," but to what extent it is "alive," "vital" (Eliade, 1963; Gebser, 1985). Myth, as a type of speech (Barthes, 1982), artic-ulates and establishes the psychology or attitude of a civilization. Myth estab-lishes various moods and emotions. These moods and emotions are manifested as the patterns that mark the comparative uniqueness of civilizational structures and the variety of cultures that manifest those structures. Cultures are the sum total of artifacts, both verbal and nonverbal. Cultures are communication (Geertz, 1973; Cassirer, 1944; Humboldt, 1973; Gebser, 1985). In order to un-derstand what constitutes the uniqueness of Western cultures, one must recog-nize the veracity of these civilizational expressions, their shared mythic establishment.

"Western" (modern) is recognizable by its comparatively (to mythic and magic) intense emphasis on spatial extension, egocentrism, competition, and hierarchical, paternal *systematization*. These characteristics are already established in Western mythologies. Ancient Greek mythology tells us that both the titans and the gods formed communities with hierarchical structures and masculine figures as ultimate authorities. This cosmology also presentiated a warring duality between these two groups of immortals.

Kronos (Time) was the ruler of the titans and father of several gods including Zeus, ruler of the gods. Time is the ever-present and indiscriminate field "against which" psyche is evinced as fragmentation (the variety of gods). The symbolic action of Kronos is to cut the nondistinction of Sky (his father Uranus) into pieces with his sickle, and to devour (consume).

Kronos was defeated by his children, the gods, who were aided by the one-eyed cyclops. The cyclops made the weapons for the three godly brothers; thunderbolts for Zeus, the trident for Poseidon, and the helmet of invisibility for Hades. This indicates the passage from a predominantly mythological world to a perspectival world, which emphasizes vision and direction. Soon the two-dimensional spectral array of the one-eyed monster would be displaced by those whom he helped ascend to power, those who saw depth-space. These were the bright and beautiful three-dimensional, two-eyed gods, including the owl-eyed Athena, shining Apollo, and traversing Hermes.

This passage from two- to three-dimensional conceptualization (spatial materialization/separation presumed by "thingism") is expressed as nothing less than a battle which culminated in a new hierarchical ordination with Zeus, king of the air (sky or heaven) and the other gods, all of whom subsequently took up localizable residences; Zeus at Mount Olympus, Athena at Athens, Apollo at Delphi, and so on. The losers, the evil preperspectival indeterminate titans (natural and chaotic forces such as earthquake, volcano, and tidal wave), were banished to the darkness of Tartarus under the earth.

Anthropomorphism, realism, and materialism won. Self-reflexive awareness, as species consciousness and arrogance, occurred. So too, the separation of culture from nature, light from dark, and the wild from the domesticated marked the beginning of the classical Western world. This is the end of the Golden Age of nondistinction, and the beginning of the Silver Age of dissociation and fragmenting alienation which emphasizes the need for communication, *sui generis*.

The emergent sense of space, as the in-between of difference, was articulated by Zeus, who was not only the most powerful god, but was also god of the skies. Zeus's sister, Hestia, was goddess of the hearth or home. Her Latin name was Vesta, which indicates the perspectival focus of a fixed position from which a privileged view originates (home culture—ethnic identity). Another titan of nondistinction, Ocean (which is indicative of subconscious preperspectival awareness), was father of Metis (Thought). Metis helped Zeus by poisoning Kronos so that he would throw up all the gods (differences) he had devoured. Metis, like the water god Proteus, had the power of formation, of "shape-shifting." Later, Zeus tricked Metis into turning into a fly, and then he swallowed her. She was reborn from Zeus's forehead, with the help of Prometheus, who split Zeus's head open with his axe.

Metis (Thought), transformed as Athena, was goddess of technical manufacture, the city, and of battle. She was fierce. In the war with the titans, Athena killed Pallas, flayed him, and wore his skin as a cloak. In her subsequent incarnation as Pallas Athena, her voice became discursive, disputative, incisive, fearsome. The names "Metis" and "Min-erva" (Athena's Latin name) are indicative of "men." This also indicates the mythic ambivalence manifested as androgyny (having two skins). The directional aim of Athena's lance is true, and her totem, the owl, perceives invisible (logical), distinct, and necessary relationships, rather than qualities. Logic becomes more clear than space, mathematical entities sharper in definition than visible objects. In the form of Victory, Athena had wings to traverse space.

Likewise, Hermes was a winged, spatial being. The semantic field articulated by the term "hermeneutics" implies the growing awareness of communication as a transference of meaning and willful intent across a gap between minds, which brought into focus the problem of communication as a dubious bridge (medium and method) over the obstacle of distorting difference. Hermeneutics encompasses the problems of translation, interpretation, as well as simple transference. "Noise" as well as "personal distance" became a recognized and integral part of message. Hermes did not simply deliver messages but translated and interpreted them, because translation and interpretation were perceived to be integral aspects of all communication. Prior to this, communication was not perceived as a process *sui generis*. Spatial separation and personal intent are necessary conditions for communication to exist as an identifiable, discrete process. To be perceived as "problems," distortion and persuasion presume personal meaning and intent.

Memory, too (as an aspect of distortion), was called into question by practically every intellectual from Isocrates and Plato on. History had already been invented by the Babylonians, Egyptians, and Jews. The advent of the desire for an enduring identity among the Greeks was also manifested as recorded history (Homer, Herodotus, and Xenophones). However, writing (recording) became a debated issue. Is it a crutch, a sign of a weak mind, or a fantastic, and even creative, tool; a poison or a medicine (Derrida, 1981)? Was it an artificial binder of individuals, a false "shorthand"? Often a little poison is a medicine. The communicative gap that threatened intent emerged as a spatialized problem of "horizon" and "semantic field." Time became spatialized and seen as a "gap" defined as forgetfulness. Society was disseminating beyond the immediate village, across space and time. Empires require records and roads (channels) (Innis, 1950; Ong, 1982). One must argue to get one's "point across," to be "clear," to win, to endure.

Zeus's son Apollo was god of light and truth. He was accompanied by the nine Muses (whose mother was Mnemosyne or Memory) that constituted the cultural arts (including singing, poetry, dancing, comedy, tragedy, etc.). Artemis, Apollo's twin sister, was goddess of wild things and the moon. Thus, a fundamental polarity was articulated between nature and culture. Dark disarray confronted illuminated order. Socrates would rather die than live outside the walls of the Greek city among the barbarian Others. Zeus sired the duality of light and dark skies.

The titan Iapetus was father of Epi-metheus and Pro-metheus. Both were endowed with *foresight*, an ability Prometheus later stripped from mortal men so that they would not suffer the knowledge of future calamities, but instead enjoy the hope of ignorant bliss. Consequently, and despite Prometheus's warning that once known, the future is closed and controls the knower, men have been struggling ever since to regain control of the future through prophecy and prediction. Prediction of a future already done presumes the notion of modern constants (absolutes). Prometheus, in his wisdom, was correct. A future already done is nihilistic and hopeless. Under such conditions, to live is to merely repeat prophecy, to be redundant, and utterly depressed. Magic and mythic humans do not see time as a line, the future as causally predictable, as already done. Instead, they venture to make it. Aperspectivity sees the mythic and magic quality of hope to be essential to human projection, and ignorance as a necessary condition for "discovery."

Prometheus was punished for bringing technology to mortal men, who had lost their full knowledge of their own future. An open future horizon that enables human projection (planning and technology) constitutes the modern sense of purpose. An unknown future was the great gift that enabled modernity. The paternal intolerance of Zeus was evinced as he sent the demons Might and Force to chain Prometheus to the Caucasus mountains on the eastern edge of the world. To the Greeks, the East was the land of the despotic Persians, of fatalism, of a future already known in the past. This is death to the Greeks.

The essential properties of modernity are thus mythologically expressed. They include an emphasis on perspectival space. Space, which is a visual phenomenon, is expressed as light, expanding dissociation, division or measurement, formalization, individuated and directional intent or will, and differential and fixed identity. The segregating mentality of paternal intolerance (opposition) is also expressed by these mythologemes. So too, is the morphological and moderating property of time (hope manifested as an open horizon enabling progressivism).

By contrast, the Judaeo-Christian contribution to Western civilization includes linear eschatological (deterministic) time, absolute law, and a consolidation of divine forces into a single, paternal ego. Individualism is manifested in the mythologeme of Jehovah. A fundamental conflict in Western culture is the consequence of the contradictory conceptions of intolerant principle, expressed by the changeless perfection of Jehovah, and compromise, manifested by Zeus, who, through experience, changed and became merciful. "In time," he released and forgave Prometheus.

The West manifests these two mutually excluding positions; fundamental principle versus compromise, absolutism versus relativity. Hence, while Prometheus was forgiven and rehabilitated, the status of Lucifer cannot change

(Mickunas, 1995). Judaeo-Christian law is absolute; damnation is "eternal," which logically must somehow already include the past and present. Western culture harbors a struggle between permanence and flux which feeds the system of binary logic and paradoxologies that mark modernity (the perspectival West), conversation, conversion, and conversionary tactics. The struggle is repeatedly expressed by opposing positions like those taken by Plato against Heraclitus, the "left" and "right" Hegelians, quantity versus quality, permanent object versus mutable subject, and modern versus so-called "post"-modern strategies (endless reversals of privilege).

TO MEAN AND TO BE (ME)AN: MAS-CU-*LINE*

Western modernity (a redundant phrase) is already expressed in mythological discourse. From Judeao-Christian mythology is prefigured the intolerance of hypertrophic perspectivism expressed as the absolute and singular male god of law and order (tit for tat). However, while the Old Testament maintains an intolerable logic, The Christ represents another, totally unreasonable, unconditional love. But in both cases, there can be only one true god, only one true reality. Such hypertrophic perspectivism attempts to suppress the realization that other, viable structures of consciousness coexist.

From time to time, mythic ambiguity dissociates into perspectival duality. Hermeneutics emerged in ancient Greece as original method/medium (Gadamer, 1975; Palmer, 1969). It became a necessity. When or wherever it occurs, the mutation in attitude which enables the dissociative distance for critical description and evaluation of communication, as such, indicates the first glimmerings of competition, directionality, probability (which presumes absolute zero and 100 percent truth so that all other "degrees" have relational meaning), and space (as a thing-in-itself) that separates positions. Under such conditions, identity, as truth, becomes a problem.

In classical Greece, communication was conceived as a means of dialogical confrontation, and thinking was equated with critique. Thus, communication became the primary curriculum. After the long "Dark Ages," two Mohammedan philosophers, one of Persia and one of Spain, reignited interest in classical modernism. They were Avicenna (Ibn Sina) (980–1037) and Averroes (Ibn Rushd) (1126–1198). It was their tendency toward Aristotle, and away from Neoplatonism, that kindled a new interest in classical mimetic method and logic, specifically in the work of the German scholar Albertus Magnus (1193?–1280) who was Saint Thomas Aquinas's professor at the University of Paris. Later, ancient modernity was promoted by Nicholas of Cusa (also known as Nicholas Cusanus 1401–1464), Desiderius Erasmus (1469–1536), and Peter Ramus (1515–1572), as they reestablished classical thinking, the "rebirth" (*Renaissance*).

Among the ancient modernists, the highest art was dialectics (rhetoric/communication). It became the method for rendering truth itself. It remains essential to the notion of a "free marketplace of ideas," which constitutes the democratic nature of scientific discourse so that a "no-name" patent clerk could successfully challenge the Newtonian world-view on the basis of ideas alone. The most advanced curriculum Aristotle taught his most brilliant students was the scientific reflection on how persuasion is done, for without that, nothing else happens, and without knowledge of it, one is unconsciously vulnerable to it.

In disputative cultures, individuals become identified with conceptual "positions." In ancient Greece, for instance, one could no longer win the day by merely emoting, by being sincere. To be was to have a position in a conversation, to formulate an argument, and marshal evidence. Still, today, to not publish is to perish. For moderns, authorship is identity. During the medieval period, authors very rarely bothered to sign manuscripts. They did not see themselves as the authority. The passion of the message was more important than who wrote it. Asking who the author is tends to lead to inferences about the intent of the source and the "true" meaning of the text. Psychoanalysis (of the author) is a modern rationalizing perspective.

For the ancient modern "pagans" of classical Greece and Rome, the study of suasive effort became the second curriculum after the art of war, because great strategy and tactics are useless without the ability to lead. This explains the advent of intense, systematic, and abstracting study of style, elocution, logic, and argumentation. Communication implied a need to express one's "self," to span space (theatrical distance), as Plato, in his *Seventh Letter*, equated soul with sky, breath, and emotion.

The first word of the first verse of the first canto of the first major work of the Western world, the *Iliad*, is *menin* (the accusative of *menis*) (Gebser, 1985: 70–78). The Greek word *menis* means "wrath" and "courage." *Menis* comes from the same stem as *menos*, meaning "resolve," "power," "conviction." In turn, the Latin *mens* means "intent," "anger," "thinking," "thought," "understanding," and "deliberation" (not liberation). Of this brief etymological survey Gebser (1985: 75) has argued that:

What is fundamental here is already evident in the substance of these words: it is the first intimation of the emergence of *directed or discursive thought*. Whereas mythical thinking, to the extent that it could be called "thinking," was a shaping or designing of images in the imagination which took place within the confines of the polar cycle, discursive thought is fundamentally different. It is no longer polar-related, enclosed in and reflecting polarity from which it gains its energy, but rather directed toward objects and duality, creating and directing this duality, and drawing its energy from the individual ego.

As expressed in the *Iliad*, the classical Greek world unfolded as an image of action that was directed, causal, and willfully ordered.[1] Having and giving direction, such as a chain of command (from first cause on "down"), presumes a perspective, distance, inequality (separation). *Menos* is the root of "men(tal)," hence the designation of modernity as a style that is mental-rational (incessantly categorizing) and perspectival.

Prior to the Greeks, the other tradition that became "the West," the Jewish tradition, "created the context for an ever-widening chasm between social time and environmental time" (Rifkin, 1989: 148).[2] The Jews replaced the cycle with the straight line, and so the notions of past, present, future, history, and progress (which presumes a *telos* or goal) were invented. The Jews imbued time with a mission (intent). History was the stage where God and his chosen people unfolded their relationship. This gave rise to the problem of hermeneutics for the ancient Jews (the Talmudic tradition). According to Frederick Polak (1961: 159), "It is through the prophet that Jehovah, ever ready with advice, aid and admonition for his people, speaks. The prophet is God's herald—more than a king, better than a priest. He is the wayshower both for rulers and ruled, and chief interpreter of the Covenant. Misfortune and divine wrath can just be averted in time by listening to the prophet's words."

Whether in trading goods or assessing appropriate punishment, the "ruler" had to be guided by absolute, not arbitrary, understanding, which was the case with all scalar attempts at objective judgement (valuation). Justice and fairness were perceived as a ratio; a scalar product of relative balance or "even-handedness."

Paternalism inoculates itself from critique by proclaiming to be the very order of the universe. Causal determinism is materialized divine intent. The chain is a very narrow line that is oblivious to the vast possibilities that surround it. For instance, from the early ancient Greek *menin* is derived "man" which becomes, in the perspectival world, *the standard* by which all other things are evaluated. (Man)uels are written to dictate the step-by-step way to achieve goals. Jewish, Greek, and Roman history, or "his-story," was conceived as a fatalistic (fatheristic) thread of yesteryear winding to the present, evincing and justifying the current state of affairs by causal necessity, thus legitimizing power relations in the ever-present "today," and preempting the dynamism of alternatives (Foucault, 1979; Kramer, 1992).

The Judaeo-Christian paternal attitude later integrated well with pagan paternalism. After the Renaissance, the Judaeo-Christian God was rationalized, and came to be perceived as the divine engineer of the cosmic machine (Husserl, 1970; Mumford, 1963; Davis and Hersh, 1986, 1981; Grant, 1977; Nietzsche, 1974). To moderns, like Galileo, Newton, Kepler, and Einstein, the book of creation was written in mathematics. The ideational process of mathematical logic gave the strictly empirical alchemists the power to become chemists, to recognize relationships, to offer hypothetical explanations, to predict states of affairs not empirically present, and to generalize.

The question science began to ask was, what is this system that gives the empirical science of things its power (Frege, 1984; Husserl, 1962, Russell and Whitehead, 1967)? Mathematics proved to be a set of necessary (intolerant) relationships, an extremely formalized language.[3] The scientific method proved to be not an empirical thing, but the expression of an "attitude," a set of rules (Husserl, 1962); a specific way to structure relationships (Bacon, 1942; Hume, 1973; Kant, 1929). Thinking itself became spatialized (systematized).

THE REBIRTH OF PERSPECTIVAL CONSCIOUSNESS

Where or whenever the perspectival mutation occurs, the mythic cycle is ruptured, disrupting the two-dimensional mythic world of imagination (Latin *imago*, "image"), emotion, and repetition. The Latin notion of *ratio* manifests the perspectival concern with reason derived from Aristotle's definition of man as the rational animal and, by ratio, the *measure* of all things. The word *ratio* means "to reckon," "to calculate," "to think," and "to understand." Recendent *"under*-standing" is reversed as explanation denotes transcendental detachment; isolation. Man "grasps" that which is now separate from him and conquers it. The world becomes resource *base* demanding *super*-vision.

During the Renaissance, the visual/spatial metaphor "horizon" became popular to express the "scope" of a person's understanding. Thus, an instrument invented to enhance depth-vision, while simultaneously narrowing the field of that same precept, came to denote comprehension itself. The Renaissance marked a rebirth in interests concerning method/medium (way of grasping). In the modern perspectival world, a common nexus of academic conflict remains method, or "ways of seeing" and organizing knowledge (the discursive formation of realities). Method is a tool, a mode of production.

Ironically, this resurgence of spatial awareness heralded a new attitude and reckoning which attempted to inoculate itself against critique by claiming to have no perspective (or bias) at all. Although transcending method claims no bias, it also insists that it presents the one and only true (most intolerantly prejudiced) perspective. However, "universal perspective" is an absurd phrase. According to Gebser (1985), the overemphasis on space and spatiality is both the greatness and the weakness of perspectival humanity.

The over-emphasis on the "objectively" external, a consequence of an excessively visual orientation, leads not only to rationalization and haptification but to an unavoidable hypertrophy of the "I," which is in confrontation with the external world. The exaggeration of the "I" amounts to what we may call an ego-hypertrophy: the "I" must be increasingly emphasized, indeed over-emphasized in order for it to be adequate to the ever-expanding discovery of space. At the same time, the increasing materialization and haptification of space which confronts the ego occasions a corresponding rigidification of the ego itself. (Gebser, 1985: 22)

Perspectival individuals tend to be suspicious, to believe only in what they can personally "see" (reliably evince), thus exaggerating their sector of experience to totality. This is religious dogma overlaid by passionate rationalization. According to Gebser (1985: 74), *ratio* presents the principal characteristic of the

perspectival world: "directedness and perspectivity, together with—unavoida-
bly—sectorial partitioning." Subdivide and conquer becomes the *modus oper-
andi* for scientific, segregating, progress.

Television is a good example of perspectivism. In many ways it is far more
accurate than any social scientific paper-and-pencil method of data collection.
Television is a child of the perspectival world and manifests that sense of reality,
that attitude (Kramer, 1993). Tele-vision, or distant seeing, also manifests the
continual pursuit of magical powers. Television generates the sense of being a
fly on the fourth, missing, wall of the world, of being present at distant events.
The animism of television also expresses this wish to "be live" at Times Square,
for instance, on New Year's Eve (even though it may only be 10:00 A.M. where
you are). The one and only "real" midnight is in New York. The urban world
is where "it's" happening.

The visiocentric modern has a tendency to confer credibility, preference, and
faith in the reliability of television news because he or she can say that "cameras
don't lie," and that they "saw for themselves" the televised event (Comstock
et al., 1978). However, the narrow cone of the camera's view tends to confer
status upon what amounts to a very tiny sector of the vast spectral array available
(not to mention the nonvisual dimensions of the world). Status conferral is
evinced by the phrase "as seen on TV," which is commonly used to promote
products. To be on television is to be, which is the point of Jerzy Kazinski's
novel *Being There* (1970). Electoral politics is now a video art.

When one watches television, the technological imperative of the camera an-
gle, like all methods and media, tremendously restricts the sense of the real. A
television signal is like a needle in a universe of haystacks, like a lone flashlight
beam in the vast ocean. Context is tremendously abbreviated, not only logically,
temporally, and spatially, but also politically, because metaphysics, what counts
as real, is power. Swimming through the virtual Internet too, is akin to groping
through a kelp forest, or wandering through a library while looking through a
tube. One is absolutely restricted to the lines (rails) on the flow chart. "Options"
are predetermined. Nothing new is discovered in the vast electronic archive. The
word "fact" means "things already done." Even with 500 channels of television, still, 500 flashlights surveying the ocean is very limited, to say the least,
especially since many of those beams are filled with contrived sitcoms and other
"fictional" fare including "pseudo-events" (Boorstin, 1964). Watching screens
makes up a good bit of modern reality.

The danger of delusion comes when attention to such a slim reality is inflated
to global import. The privileged perspectives that survive the shot selection and
editing process serve specific interests and values, like "news worthiness" and
commercialism. We work to buy the stuff we watch, including entire lifestyles.
Survival of the fittest means that the images that fit certain desires are the ones
disseminated. The deeper one's faith in what one sees (empiricism), the more
one is fooled into participating in the hegemonic process of truncating reality.
This hypertrophic condition has, for many, erased the boundary between wish

and reality, the actual and the virtual. Agenda-setting systematically generates the limits of the empirically possible (Nessen, 1980; Parenti, 1993).

As mythic polarity fragments into duality, a new awareness emerges; that of space as such. The perspectival analysis of everything, including communication, invariably includes haptification of directionality expressed by "empirical" models that depict "arrows" and "loops" to represent the "path" in-formation "follows" "between" the "source" and the "receiver," as though such phenomena empirically exist. To be "in the loop" means to be systematized and in-formed.

As the awareness of space was reborn from about 1200 A.D. on, the modern individual solidified into an egological monad with an emphasis on "direct(ional)" personal experience (empiricism) and presumed rights/responsibilities. The mind became either a passive (a la the early Locke) or active (a la Kant) process. But, regardless of this duality, both kinds of "mind" depended on a more fundamental duality which posits stimulus "in"-put from "out there." Modern individuals such as Gottfried Leibniz, Francis Bacon, René Descartes, Niccolò Machiavelli, Galileo Galilei, and Thomas Hobbes articulated this new world of dissociation, isolation, communication, and competition.

Understanding became synonymous with dismembering and observing, as much as thinking (Gebser, 1985; Gadamer, 1975; McLuhan, 1964). Concentration (of conscious awareness) became synonymous with "focusing," which indicated a narrowing of "horizon" proportional to depth perception. Consciousness is thus reduced to a channel that abhors "interruption." Privacy becomes highly valued. The greater one's knowledge of a subject, the more "specialized" one becomes so that Folkmann Schluck (one of Edmund Husserl's brightest students) once commented that moderns aspire to eventually "know everything about nothing" (Mickunas, 1978). As one's "scope" (interest) narrows, history and context become impractical and eventually irrelevant.

Via the modern metaphysical prejudice of spatializing materialization, meaningful (valid and legitimate) description is limited to physical extension in space. To make sense means to originate in the senses. A strange irony arises here. The modern world is deemed sensical only insofar as it can be fragmented into uniform units without unique qualities. At the same time that perspectivism became dominant, the search for a unifying principle commenced with the metaphysics of isolation and isomorphism (unitization). The seamless world of direct experience gave way to a dissected and dissociated world that offered more control.

The primitive scale invented value and justice as exchange and balance. The thoroughly arbitrary spatial phenomenon of the scale became the essential requirement for meaningful statements, and paradoxically, the seed of deconstructive nihilism. "Arbitrary meaning" is an absurdity. Furthermore, the scale, or balance, has only two sides. The line and measurement gave birth to progress, pragmatics, and a new sense of knowledge and justice. Truth itself became, for some, a thing (some place?) in space, implying that it was somewhere, such as in a box, or in a library. Truth became "empirical" knowledge.

In such a world, communication becomes rationalized and reduced to being a sequential exchange, and strictly informative. Perspectival informatics is instrumental. Information is conceived as asset, and commodity, with its own channel and finally "highway" (Wiener, 1954; 1961; Shannon and Weaver, 1949; Broadhurst and Darnell, 1965; Krippendorf, 1975). Reciprocity is reduced to stimulus/response, which is heralded as "interactivity." Redundancy, as in the chorus and the narrator, are not valid in a world exclusively concerned with spatial movement (efficiency/speed) (Mumford, 1963; Ellul, 1964; Gebser, 1985; Wright, 1992; Rifkin, 1989; Aveni, 1990; Kula, 1986). Besides, no *two things* can occupy the same space at once. Binary opposition, as in digital reasoning and encoding/decoding, manifests the modern power formation. The whole world is identified as a system of operations and functions.

GALILEAN OTHER-WORLDLINESS

Mathematical Colonialism

Edmund Husserl's (1970) exposition of Galilean-style dissociative science (the two-world theory), has inspired practically every "postmodern" writer.[4] Galilean-style metaphysics constitutes the modern style, whereby direct experience is displaced by an ideal mathematical rendering of the universe (Husserl, 1970). The creation of this mathematical manifold posits a second universe that presumes to "mirror" the first. The "secondary" mathematical mirror presents itself as an accomplishment, rather than as a naturally occurring phenomenon. And, as its "reflections" are integrated "back into" the lifeworld, the "mundane" life of everyday experience is altered so that the Galilean style increasingly colonizes life, becoming the only valid experience (even in casual interactions). For instance, as systematization and standardization (from industrial and military ordination to moral education) was promoted and adopted in the interest of power, then is it any surprise that subsequent research would "discover" systemic relationships in organizations? What is strange is that such empirical "discoveries" were then labeled "naturally occurring."

Hence, we come to see ourselves as living in a time and place increasingly defined by the simulacra and other technologies we create. Our whole world becomes narrowly defined by machines as evinced by such phrases as the "jet age," the "automobile age," the "atomic age," the "computer age," the "corporate age" (bureaucracy and "organization" being the application of means/ ends technique to human bodies in motion reduced to "function"), and so on. In the modern world, we not only argue in a formalized way (debate), but make decisions, dance, sing, exercise, "play," and even cheer in strict form-ation.

Every aspect of life can become a formalized competition. The stricter, or more conformist and precise, the "better," or "more" ideal. Segregation strives for ever more minute distinctions (hair-splitting). Precision strives for the smallest bit yet measurable (definition).

At about the time that debate, rhetoric, and pro-positional logic (method) emerged in the form of explicit rules, the chorus was invented. The West emphasizes explicit verbal and written communication (rules, laws, instructions), while the non-Western (unmodern) style is less explicit, relying more on non-verbal means to communicate feelings than pro-positions. For instance, symphonic coordination and the waltz are fundamentally different from jazzy improvisation and aperspectival spontaneous dancing.

The West is a noun civilization that talks/thinks in terms of fixed things (constants), while most of the non-West is constituted of verb (process) civilizations that are neither materialistic nor means/ends oriented. However, Westernization, which defines development itself as constant material progress (progress itself being a constant), is spreading very rapidly. It spreads because it is goal-oriented, linear, and not just a-ggressive, but pro-gressive.

Where modernity predominates, people conform to, and manifest, these technologized environments as indicated by shifts in emphases (valuation) toward formal education and curricula that enhance digital thinking (''computer literacy'' and ''accounting,'' for instance). Spontaneity is replaced by ever-more planning. To the modern, uncertainty (open time) is experienced as an anxiety that can only be ameliorated by prediction—control. Systematization facilitates prediction. The future is ''charted'' by imaginal means such as calendars and flow charts. Plans are articulated with imbedded rhetoric (deadlines), and ''executed.'' The future is certain because it is made. As little as possible is left ''up to'' chance. The modern world is so intolerantly synchronized that when something unscheduled happens, like a death or sickness in the family, interruption of the structure causes guilt and frustration.

Life-time is increasingly reduced to a means toward infinite progress—endless preparation. ''Work'' is a modern malady instead of a means to leisure. Work is never finished, and growth is never complete. Those who conform the most completely (including thinking in particular concepts, in terms of a particular vocabulary and grammar, and within certain prescribed expectations) are rewarded. Modernity presents a techno-economic power formation that makes it identifiable from other modes of being, such as societies where even ''unproductive'' people (the elderly for instance) still have value and prestige, and where people appear (from the modern perspective) to be ''going nowhere fast.'' The person is not split into private and public selves, so that if public performance suffers due to a private ''problem,'' the private issue is not marginalized as irrelevant by phrases like ''just handle it.'' The modern strives to perpetually rush headlong into a dead, predictable future.

The second-order mathematical universe (*mathesis universalis*) is a modern cultural artifact that establishes a cleavage between the world as experienced in everyday life and the world as it is in scientific truth (''in reality''). Mathematical science proclaims itself to manifest the truth, while denigrating direct personal experience to "mere appearances." What is wrong with the subject is contingency. True truth is a constant. Yet, truth is something always to be accomplished in the future. Truth keeps getting "truer" and "truer." Each generation is "smarter" and "smarter." The modern style manifests a fundamental contradiction. It refuses to accept the perceptual world at face value, while worshipping progress. For the modern scientist (and in classical Platonic style), the imperfect world of contingencies is believed to conceal a permanent mathematical structure. The effort of the modern "methodical" style is to pierce the veil of appearances in order to reveal the true nature of the universe which is "rational," "linearly causal," predictable.[5]

Truth is not given, but must be "tortured from the bosom of nature," as the royal inquisitor himself put it (Bacon, 1942). Truth is a production. One must work to render truth. Bacon is a fine example of "hermetic semiosis" (Eco et al., 1992: 45). Umberto Eco (Eco et al., 1992: 54) has traced this faith throughout the history of the "followers of the veil" (*Adepti del Velame*). Likewise, Paul Ricoeur (1974) drew a similar distinction years earlier when he labeled this duality the "hermeneutics of suspicion" and the "hermeneutics of faith" (1965: 258). Discovering some "thing" or meaning, behind the veil of cognitive distortion or mental faculty (or some other neo-Kantian split between the phenomenal "image" and the noumenal "reality-in-itself"), is essentially invention ("constructivism"). It also raises a serious problem. If, in principle, sensory-based knowledge is flawed, and with equal conviction it is posited that this is the only access one has to the world ("out there"), then one is caught in a paradox. If one can have no supersensory "direct" access to the world (what Maurice Merleau-Ponty called "immaculate perception"), then one cannot know that one's sensory-based knowledge is in fact distorted (Merleau-Ponty, 1962). Distortion is evident only when one can make a comparison between immaculate and maculate versions of reality. Otherwise, distortion and truth are products of interpersonal communication. Facing this problem, either one must abandon the premise that the world is different from what one perceives, or abandon the principle of apodictic knowledge and embrace the hermeneutic principle that "objectivity" amounts to replicable intersubjective agreement, which then opens epistemology to the politics of discourse, the babbling herd (precisely Friedrich Nietzsche's contention). Furthermore, this dilemma exposes epistemology to time, because people change their minds and (brute-power) interests.

The etymology of the word "method" connotes access and way of approach. However, the contention that the world is not in reality as it looks, but that its true condition and constitution must be disclosed and discovered by means of experimental manipulation and mathematical construction, is not retrospectively formulated on the basis of results attained. On the contrary, it is the guiding principle of science which is always and still to be developed. The principle of method institutes development (Gurwitsch, 1974: 35).

In the modern hierarchical world, physics establishes the most "true," the most "hard," and "fundamental" of all materialistic discourses. Physics is the "king" of the sciences. By comparison, all other disciplines lack discipline. As physicist Fred Hoyle put it, fields like biology and geology do not really "prove" theories. Instead they network "scenarios." "It's a kind of herd instinct; I think it probably dates from the days when man was a hunting animal, and the worst thing you could do if you were in a community of, say, twenty men was to disagree about the direction in which you should hunt for the animal; it was better to choose one direction at random and all go in that direction than to split up and each go in a different direction—they needed the whole party to be successful" (Hoyle, 1992: 61). Thus, knowledge is reduced to gang politics and networking ("mainstreaming").[6] But, battles over the interpretation of data rage in physics too (see Chapter 7).

The fact that such a manufactured world no longer seems to require any justification, that the processes of idealization and formalization are self-evident, that presuppositions are forgotten, Husserl called uncritical "traditionality." The cloak, or "tissue of ideas" (*Ideenkleid*), that the mathematical manifold presents, is a mental product that extends rationalization to all observed phenomena, as though trees grow rationally. All worlds posit difference, but only the modern perspectival world exclusively rationalizes segregation as intolerant, two-valued opposition. While Galileo inherited the idealized universe of Euclidean geometric perfection, formalization soon commenced with the algebrazation of geometry by Fermat and Descartes, and later differential calculus invented by Leibniz and Newton. This progressive formalization (dissociation from "mere appearances") extends to contemporary axiomatics and the geometry of abstract spaces culminating in group theory, whereby all intuitive content is emptied, and "objects" are defined by the relations that obtain between them and the operations which can be performed on them. A tightly closed, tautologically definitive circle is the result. Scientific "objects" are conceived (articulated and established) as operational "in nature" (actually by definition). Such abstract entities take on a semblance of independence from the lifeworld of direct experience. They present themselves as being self-evident and self-sufficient in the form of the algorithm, which *establishes* systems of symbols and rules for their operation. The scientific world is an artifact that only one civilization developed. It privileges itself, denying in the most ethnocentric of ways the validity of any and all other worlds.

According to Aron Gurwitsch (1974: 43), this autonomy posits a world where "The operations can be performed 'blindly' and mechanically; the only requirement is that they conform with the operational rules." Methods insure reliability, which means automation. No matter by whom, or how many times the operation is carried out, so long as the same "raw data" are processed by the same "test," the same results *must* occur. To be reliable means to be unchanging, uncreative, unconscious (like a mindless object, "objective").[7] This is the essence of uniform mass production.

There are several consequences of this hypertrophic Platonism. One is the colonization of the world by a quantifying metaphysic (rationalization). The emotional basis of this process is desire for power and control—technologization. Another is the conceptualization of what Husserl called "ideal limit-poles" located at infinity, so that all perceptions are like the mere reflections of ideal objects in water (to use Plato's analogy). Perceptions are merely approximations. The establishment of ideal limit-poles leads to a growing discrepancy between perceptual content and formal entities.

Epistemologically, the relatively indeterminate, variable, and inconsistent (arational) everyday lifeworld pales in comparison with the ideal mathematical manifold, and its totalitarian, closed, internal criteria of reality (self-defining apodictic certainty). The former is only probabilistic, the latter absolutely consistent and predictable (although, and as discussed below, even the human artifact of the mathematical world has shown itself to harbor "internal complications"). The ideal is much more "knowable" (predictable) than the contingent lifeworld, what Nicolas Malebranche meant by "*illusions naturelles*" (1992), and what the mathematician Alfred Renyi was mesmerized by when he queried, "Is it not mysterious that one can know more about things which do not exist than about things which do exist?" (Renyi, 1967: 11).

The virtual displaces the actual in the service of controlling interests. Conformation and conformity are promoted. The creation of the virtual is hardly dispassionate or value-free. It serves to ameliorate the temporal anxiety (or chronic sense of urgency) that plagues the modern, to reduce dreaded uncertainty, a pathetic attempt to conquer or escape time. The virtual also constitutes the source of expert power. The expert is that person who is constituted by, and maintains, the system of knowledge. He or she knows the system because she creates and "practices" it. Engineering and jurisprudence are good examples. Since such virtual systems are deemed to be more fundamental and explanatory of the world, such experts and their discourses have supernatural status. Doctors do miracles, physicists can create suns on the surface of the earth and elements that never existed before. This is powerful magic, for it creates what never was before.

Consequently, what is posited is a two-world theory, where the two worlds are distinguished by unequal ontological status. One domain, the world as it gives itself in direct perception, must be explained in terms of the domain of higher order which persists forever in strictest self-identity. Thus, true knowledge of the unchangeable (*episteme*) which is per(man)ent and universal, displaces the relativity of knowledge of appearances (direct personal observation) (*doxa*). Hence, the replacement of qualitative differences by quantitative ones. Even meaning is replaced by statistical significance (a number), and values are equated with numbers (as if by magic). Value however, is nothing but the relationship of exchange (difference, absence), while numbers presume to present thingness (identity). They are essentially different. The disease of flux is presumably permanently "cured," as when we preserve meat. But consuming this concoction may make one sick.

With the positing of ideal limit-poles, the conditions of what Husserl called the "horizon of infinity" are established (1970: 346). The perfectability of measuring techniques now begins in earnest and with no limitation. Idealization precedes and inspires an endless drive to evermore approximate (but never exact) measurement, constituting a horizon of infinite progress, permanent accomplishment. It presents a kind of mad obsession, or temporal anxiety, or permanent state of urgency without rest. It is a totalitarian dream to conquer, by means of mathematized prediction, not only the here and now but the future too. Thus, the expert not only identifies who you are, but who you will be. (S)he makes it so.

NOTES

1. Such a world was expressed earlier by the Jewish dissociation of human events from the natural rhythm of cyclical periodicity and repetition. Incipient dissociation is also found in the Oriental notion that all the world is made up of consistent units (numbers), which the mystical Pythagoras brought from the eastern Mediterranean island of Samos to Croton (on the east coast of modern Italy) in the sixth century B.C. This included his doctrine of eternal souls, harmonics, and his belief that "number is all."

2. Prior to the Jews, cyclical time was based on the direct observation of naturally recurrent events such as the seasonal migration of birds and fish. Magical ritual often manifested the process of regeneration.

3. With the advent of so-called postmodern science comes a shift from thing to information. It is so-called because modernism is characterized by reductionism (historicism and materialism) which is yet the dominant approach to explanation. All "things" are reduced to information. Subatomic particles are defined as being equal to the information that defines their characteristics, and culture, too, is reduced to communication (Heisenberg, 1958; Ruesch and Bateson, 1951; Hall, 1966; Geertz, 1973). "Man" is redefined as *homo symbolicum* by Ernst Cassirer (1944) whom Clifford Geertz, and most cultural anthropologists, follow. Lingualism (the reduction of the world to language), most radically espoused by poststructuralists like Heidegger (1962), Gadamer (1975), and Roland Barthes (1982), is merely an extension of this trend toward late-modern cybernetics.

4. It is noteworthy that Husserl held a doctorate in mathematics.

5. In this sense, Albert Einstein was the last great modern scientist. He was disturbed by the aperspectival science of quantum theory.

6. Some journal editors encourage this by turning to the references of submitted manuscripts first to see if there are any references older than five years. If so, they reject the piece. Such a policy assures the promotion of very short-lived fashions; what some call "headline social science."

7. Science has breakthroughs when inconsistency occurs. When the system is violated by free association, inspired daydreaming, hunches, accident, and "strokes of genius," then an opening for change is enabled. The liminal threshold between something and nothing appears just as it is crossed with a new idea, invention, or "discovery" (often by using other inventions). Science, after all, is just like the rest of life, indeterminate. Scientists cannot predict the future of science.

REFERENCES

Aveni, A. (1990) *Empires of Time*. London: I. B. Tauris & Company.

Bacon, F. (1942) *New Atlantis*. New York: Classics Club, W. J. Black.

Barthes, R. (1982) *Mythologies*. New York: Hill & Wang.

Boorstin, D. (1964) *The Image: A Guide to Pseudo-Events in America*. New York: Harper & Row.

Broadhurst, A. R., and D. K. Darnell. (1965) ''An Introduction to Cybernetics and Information Theory.'' *Quarterly Journal of Speech* 51, no. 4: 442–453.

Cassirer, E. (1944) *An Essay on Man*. New Haven, CT: Yale University Press.

Chomsky, N. (1972) *Language and Mind*. New York: Harcourt, Brace, Jovanovich.

Comstock, G., S. Chaffee, N. Katzman, M. McCombs, and D. Roberts. (1978) *Television and Human Behavior*. New York: Columbia University Press.

Davis, P., and R. Hersh. (1981) *The Mathematical Experience*. Boston: Houghton Mifflin.

———. (1986) *Descartes' Dream: The World According to Mathematics*. Boston: Houghton Mifflin.

Derrida, J. (1981) *Dissemination*. Chicago: University of Chicago Press.

Eco, U., R. Rorty, and J. Culler. (1992) *Interpretation and Overinterpretation*. Cambridge, England: Cambridge University Press.

Eliade, M. (1963) *Myth and Reality*. New York: Harper and Row.

Ellul, J. (1964) *The Technological Society*. New York: Vintage.

Foucault, M. (1979) *Discipline and Punish: The Birth of the Prison*. New York: Vintage.

Frege, G. (1984) ''On Sense and Reference.'' In *Readings in Semantics*, edited by F. Zabeeh et al. Urbana: University of Illinois Press (pp. 118–140).

Gadamer, H. G. (1975) *Truth and Method*. New York: Seabury Press.

Gebser, J. (1985) *The Ever-Present Origin*. Athens: Ohio University Press.

Geertz, C. (1973) *The Interpretation of Cultures*. New York: Basic Books.

Grant, E. (1977) *Physical Science in the Middle Ages*. Cambridge, England: Cambridge University Press.

Gudykunst, W., and Y. Kim. (1992) *Communicating with Strangers: An Approach to Intercultural Communication*. New York: McGraw-Hill.

Gurwitsch, A. (1974) *Phenomenology and the Theory of Science*. Evanston, IL: Northwestern University Press.

Hall, E. T. (1966) *The Hidden Dimension*. New York: Anchor Books.

Heidegger, M. (1962) *Being and Time*. London: SCM Press.

Heisenberg, W. (1958) *Physics and Philosophy: The Revolution in Modern Science*. New York: Harper & Row.

Hoyle, F. (1992) Essay in *Stephen Hawking's ''A Brief History of Time''*: A Reader's Companion, edited by S. Hawking. New York: Bantam.

Humboldt, F. W. (1973) ''On the Historian's Task.'' In *The Theory and Practice of History: Collected Manuscripts from 1829–1880*. Indianapolis: Bobbs-Merrill.

Hume, D. (1973) *A Treatise Concerning Human Understanding*. London: Oxford University Press.

Husserl, E. (1962) *Ideas*. New York: Collier.

———. (1970) *The Crisis of European Sciences and Transcendental Phenomenology*. Evanston, IL: Northwestern University Press.

Innis, H. (1950) *Empire and Communication*. Oxford, England: University of Oxford Press.

Kant, I. (1929) *Critique of Pure Reason*. New York: St. Martin's Press.

Kazinski, J. (1970) *Being There*. New York: Harcourt, Brace, Jovanovich.

Kramer, E. M., ed. (1992) *Consciousness and Culture*. Westport, CT: Greenwood Press.

———. (1993) "Mass Media and Democracy." In *Open Institutions: The Hope for Democracy*, edited by J. Murphy and D. Peck. Westport, CT: Praeger.

Krippendorf, K. (1975) "Information Theory." In *Communication and Behavior*, edited by G. Hanneman and W. McEwen. Reading, MA: Addison-Wesley.

Kula, W. (1986) *Measures and Men*. Princeton, NJ: Princeton University Press.

Malebranche, N. (1992) *Philosophical Selections: From the Search After Truth*. Indianapolis: Hackett Publishing.

McLuhan, M. (1964) *Understanding Media: The Extensions of Man*. New York: Mentor Books.

Merleau-Ponty, M. (1962) *Phenomenology of Perception*. London: Routledge and Kegan Paul.

Mickunas, A. (1995) personal conversation.

Morris, D. (1967) *The Naked Ape*. New York: McGraw-Hill.

———. (1969) *The Human Zoo*. New York: Delta.

Mumford, L. (1963) *Techniques and Civilization*. New York: Harcourt, Brace and World.

Nessen, R. (1980) "Now Television's the King-Maker." *TV Guide*, May 10 (p. 4).

Nietzsche, F. (1974) *The Gay Science*. New York: Vintage.

Ong, W. (1982) *Orality and Literacy*. London: Routledge.

Palmer, R. (1969) *Hermeneutics*. Evanston, IL: Northwestern University Press.

Parenti, M. (1993) *Inventing Reality: The Politics of News Media*, 2nd ed. New York: St. Martin's Press.

Polak, F. L. (1961) *The Image of the Future*, 2 Vols. Leyden, Netherlands: A. W. Sijthoff.

Pribram, K. (1971) *Languages of the Brain: Experimental Paradoxes and Principles of Neuropsychology*. Englewood Cliffs, NJ: Prentice-Hall.

Renyi, A. (1967) *Dialogues on Mathematics*. San Francisco: Holden-Day.

Ricoeur, P. (1965) *History and Truth*. Evanston, IL: Northwestern University Press.

———. (1974) *The Conflict of Interpretations*. Evanston, IL: Northwestern University Press.

Rifkin, J. (1989) *Time Wars*. New York: Henry Holt and Company.

Ruesch, J., and G. Bateson. (1951) *Communication: The Social Matrix of Psychiatry*. New York: W. W. Norton & Company.

Russell, B., and A. N. Whitehead. (1967) *Principia Mathematica*. Cambridge, England: Cambridge University Press.

Shannon, C., and W. Weaver. (1949) *The Mathematical Theory of Communication*. Urbana: University of Illinois Press.

Wiener, N. (1954) *The Human Use of Human Beings: Cybernetics and Society*. Boston: Houghton Mifflin.

———. (1961) *Cybernetics: Or, Control and Communication in the Animal and the Machine*. Cambridge, MA: MIT Press.

Wright, L. (1992) *Clockwork Man*. New York: Barnes and Noble.

4

Modernity

Waste not your time, so fast it flies;
Method will teach you time to win;
Hence, my young friend, I would advise,
With college logic to begin.
Then will your mind be so well brac'd,
In Spanish boots so tightly lac'd,
That on 'twill circumspectly creep,
Thought's beaten track securely keep,
Nor will it, ignis-fatuus like,
Into the path of error strike.
Then many a day they'll teach you how
The mind's spontaneous acts, till now
As eating and as drinking free,
Require a process;—one, two, three!
                    —Goethe's Mephistopheles to the Young Student

PRELIMINARY NOTES

Under the purview of modernity, magic correspondence and mythic complementarity no longer apply except as "superstition" and "fantasy." In accord
with the dominance of a spatial/material metaphysic, "the message" is seen as
a reified thing-in-itself that is "exchanged" across space without interpretation,
motive, or emotion. In an address given on top of Pnyx Hill in Athens in 1964,
Werner Heisenberg noted that after searching for an understanding of our experience of patterns (what Plato called archetypes), mathematics could not describe them. He said, "Whatever the explanation of these other forms of
understanding may be, the language of the images, metaphors and similes, is

probably the only way to approach them'' (1970: 45). What he came to understand was that mathematics, too, is a metaphorical system of expression that itself manifests a particular consciousness structure, which distinguishes modernity from other worldviews.

The impulse to create mathematics, science, and technology cannot be explained by mathematics, science, or technology. The impulse is neither mathematical nor scientific, indeed not logical. The great logician of quantum mechanics, C. F. von Weizacker (1949: 190) has written that ''The scientific and technical world of modern man is the result of his daring enterprise, knowledge without love.'' Friedrich Nietzsche (1973: 114–116, *Beyond Good and Evil*, sec. 207) referred to so-called disinterested objectivity as ''pure will-less knowledge.'' The ''objective man'' turns himself into an instrument, a ''self-polishing mirror'' of Reality, as if this is an end in itself, indeed the salvation of man from himself, achieving the *caput mortuum* of all virtue. But it ends up being the *tour de force* of both vanity and slavery at once. The ''objective man'' merely reflects, and is unmoved. If this were accomplished, (s)he would be utterly redundant (dead). The dream of pure disinterestedness exaggerates into the scientific narcissism of self-transfiguration, a form of self-captivity taken from the religious belief that humankind is atop (caps the pyramid of) all creation. The story of Darth Vader, in the George Lucas film series *Star Wars*, is a retelling of Mary Shelley's *Frankenstein*. Vader has become as much machine as man, and a slave to external forces (the ''Emperor,'' which is the essence of causal determinism). In *Frankenstein* the real monster is the doctor.

Modernity stresses spatial coincidence, absolute arbitrariness. Things lose their connectedness; their mutual relatedness found in mysteries and magical unity. For instance, Aristotle's enthymeme expressed a new attitude that reduced knowledge of the real to probability. The Latin *arbitrarius* is derived from *arbiter*, signifying law and dictatorship. According to the modern perspectival consciousness structure, mediation between separate positions became the source of method and media. Method and media presuppose modern space. Because of separation, knowledge of the given became unsure, suspect, debatable.

In the allegory of the cave, Plato's hapless spelunker went out into three-dimensional space, the noumenal realm, and then returned to the two-dimensional cave, the phenomenal realm of ambivalent opinion, becoming the prototypical intellectual hero (due to his sacrifice) for Western culture. This story indicates a conflict between emergent perspectivity and relatively submergent mythical awareness. Even the way the story is told expresses an awareness in transition, for Plato told the story in a mythical way, relying on dialogue and the ambivalent discourse of allegory and metaphor.

The prototype of modern (presumably) nonfigural scientific discourse, with its pretension of being a perfectly referential language, appeared a generation later with Aristotle's analytic monologues (Gebser, 1985; Husserl, 1970; Merleau-Ponty, 1964; Heidegger, 1971; Gurwitsch, 1974; Derrida, 1973; 1978; Rorty, 1991; Baudrillard, 1983). It was Aristotle's new ''disturbing'' attitude, or perspective (method), that caused him to be passed over as leader of the school established by Plato. Hence, he left Athens for the court of King Philip of Macedon, where he created a monster.

MODERN AND WESTERN

Despite calls for an alternative modernity from the formerly "nonaligned" policy makers of the world, for most (popular) discursive uses today, "modern" is synonymous with "Western" (which in this context includes Soviet and Chinese systems of centralized planning). However, modernity presumes mythology, be it Confucian heavenly justification for order, or purpose-oriented progress. "Ideology" is a mental-rational phenomenon that transforms mythology. An ideological (or metaphysical) treatment of myth is exemplified by Thomas Jefferson's rewriting of the Bible, by which he attempted to remove all the miracles and retain only that which made sense in his mind, empirical statements and logically consistent positions.

Marxism, capitalism, democratization, and other totalizing programs are forms of Western perspectivism. "Modernization" is practically identical with "Westernization." The civilizational values of the West constitute modernity. Insofar as "West" and "modern" are interchangeably used, "West" has no geographical import. Instead, "Western" and "modern" denote an attitude, a consciousness structure. Perspectival mental-rationality is not restricted to a certain time or place, but constitutes a unitized style of space and time. Confucian China was holistic. The "logic" of holism is fundamentally different from unitary logic, which presumes partitioning (unitization) which enables systematic interconnections between parts. Medieval Europe, for instance, did not exhibit what we would call "Western" or "modern" tendencies as much as the Arab world or Confucian China during the same period. Consequently, one could say that as cultures around the world "modernize," they exhibit more and more materialism, grand-scale hierarchization/coordination, technological prowess, dissociation, a schism between individual and mass, and faith in "progress" or "development."

As "developing" nations come "on line," it is presumed that they abandon their deranged ways and become arranged (domesticated). In this sense, the mad rush to become modern, to westernize, to mimic and imitate the West, is itself already the triumph of Western values, including *mimesis*, progress and vertical evolution. Imitation is the essential behavioral mode of commercial culture. The urbanization of mass populations around the world is indicative of the seductiveness of the Western concept of time, especially the idea of having a "future" that is different from the "past." Around the globe, intergenerational and class conflicts are also signs of this fundamental shift in attitude. The generation "gap," and clash of "traditional" and "modern" values is painfully evident throughout the "developing" world.

In the Mediterranean region, this fundamental change toward a perspectival world is evinced by countless examples, including the value of spatial *mimesis* in classical Greek art, Aristotelian variable analytics, the mathematical modelling of Archimedes and Euclid (Pythagoras presented a magical attitude whereby numbers were neither referential nor arbitrary but identical with the world), "realism" in the theater (which switched subjects from gods and spirit beings to men), and the murals of Pompeii. For instance, the latter *artifacts* depict landscapes, as such, and "still lifes," both of which indicate "realistic" representation (control). Realism and *mimesis* presume a fixed, stable truth, a changeless "point of view." This shift to modern perspectivism is also expressed in Roman garden designs and the pastoral scenes of late bucolic poetry such as Virgil's *Ecloges*.

Since the current world condition is dominated by the value of becoming "modern," "modernizing," "westernizing," "developing," in a word perspectivism (perspectivally educated elites around the world), it is important to clarify the terms "modern" and "modernity." They are not used to denote a specific span, or position in conventional geography or history. In fact, history, as a recorded time-line, is itself a modern, spatialized phenomenon. Rather, following Gebser's (1985) acceptation, "modern" is a mode of thinking and expressing. The phrase "civilizational expression" indicates that all behavior can be seen as communicative, a theory not unlike that promoted by the hermeneutics of Wilhelm von Humboldt (1973), Ernst Cassierer (1944), Martin Heidegger (1971), and Hans-Georg Gadamer (1981), the semiotics of Charles S. Peirce (1940) and Ferdinand de Saussure (1974), the ethnolinguistics of Benjamin Whorf (1956), and the ethnography of Clifford Geertz (1973). However, this author agrees with Gebser that expression is not limited exclusively to the domain of lingualism, so popular among the students of many of these scholars.

Communication tends to be reduced to either brute behavior or language. To exclude interpretation, as many behavioralists do, seems patently absurd. Language (talk) and behavior are strictly separated from each other, as in the case of pornography, where many believe that depictions of rape are not the same as "real" rape. Neither ontology is exhaustive, yet proponents of both behaviorism and lingualism tend to argue for a totalitarian scope of explanation. In other words, everything is either behavior or language, and each claim is mutually excluding (reductionistic). As is typical of all master narratives (intolerant, mutually excluding "regional ontologies," to use Edmund Husserl's terminology from *Ideas I*, 1962), language and behavior attempt to ground each other, to explain each other out of existence. Speech becomes merely behavior, and "behavior" becomes merely a word. Under the intolerant attitude of master narratives, everything is discourse, everything is language, everything is writing, everything is response, and so on. This is the nature of the messianic obsession that fragments the world into warring camps of mutually excluding, but all encompassing, truths. But of course, a category of everything is senseless.

Each consciousness structure (magic, mythic, and perspectival) exhibits a different mode of expressivity including dissociation (see Chapter 2 for further explanation of magic and myth). Artifacts cannot hide from themselves. Renaissance painting, for instance, does not represent three-dimensional space, it originates it, as such. It established different criteria for rendering a different kind of relationship. If one does not follow those criteria, then one has failed to create "correct" perspective, according to the Renaissance cannon. Criteria are not "elsewhere," anymore than logic is to be found in a specific place (like the contingent tissue of a brain). Criteria are manifested in the expression (artifact or behavior) itself.

Magic peoples, who live a predominantly one-dimensional sense of spaceless and timeless identity, exhibit idolatry. Hence, to steal a talisman is not to steal a *symbol* of power, but to steal *the* power. Magic incantation is not symbolic, but idolic. Identity is presumed. Words are generative. For instance, to know someone's name is to gain control over her. For this reason, many predominantly magical peoples, like the original Powhatans of North America, named members of their society twice; one name for "public" use, and the other a secret, "true name." This issue is exhibited in the trial of Shoko Asahara in Japan. Asahara is the leader of the *Aum Shinrikyo* (Aum Supreme Truth) cult that put sarin poison gas in a subway in Tokyo, killing many and injuring hundreds. During the trial, the prosecution has insisted on calling Asahara Chizuo Matsumoto, which is his original name. By so doing, the prosecution is denying his power to rename himself, to don a persona that may protect him from social/moral forces. The prosecution insists on treating him like other "common" criminals, to demythologize him. Name-changing is a magical process common for would-be mass leaders such as Herr Führer, Rock Hudson, John Denver, Prince, Marilyn Monroe, Trotsky, Stalin, David Koresh, and so on. Name-changing is an expression of incantatory power and a magical attempt to transform oneself. This often takes the form of identifying oneself with other forces and meanings like bombs, ideas, and animals. Each pope takes a name, and in the secular world titles abound. Rock bands, corporations, athletic teams, and military squads carefully choose names which often outlast the original members. A great deal of care is taken in choosing the names of machines like fighter jets and automobiles. Iconic insignias also mark identities, from high school "letter jackets" to military patches which usually include lightning bolts, stars, and eagles. "Hand signs" and colors mark urban gang membership just as a subordinate in the military must salute first. Graffiti marks territorial claims just like national flags. All such markers of identity are idolically magical and symbolically mythical. Depending on the degree of identity with the markers, a person may go so far as to kill and die to protect the integrity of a marker. Under magical awaring, disrespect for the marker means disrespect for the person/group.

But, as mentioned above, civilizational expressions cannot hide. For instance, when Iosif Vissarionovich Dzhugashvili took the name "Man of Steel" ("Stalin") it tells us less about his mettle and more about his magical and mythic fantasies, and the fantasies those around him shared. His portraits never aged, and his name sent shudders even through the highest-ranking Soviet leaders. Those who actually met him were very often astounded to find a chubby, graying, five-foot-two-inch man that reminded some of a "waiter." Names are transformative, like "doctor" and "vice president." For a woman to "take her husband's name" is an incantatory change of identity.

By contrast, mythic consciousness exhibits a tendency toward dissociation so that communication is ambivalent and symbolic, as in allegory and metaphor, which calls into being the need for interpretation (hermeneutics, protomethod, oracles, and "channelers"). For example, to steal someone's crucifix may be sacrilegious, but it is not the same as stealing her god. The crucifix is only a symbol that "stands in for" the deity. This indicates a nascent spatialization which enables an ontological (and for many literally a physical) gap to open. However, in the mythic world, ambivalence predominates so that the crucifix is not totally arbitrary either, but presents a highly motivated association that can inflame great emotional expression.

Another good example of mythical and magical reality is the case of the highly violent clashes between Hindus and Muslims in Northern India. Periodically, these two worlds clash as they attack each other and each other's sacred places. For instance, in 1992, tens of thousands of Hindus rioted and destroyed Muslim mosques in retaliation for the destruction of a Hindu temple that marked the very spot where the Lord God Rama was born. This temple did not merely symbolize a place, but concretely marked *the* place of Rama's incarnation in human form. Such profound emotion may one day exploit nuclear technology for its expression. Technological behavior is always an expression of a more fundamental want. Magical and mythic attitudes are not extinct, but express themselves in many ways.

An example of emergent perspectivism is the ancient Greek "amphitheater," which initiated theatrical distance. "Amphi" means "both sides," as in "amphibian."[1] The theatrical distance, now so rigid with television and movies, was ambivalent in the ancient Greek theater. The amphitheater (like Plato's dialogues on the way to Aristotle's monologues) is an expression that is on the cusp between mythical participation and perspectival spectatorship.[2] But even television viewing is understandable only if emotional desire is taken into account, which Elihu Katz's (1974) theory of uses and gratifications does. As Jib Fowles, in his 1992 book *Why Viewers Watch*, argues, they do so because they like it, and want to. For the viewer, television is "good." The earlier direct effects, or "bullet" theory suggests a magical prereflective identity between the viewer and the viewed (Schramm, 1971). Even though the experience of viewing is not so simple, imitation would seem to evince this dimension of viewing. Hundreds of millions of "moderns" sit in a perspectival posture facing a screen for hours every day. As Nietzsche (1966: 258, *Thus Spoke Zarathustra*, section 4, "The Magician," part 2) said, "Today belongs to the mob." They are not pursuing symbolic logic, they are converging on shared fantasies which they enjoy (Bormann, 1985). Whether this is a good or bad thing is another issue. The point here is that technologies are conceived for a purpose which is a want or need. Modernity presumes magic and mythic consciousness. Technology is concretized (expressed) magical desire and mythic imagination (*imago*—vision).

In modernity, the mythic polar ambivalence (expressed in the ancient amphitheater) between participant actor and passive spectator is sundered into a dissociated duality. Hence, many modern thinkers have acknowledged Hegel's accuracy in identifying a dialectical structure of contradicting formations. This modern duality emerged from the church mass, with its intense emphasis on conformism and ordination, and romantic individualism. The age of the troubadours (1200) heralded the modern individual subject who would demand self-expression and self-determination in the face of medieval dogma. This self-assertion was articulated in the demand to choose one's own mate, even at the peril of eternal damnation. The story of Tristan and Isolde's love epitomizes this shift in power, a new awareness of a self-possessed individual with the liberty of discrete judgement (discretion and evaluation).

Immediately the two opposing orientations (mythic unperspectival and modern perspectival worlds) clashed, as the church launched the Albigensian Crusade in 1209, what Joseph Campbell (Campbell and Moyers, 1988: 186) has called ''one of the most monstrous crusades in the history of Europe.'' Of all the crusades, this one indicates that the church understood (as Plato had earlier with his advice in *The Republic* to expel poets) the profound danger individualism would pose for it. Individual passion is dangerous to dehumanizing systems. It was more threatening to the medieval church than Ottoman invaders, who could be stopped by force of arms. In fact, with the fall of Grenada, the Muslims (''Moors,'' which is the Berberized pronunciation) left behind a ticking time bomb in the form of books including romantic poetry and Aristotle.

The troubadours (who were mostly of the Iberian Peninsula) initiated an ontopolitical conflict, from the ''ground up,'' so to speak. Individual desire and judgement would constitute the new ground for knowledge and action. Platonic principle would be displaced by Aristotelian probability. Egoistic pragmatism, which favors material results over spiritual growth, would express a profound prejudice by labeling the entire era of religious civilization ''dark'' and ''medieval.'' In retaliation, church leaders would call the descent into the values of materialistic pragmatism a ''culture of death,'' a dispirited world of vibrating atoms and nothing more.

Church/state power (including divine right of kings rooted in ancient Jewish paternalistic hierarchy—aristocracy) depended on dogmatic ''blind'' faith, and the maintenance of a system of esoteric knowledge. Once the romantic subject came into being, demands for direct personal verification of claims (empirical observation) completely undermined the miraculous power structure of medieval Europe. Induction supplanted deduction. The split is traceable to the conflict between the Socratics (the pragmatic ''Socratism'' of ''Alexandrian Man,'' as Nietzsche put it [1967b: 87, 109, *The Birth of Tragedy*, sections 13–18) and pre-Socratic Dionysian creativity. The split or tear in the ontological foundation of Western thought progressed from Platonic unperspectival allegorical dialogic to Aristotelian analytical monologic. Plato posited massive (generalizable and totalitarian) formalism, while Aristotle turned toward contingent individuation and probability. These two distinctly Western principles (fundamental orientations) have continued to battle each other in various guises such as conservative/ liberal; science/rhetoric (power—technology); description/manipulation; private capital/communism; public structure/private freedom; corporate giantism/entrepreneurialism; and permanence/flux. To understand modernity, one must understand this fundamentally dualistic structure of consciousness which marks mental-rational perspectivism. This dualism is at the core of Hegel's (and later Marx's) contention that Western culture contains contradictions. According to Gebser (1985: 3):

The current situation manifests on the one hand an egocentric individualism exaggerated to extremes and desirous of possessing everything, while on the other it manifests an equally extreme collectivism that promises the total fulfillment of man's being. In the latter instance we find the utter abnegation of the individual valued merely as an object in the human aggregate; in the former a hyper-valuation of the individual who, despite his limitations, is permitted everything. This deficient, that is destructive, antithesis divides the world into two warring camps, not just politically and ideologically, but in all areas of human endeavor.

Modern empiricism presumes subjectivism and, as Max Weber (1949) noted, it romanticizes numbers, which are not empirical things. With the rise of the modern individual, interest in communication was reborn. In a world where knowledge begins with individual sense data, a necessary condition for transcending knowledge is formal structures of intersubjective communication. As ways for the individual to interact with others and the world, method and mediation became prominent concerns once again. The invention of method has been a *cause célèbre* because it has meant the path to the new reality, the ''new world,'' the ''new Atlantis'' (for instance) (Bacon, 1942).

Because methods present new ways of seeing (new realities), they generate whole new fields of research, and their inventors often become targets of great (almost religious) admiration as well as consternation. Examples include Newton, Husserl, de Saussure, and Skinner. Formal debate, disputation, and ''cross'' examination of incompatible individual interpretations (perspectives) constitute the modern mode of ''refereeing'' the birth of knowledge. But such contentious interaction presumes a shared ''hermeneutic horizon,'' shared language, and topical theme. Argumentation, understanding and misunderstanding, presumes a communicative ground that is more or less shared.

Against such a shared horizon which is basically magical (making sense and nonsense), the perspectival modern world exhibits a high degree of dissociation. According to its credo, signs and signals, such as mathematical notation and digital coding, are *totally* arbitrary. Hence, modern hermeneutic theory is obsessed with distinguishing the necessary conditions for convention to exist, for arbitrariness to be limited so that communication and mutual understanding and misunderstanding are possible. In modernity, signs tend to displace analog symbols and the identity of idolatry. "Modern" is manifested as a privileging and supersession of mental-rationality over emotion, information over communication. The ideal of the modern citizen is to be "informed." According to the modern worldview, reciprocity, which has been regarded as a necessary condition for communication, is not necessary for being informed. This is the basic difference between the mass audience member and the conversationalist.

MODERN MASS: AGGREGATE, NOT COMMUNITY

The origin of method lies in classical Greek thought which the Romans systematized before it went into hibernation, or suspended animation (an oxymoron) within monastery walls, for about one thousand years. Medieval monastic discipline was methodically conformist (i.e., the fool-proof plan to salvation offered by the modern "Methodists"). Monastic discipline shunned all "impurities" (or forms of untameable wildness such as women and snakes) that could be disruptive. Disruption means change, difference, choice, *Time*. Disruption of order was a punishment for mortal men expressed as woman (Pandora) in classical Greek mythology. Pandora (not unlike Eve) chose to open the forbidden box of agonies that belonged to Prometheus. The word "heretic" is derived from the Greek "*hairetikos*" meaning, "being able to choose." Method epitomizes patriarchal intolerance. The purpose of method is to systematize the very process of investigation and thinking. This is done in the interest of reliability, which is an effort to replicate "the same," to arrest criminal time and promote permanence. A fact must be fixed. Difference equals maculation.

The heresy of the Gnostics was their faith in knowledge and freedom, which imposed the burden of reasoned responsibility on individuals. A necessary condition for freedom is change—time. In the Garden of Eden, time was not known. Aging, disease, and death did not exist. The bliss of ignorance was expressed as a kind of automation or method (specific way) of being, a perpetual state without beginning or end, without maturation or awareness. When Adam and Eve exercised individual choice and ate the fruit of the tree of knowledge, they fell into time, which is an agony of perpetual loss. The snake in the tree, like all snakes, sheds its skin signifying temporality. Their punishment for growing up was to know pain.

The Renaissance presented a world of choices. With the reemergence of the individual came a new, more sympathetic reading of Aristotle. The traditional saintly heros were rejected for a new type exemplified by Aristotle. Aristotle did not cause the Renaissance anymore than Plato caused the Middle Ages. Instead, we choose our histories and select those who personify what we want. We select those figures who agree with us and can act as legitimation for our desires. Aristotle's rebirth (the "Renaissance") added credence to a new notion

of knowledge, which cast doubt on testimony in favor of direct personal observation, and the methodical replicability of events. The compulsion to find a
champion, especially one with antique credentials, evinces the need to find an
alibi, or cover, for one's beliefs and desires. The rhetoric of citation, the phrase
"according to . . ." allows one to say what one wants without taking all the
blame for it. It is a rhetoric of the inevitable, the ultimate master. The Renaissance man could say Aristotle made me do it.

Method surpasses supernatural mystery (mythical imagination), which rapidly
lost its relevance after the Renaissance; nor was magic very reliable. Power is
emasculated and humiliated when it fails unexpectedly. Physical deeds and
graphic accuracy increasingly became the focus of artists' attention. History
changed from being a paroler hobby to a founding discipline that generated
master narratives of the world. An emphasis on memory, as a boundary against
changing mind, characterizes modernity, as in the rhetorical training of Isocrates,
who believed that memory and memorization manifested power. Bureaucracy,
which is institutional memory, grows so that surveillance can gain power. This
in turn has driven the quest for ever more powerful computers to store and
process more and more information. Recording technologies have expanded rapidly. Managers (law enforcers and system guards) charged with "over-sight"
clamor for ever more powerful technologies that enable instant recall of biog-
raphies to help justify evaluations. From scholastic to credit and penal data-
"bases," memory acts as foundational power to legitimize decisions. Memory
is essentially the attempt to enhance permanence. This is technological determinism, the formative will behind the ever-changing shadows.

Likewise, the post-Renaissance exhibits the aspiration to create memory that
is "photographic" (visiocentric). With modernity, recording becomes a central
concern in order to justify present conditions, as in institutional memory and
other forms of memorial culture. Surveillance takes a quantum leap as everyone's actions are dutifully recorded and accounted for (evaluated as in financial
records, consuming records, resumes, vitas, medical records, "rap sheets," etc.).
Inquisitorial interest is preserved in modern bureaucracy. We are all surveyed
and "on line." Modernity celebrates the individual with biographical identity.
Our identities are increasingly hard to shake. They follow us everywhere as
systems of monitoring become more powerful. Our record is our virtual self.
To whom it may concern, our record is more trustworthy than we are. For
instance, in May of 1996, the U.S. military proudly announced that commanders
could finally access personnel files, including enlisted evaluation reports and
enlisted duty history, from anywhere in the world. "The goal is to give commanders themselves this worldwide direct access at their desk" ("More Personnel," 1996: 14). This information will be used for promotional decisions and
to increase efficiency and decrease assigning the "wrong" person for a job
(information from the *Tinker Take-Off* newspaper for Tinker Airforce Base,
Oklahoma City, Oklahoma). The narrowing of expertise and function within the
larger system continues. The possibility to change, to "turn over a new leaf,"

is being expunged from the system. The penultimate interest is that which en-hances the efficiency of the system, and efficiency abhors second and third chances. One must mind his or her "p's and q's" like never before, because the system has an unforgiving memory and an increasingly powerful surveillance feedback control. To successfully "move on" and "start over," one must have good "references." The past is becoming ever more sticky.

The flip side of modern individual identity is the mass human who is factored into large number calculations in the interest of social, economic, political, and commercial engineering. The ego-hypertrophy of the celebrity stands opposite the masses. Both are thoroughly modern phenomena. They are co-constituting binary phenomena. By contrast, in the magic world, text and context (which are also co-constitutional phenomena) did not exist. Interpretation is a problem in the mythic world where texts emerge as semi-autonomous messages "about" (ab-out). Ironically, in the modern world, where it is assumed that messages are most autonomous (arbitrary), interpretation is not more of a problem, but sup-posedly no problem at all. This is because, though absolutely arbitrary, codes are semantically primitive—unambiguous such as on/off.

The medieval monastic world was one preoccupied with mythic orality, ex-pressed by sacred and synchronized chanting, homiletics, epidectic speech, in-cantation, trappism, and "the Word." This emphasis on audition, and the cave-like interiority of Romanesque churches, displaced the previously dominant pagan stress on sight and open temples, and its inherent democratizing tendency. The democratizing nature of sight is expressed by the phrase "The ayes have it." "Further-more," modern democratic tendencies presume quantification. The phonetic identity of self-expressed "I" and "eye" is significant. To "Eye" (to "observe") also indicates a manner or way of looking (through space), and, in nautical terminology, the precise *direction* from which the wind blows.

Direction is a choice, and choice is the essence of the democratic cosmos. Moderns perceive, with exclusive validity, an extensive world of spatial (visual) relationships such as linear sequentiality, physical surfaces, and measurement. "Sur-face" means that the world presumably presents an "over" face, common to everyone, which opens the possibility for modern democratic behavior. Each individual can see "the truth" for him- or herself. For instance, in modern jurisprudence "materiality" means relevance.

While the mona-stery ideology of Thomism (Platonic formalism) kindled the smoldering embers of perspectival culture, romanticism added libidinal fuel to it, thus giving rebirth to full-blown and revolutionary mental-rational modernity. But as Marx understood, modernity carries within itself the seeds of the post-modern. Democracy presumes a revolutionary realization that the world is not fixed but rather *(con)ventional*. It does not have to be this way, that way, or any *way*. This has made all the difference. In a world of fixed facts, where the law of noncontradiction and the mutual exclusion of binary opposites on a var-iable analytic line prevails, there is no room for "reasonable persons to dis-agree." Conformism is a prerequisite to methodical progress. Thus, even democracy can lead to the tyranny of system, the tyranny of the systematically established majority. The postmodern impulse is to reverse this systematic privileging and to champion the marginal voice. This tactic enables the projection of an alternative future/interpretation from a peripheral vision (source). In this way, alternatives can emerge. This is the essence of creative pluralism. Though championed by Jacques Derrida (1978), it is hardly new.

Modern perspectivism (visiocentrism), like ancient perspectivism, stresses the visual dimension of space and light which is why Gothic and Renaissance cathedrals abandoned the Romanesque enclosure and strove for new architectural forms, like the flying buttress, that enabled the construction of walls of glass. Just as light leads to the development of the eye (or darkness leads away from it as in cave fish), the desire for a transparent solid inspired inventive experimentation culminating with glass. The precursor to modern movies and television is the public display of stained glass windows which established a visual narrative for illiterate, indiscriminate masses. The concept of "illuminated" words comes from the heavenly light that streamed through the medieval glass walls bringing to awareness a new understanding of the Christian universe (story).

During the "Dark Ages," spiritual relationships, which are for moderns not so readily perceivable as physical surfaces (and are therefore the purview of religious elitism), took precedence over relationships between things. What may seem to be an incompatibility between auditory and visual emphases is explainable by the fact that the early Christian church organization was largely enabled by its adoption of the pagan Roman infrastructure (especially the postal service and roads), which was very much modern-rational, and pragmatically useful.[3]

During the period of mythological domination, the organizing impulse and compulse of antique modernity was kept alive within the secure walls of the medieval monastery. "Orders" were established, as well as "missions" throughout the spatial world, in conventional patriarchal fashion. The walls were ramparts that segregated the chaos of a collapsing empire (into wild barbarism) and domesticating culture (law).

Techniques of behavior modification in the interest of "corrections" (which means alignment with the maintenance needs of the system) became institutionalized (rationalized). From the beginning of the "Age of [spatial] Exploration" (and partly due to the fragmenting tendencies of the Re-formation), the Catholic Church was in the forefront of expansion. As the intensity of time became more evident, the orders established schedules and schemes for the regulation of bodily functions and religious "observances." Later, such conventional power relations were "naturalized," or inoculated from reflexive critique. The system is what is the case. Facts are things already done, with the consequence that debate is preempted.

This emphasis on the politics or control of the body achieved sublime proportions in the scientific management of Fredrick Winslow Taylor's time-and-motion studies, Henry Ford's assembly lines, and current keystroke surveillance to which computer operators fall victim.[4] We all work with "monitors."

Instrumentalism is the primary value in a materialistic form of pragmatism. By contrast, in a mythic or magic society, even if someone does not present materially exploitable skills (productivity), she may still have value. Value is not reduced to material measurement. In the modern world, we warehouse unproductive people such as the elderly, children, delinquents, and other "offenders." In the most modern of Asian societies, Japan, such people are called "bulky garbage," which, like a dilapidated refrigerator, is difficult to dispose of. While elderly who can produce something unique are called "national treasures," the vast majority of aging Japanese are victims of the new system of modern mass production. Rather than preserving an old way to produce, for instance, textiles, they find that they cannot "keep up" with industrial progress. In many modern totalitarian systems such as Communist China and the old Soviet system, "delinquents" have suffered "reeducation" by means of the "nobility of labor," which is a euphemism for slavery.

SECULARIZATION OF ORDER

Monasticism constituted both the germinal seed of postmedieval modernity and also the nascent expression of aperspectivity such that time (relativity), which is an essential aspect of systatic awareness, first makes its presence felt in the monastery as an anxiety (as evinced in Augustine's writings). Wild time threatens the permanence of order. The protomodern medieval monks spatialized time into numerical ordination. The birth of domesticated clock-time, as sequential punctuation (around 1200 with Pope Sabinas's order for hourly bell-ringing), is the modern way of expressing and dissociating time as a spatial constant (Mumford, 1963; Gebser, 1985; Kramer and Ikeda, 1996). Time was removed (abstracted) from lackadaisical flux.[5] A cosmic reversal occurred whereby nature, which exhibits constant variety, became refined as a set of "constants." The establishing of clock-time is an expression of modern pragmatism.

The first machine that used proportional gearing and precise leverage was the clock. Clockwork became the model for all subsequent machine development, including the factory and the bureaucracy. A moral person became a person who was organized, prompt, and punctual, "just like clockwork." Sanity became equated with "stability" and regularity, while "deranged" (as opposed to arranged) emotion and passion became a "mental illness" (hysterics for instance, as when a machine "breaks down"). Changing one's mind became a disease. A dependable, "steady" ("steadfast") person is "good."

The machine expresses four fundamental aspects of the modern world: mindless automation, absolute control expressed as self-contained feedback (surveillance) in the interest of regulation to maintain status quo (homeostasis or equilibrium), obsessive reductionism (in the form of simplifying fragmentation), and anxiety (to the point of hysteria) in the face of time. Qualitative difference and complexity are abandoned for quantity (efficiency) and uniform physical precision. It also enhances power/control. Craftsmanship gives way to anonymous and fragmented mass production. Consistency for its own sake ascends to be an important value.

According to Nietzsche (1974), the desire to conquer nature includes the attempt to control or transcend time. This process includes the compulsion to isomorphize the mediation of "things-in-themselves," and thereby create a purely quantified "world." Nietzsche (1974) argued that this desire, or "will-power-drive," manifests, like all emotion, illogic. Rationalization is a defense mechanism. Dissociation, and the consequent desire for representation, is born of emotions such as fear, and desire for power.

The dominant tendency, however, to treat as equal what is merely similar—an illogical tendency, for nothing is really equal—is what first created any basis for logic. In order that the concept of substance could originate—which is indispensable for logic although in the strictest sense nothing real corresponds to it—it was likewise necessary that for a long time one did not see nor perceive the changes in things. The beings that did not see so precisely had an advantage over those that saw everything "in flux." (Nietzsche, 1974: 114, *The Gay Science*, sec. 111)

Hence, the desire of science to grasp reality as a causal chain of "iron necessity with eternal clamps" is quite illogical (Nietzsche, 1974: 111, *The Gay Science*, sec. 46). Such an attitude indicates an anxious search for secure ground, a fleeing from the compulsion to "live dangerously," to build one's city on "the slopes of Vesuvius," as Nietzsche put it (1974: 228, *The Gay Science*, sec. 283).

Comprehension becomes apprehension with simulation being confused with explanation. The desire is for a "second-order" synchronic universe which claims to be the best model for the "primary" diachronic universe (see the discussion of Galilean stylistics in Chapter 3).

Because of the overwhelming nature of pragmatic interest and valuation (greed in the guise of collectivized mass production), time itself had to be organized and made into a constant so that anxiety and uncertainty could be allayed. Consistency assures predictability. Systematization enhances reliability. Fluctuation is the enemy of time "keeping." Since people tend to change their minds and cultural expressions, the more autonomous the clock, the better. Hence, the drive to create the automated clock, which forms a permanent structure against "unstable" flux. Time must become transcendentally dissociated from the contingent flux of everyday life. Indeed, everyday life would become ordered by the new clock-time.

Flux and clock-time are qualitatively different. Sundials, and early, manually adjusted clocks, indicate cosmic variance rather than abstraction from it.[6] Once a dissociated system was established, reliable sources of artificial light were necessary, and the laboring day was extended "around the clock." The development of technologies of artificial lighting, such as gas lights and electrical lighting, is an expression of a directly felt need and want. It is the clock that now orders our universe and it is time we fear and worship.

Automation: The Technique of Making Reliability Happen

Mapping Time: Including the Self

In the interest of utilitarian pragmatism (practical power), the machine clock created a constant time dissociated from the direct experience of variation, such as the seasonal change in length of day and night. Interest shifted from magic identity and mythic harmony to willful and arbitrary ordination. The clock has become divine-like, since it is stable and utterly disinterested in vagarious contingency. The more stable the clock, meaning the more identical its repetitious "beats," the more precise and reliable; the "better."

"Reliability," like "validity," is a product of method. Reliability means monotonal (monotonous) replication. In order to achieve this, consciousness (subjectivity) must be banished from the system of ordination. Reliability is built into the method of the clock which measures (makes) time. Thus, the most stable (monotonous) time "pieces," like atomic clocks (that count the frequency vibrations of atoms of cesium or rubidium), which are accurate to within one second in 30,000 years, are esteemed as "Master Clocks." "Universal time" is "arrived at" by calculators at the International Time Bureau in Paris, who correlate astronomical measurements and atomic clocks from around the world in order to order. Precision and dependability are moralized as the most valued "personality traits" in "professional" modernity. The more like a machine, the more dependable and efficient (competent) someone is, the "better."

The modern world is recognizable as a world that has been colonized by mathematical operation. The whole modern world presumes numbers, and runs by the clock. Conforming synchronicity is the essence (the "nature") of modern mass society. For moderns, horographic entrainment is the mode of being. Scales exercise the power of conventional (yet arbitrary) behavior inflated to absolute truth (hypertrophic perspectivism). The invention and dissemination of clock-time demonstrates a form of groupthink and convergence that is so naturalized and global that neither Irving Janis (1982) nor Ernest Bormann (1985) could see it as such, although Gebser (1985), Julius T. Frazer (1981) and Edward T. Hall (1983) have recognized the essential importance of temporal synchronization to social cohesion.

The modern stress on time has reduced the self to memories. Biography is the final fixation of the modern ego-self. And, although it cannot be proven, since it is assumed that no one else shares my world, my sensations, my experience, my life, then I am the sum total of my memories, which are absolutely unique. The modern strives to produce more and more "accurate" techniques of recording in order to preserve the past, to defeat flux. For instance, following from the "still life" realism in painting and portraiture, "still" photography offers bits of frozen time. The most cherished possessions of a family or individual are their videos and photo albums. When the house burns, these, along with the pets, are what moderns first try to *save*. They are most important. Pets and photos are the repositories of sentiment. Bureaucracies go to great "lengths" to safeguard their records. People take pictures almost as a way to prove that they existed, and to mark "progress." It is important to record the growth of one's children. Self-recording is a fundamental aspect of the fixating tourist gaze. Tourists want their pictures taken with . . . to prove that they were there.

With digital technology, soon this form of proof will be jeopardized because "I" could be "anywhere." So genetic "fingerprinting" will become the next recording technique that resists ambiguity of the self. Social scientists too, make careers of attempting to preserve ruins and record the passage of vanishing cultures and languages. Recording and correlating is the modern's mode of self-preservation.

Mapping Space: Including the Self

The conscientious coordination of masses of people is the hallmark of modernity. To make mass production economies or to make massively destructive war is the forte of modernity. Coordination and correlation of behavior was made possible by the clock and the modern map. Just prior to the fall of Constantinople to the Ottomans in 1493, a Greek sailed to Rome to ask the pope for help. The pope refused, and so the Greek found himself unable to return to Constantinople. Consequently, he began to teach Greek in Italy.

Italian merchants and traders who had begun to amass great fortunes (thanks in part to the invention of double-entry accounting) had already been searching for a justification for their wealth. These *nouveaux riches* were not aristocrats and did not trace their power and station in life to the church and its teachings. Instead, they had been drawn to the pagan hedonism found in the ancient Greek writers.

In their desire to be recognized as just as civilized as the aristocracy, they began to patronize the artists and academicians of the day. They also took classes in Greek. The fellow who had come from Constantinople found himself the darling of this new class of students. After some time he organized a sort of field trip to Greece for his wealthy students who were eager for the opportunity to visit the land from which their new lifestyle drew its legitimacy. While there, they bought everything in sight including a map that had been made by a Greek who had been a Roman citizen and who had lived in Alexandria, Egypt, Claudius Ptolemaeus ("Ptolemy," A.D. 100–170?). When they returned to Italy with this souvenir, some university teachers who had been racking their brains about the problems of navigation, and who had also been studying the Muslim scholar Alhazen's (Ibn-al-Haitam) (962–1038) ideas about optics, immediately saw the significance of Ptolemy's map—global perspective. Space suddenly expanded to encompass everything.

Perspective is the projection of imaginary lines from the eye into space. There are several perspectives that have been exploited in mapmaking. Examples include Lambert's conformal conic projection, polyconic projection, Goode's Homosline projection, azimuthal and zenithal projections, cones, planes, and cylinders. The problem is that all perspectives distort. All perspectival awaring projects itself from a fixed point so that everything else one perceives depends on one's own identity, orientation, or location of the privileged point of origin (usually the self). "Attitude," which means the position of an object in space relative to its line of travel or the horizon, and one's bearing or disposition, is a modern issue.

The Mercator map (designed by the Flemish scholar Gerardus Mercator) presents an accurate rendition of relationships at the equator but increasingly distorts proportions as one moves North (up) and South (down) on the map. This is so because the point from which the rays of projection originate is at the equator. Mercator projected a sphere onto a cylinder, tangent to the surface of the earth at the equator. Azimuthal maps present a gnomonic projection which takes as its point of origin the center of the earth. In other words, in gnomonic projection, all rays are presumed to be projected from the center of the earth, with corresponding distortions. Orthographic projection, by comparison, presumes that the source of the projecting rays is at infinity. Stereographic projection posits the source of projecting rays to be a point diametrically opposite the tangent point of the place on which projection is made.

The mapping of the self, which for the modern physicalist equals the brain and which began with Paul Broca, continues today. The spatialized self is well expressed by Carl Sagan (1974: 9) when he says, "And here was Broca's brain floating, in formalin and in fragments, before me.... It was difficult to hold Broca's brain without wondering whether in some sense Broca was still in there—his wit, his skeptical mien, his abrupt gesticulations when he talked, his quiet and sentimental moments." Sagan, the physicist, as should be expected, is confusing mind with brain, just as a mourner claims that a corpse is sacred, and visits not a grave, but a "loved one."

For the modern, space, history, meaning, significance, friend, enemy, everything is determined by an arbitrary point of reference, the point of origin. Depending on which point one chooses, everything else is altered accordingly. Gebser (1985) deconstructed this notion of origin, from which everything gains its *subsequent* orientation (identity) by using the paradoxical phrase "ever-present origin" to describe integral awaring.

According to Nietzsche (1974: *The Gay Science*, sec. 354), after absolute and infallible truths (like the voice of God) had been relativized by science, "Insofar as the word 'knowledge' has any meaning, the world is knowable; but it is interpretable otherwise, it has no meaning behind it, but countless meanings— 'perspectivism.' " This includes various identities such as philosophical, ideological, occupational, racial, ethnic, and national. Nietzsche's conviction that we are interpreters of our experience, and that this honest concession is "alien to all founders of religions and their kind" (1974: sec. 319), led him to refer to science as a "mechanical prejudice" and "one of the most stupid of all possible interpretations of the world," because it is "one of the poorest in meaning" (1974: *The Gay Science*, sec. 373). In his distaste for nihilism, Nietzsche rejected the notion of a "pure will-less knowledge," derived from a single absolute perspective. He also, therefore, rejected the idea of the scientist as instrument, as self-polishing "mirror" (1973: *Beyond Good and Evil*, sec. 207). The master narrative, or immaculate perspective, makes difference (meaning) superfluous. Under such totalitarian power, "alternatives" are "entertained" and selected according to the criteria or interests of the dominant reality.

The rational perspective, too, begs the question: What are our reasons for being rational? What is it that we want? To destroy culture? Science cannot supply goals. Thus, Socratism ("theoretical optimism") constitutes the delusion of limitless power, the comprehensive view of the world, and the "tragic insight" of the "shipwreck" of logic (Nietzsche, 1967b: *The Birth of Tragedy*, sec. 15). The question goes begging because Nietzsche does not hold out the hope of messianic redemption by a single right answer. But once difference is not suppressed, then we can finally see each other, and real alternatives (life-potential) are freed.

But as one picture of the world gains prominence via institutional and official sanction and dissemination, the consequence is the origin of the herd mentality. Mass men share a common perspective and because they do, they confer the mantel of Reality onto it. Decades before Walter Fisher (1987), Robert Bales (1970), Bormann (1985), and Janis (1982) generated theories about people converging on a common fantasy-theme or narrative (groupthink), Nietzsche (1974: *The Gay Science*) and Gebser (1949), and one might add Kenneth Burke (1962), had identified the essential nature of mass perspectivism.

Ptolemy's maps, which had been published in his *Geography*, were not the first. The earliest maps known were land surveys recorded on clay tiles by Babylonians about 2300 B.C. The utilitarian motive for such "scaled" representation is self-evident from the start. The ancient Chinese made silk maps of regional interest about the second century B.C. The Inca and Maya also made maps, mostly of conquered territory. However, the first physicalistic (as compared to cosmological renderings like mandalas) map of *the world* was made by Anaximander in the sixth century B.C. Cosmological systems had been represented before but not in a strictly physical sense. In fact, Ptolemy was not even the first, or exclusive source, to use imaginal meridians. Marshall Islanders in the South Pacific made chart maps that consisted of a gridwork of cane fibers to locate islands. Likewise, around 200 B.C., Eratosthenes founded the discipline of "geography," which means "earth description." Eratosthenes was the first to use transverse parallel lines to show equal latitudes. He also established meridians for longitude, but they were irregularly spaced. Modern mapping is marked by its stress on proportional relationships and regularity of units of measure.

Ptolemy's contribution to mapmaking was his use of trigonometry and consistent scalar ratios to "accurately" form conic projection. The word "accuracy," though commonly used, is not quite correct. Rather, Ptolemy's systematic approach maintained an internal consistency to his cartographic logic. Ptolemy laid a coordinate grid (which Descartes would later plagiarize) over a drawing of the known world. This grid established a new kind of space with imaginary relationships created by uniform units.

Meanwhile, sailors, for the most part Portuguese, had been attempting to sail around the Ottoman Empire to get to Eastern traders. Their problem was that as they sailed south, hugging the coast of Africa, they risked getting hopelessly lost. This threat was based on the fact that they navigated by the one constant, the Pole Star, Polaris, which sits atop the imaginary axis of earthly rotation. The problem was that the farther south they went, the lower on the horizon Polaris sank, and at the Equator the terror of terrors occurred, it disappeared altogether below the horizon, thus making rudimentary navigation impossible. This point of no return occurred at a spot the Portuguese named Sierra Leone.

But as news of Ptolemy's map spread, people like Henry the Navigator and Christopher Columbus reasoned that navigation could be possible via an imaginary coordinate system, a system still used by global-positioning satellites today. The key was the establishment of imaginary points that would enable calculation of position. As sailors made their way they could use the stars to measure latitude and speed to measure longitude. They measured speed by letting a rope drift off the side of the ship with knots in it at "certain" intervals (hence the unit of nautical miles). But the problem of navigating longitude would remain a very rough estimate until the invention of an accurate timepiece.

The Synthesis of Space and Time

Although many participated in the effort to create a timepiece durable and accurate enough for nautical navigation, it was three British citizens who first succeeded. They enabled the British navy to sail at will by use of an accurate timepiece by which to measure the degrees' arc in terms of minutes and seconds (given a standard "Mean" time arbitrarily and nationalistically established at Greenwich, England). Robert Hooke invented escapement, which permitted the use of a pendulum with a small arc of oscillation; George Grahm improved escapement technology; and finally, in 1761, John Harrison succeeded in producing a chronometer reliable enough to be used for navigation. Harrison found a way to compensate for variations in the length of the pendulum due to temperature changes.

Thus, the unitizing systems of time and space would come to be correlated, making possible the modern world of global colonialism and industrial expansion. The fact that a British citizen (Harrison) was the first to perfect the use of different alloys that would offset variable expansion and contraction in his clockwork, thus assuring great reliability (redundancy of motion), enabled the British navy to rule the seas for over one hundred years. During the late eighteenth century in Europe, nations began to produce extraordinarily detailed national topographic surveys to establish their territorial integrity and interests. For instance, France completed its survey in 1793. The result was a map that was roughly square, measuring 11 meters (about 36 feet) on each side. Mapmaking expresses and helps to establish nationalism, which is uniquely modern. The legal notion of a nation-state is new with the Renaissance.

Ptolemy's imaginary grid enabled the mathematization and unitizing automation of space. His coordinate system created modern space just as the clock had created modern time. The correlation and coordination of the two (space and time) constitutes the basis of the modern world, including its way of thinking, its dreams, identities, and expectations. Armed with such new instrumentalism, Europeans became energized, adventurous, optimistic. Thus was born the philosophy of positivism. A whole new culture based on imaginary relationships emerged. We can know the world through method. These imaginary relationships became more real (virtual) than the real (actual), because they lent themselves to manipulation and pragmatic interests. They were utilitarian, meaning dependable.

But the story of Ptolemy's system does not end with global empire. Another Italian, Leon Battista Alberti, had adapted the systematizing grid to art. In his classic book *Della Pittura* (*How to Paint*), first published in 1436, he described a method (specifically the chapter entitled ''Della Prospettiva'') that could be applied to any and all subjects by any and all painters. He described how to construct a wooden frame and then create a grid with string in the frame. He would sit this instrument up next to his canvas, and then, on the canvas, he would draw an analogous grid.

As he viewed the world through the framed grid, he would copy, square by square, unit by unit, what he saw. Painting thus became more controlled and automatic, the first painting by units or numbers, as it were. The grid greatly enhanced the reliable copying of the variable size of distant objects, and thus the illusion of three-dimensional depth on a two-dimensional canvas. The grid also simplified and systematized painting so that subjective differences like talent could be minimized.

Alberti had found a methodical shortcut to realism. The shortcut constituted enhanced efficiency, reliability, and accuracy by minimizing subjective variance (consciousness). One no longer needed to grasp the whole scene, but instead could break it down into more manageable parts. Thus was born an approach to the world that would influence all modes of production from the assembly line to science and engineering. Ptolemy's system enabled perspectivism, which swept through Europe. With simple geometry, and using the grid as a foundation, additional relationships could be created. The Renaissance imagination took off. It now had power over distant objects. Triangulation made modern artillery from the rifle to the missile painfully accurate.

During this time, several artists, such as Lorenzo Ghiberti and Alberti had struggled to find the best way to present three-dimensional depth-space on a flat surface. By formulating the geometrical relationships based on the simple grid, Leonardo da Vinci finally formulated the ratios for general and aerial perspective which revolutionized painting and technical *drafting*. Leonardo is often thought of as an artist (which is true enough); however, he only executed twelve paintings in his lifetime (one being lost), while spending most of his time drawing military machines and architectural plans for fortresses (he was also director of water management for Milan). His new kind of technical drawing (which influenced his art much more than his art influenced his ''drafting'') also established a new way of seeing.

Modern dissociation was enhanced as drawing literally became ''mechanical,'' formulaic. One no longer needed to imagine the final product, but simply follow the steps of technical drafting (drawing ''by numbers''), which has its own preestablished imperatives (reasons), regardless of the artist's individual qualities such as talent or intent.

SYSTEMATIC NONTHINKING

''Methodical'' (mechanically automated) means that if you follow the steps according to preestablished rules, the picture *must* turn out the same way, regardless of who does it. One need not understand what one is doing in order to be correct. Method is a hallmark of the modern mechanistic world, and its flight from consciousness (valid subjectivism). Method enables massification, such as mass production, consumption, and predictability. Mechanical drawing is, in a word, mindlessly methodical, automatic. That's why dead computers can do it so well. Unlike ''open'' (creative) painting, we know when a mechanical drawing is ''wrong,'' by retracing the steps and recognizing ''error'' betrayed by preestablished rules that were not followed, conformed to, or repeated without subjective whimsy. Method strives to escape time, it does not have a mind to change. Method presumes total conformity which also identifies the modern world and enhances predictability (reliability) and minimizes uncertainty. The flight from consciousness and time make ''bunk'' of history and context.

In this way, ''reality'' became identified with what one could control (operate) *by definition*. The vagaries and irregularities of the world, such as subjective uniqueness, which resist control and prediction (cybernetics) must be banished from existence altogether. Vagaries represented the existence of subject-wills, other than the *one* Divine Will. Modern egocentrism and will-power-drive are thus expressed as surveillance. Super-vision is more accurately rendered ''over-vision'' because ''sur'' means ''over.''

While a tool, such as a knife, can be used in a myriad of ways (to cut, pry, spread, sculpt, kill, etc.), the machine is very narrow in its focus (perspective), and very resistant to creative adaptation (change). The more complex the machine, the less adaptable it is.

Self-Imposed Ignor(ing)ance

The spatial preoccupation of modernity is expressed by ever-greater precision, which means ever more minute subdivisions of the world. Quantification expresses this desire. These subdivisions are then arranged in hierarchical schema which pretend to operate automatically, methodically, and, irony of ironies, "naturally." Even modern evaluation and judgement strive toward mechanization; to be autonomously "im-*part*ial." Autonomy of method is an attempt toward objectivity and freedom from awareness (subject-consciousness). Method, like lady justice, pretends to embrace blindness. But the very structure of the scales she holds incorporates and introduces an inherent bias in favor of binary "impartiality" (Western-style democratized justice). The blindfold also expresses a bias in favor of decontextualization as often embraced by "objective" Western-style news reportage and context-free social science.

Most of the mythical world, by contrast, perceives such a high premium placed on blindness to be foolish and ignorant (self-imposed ignoring). For instance, in collectivistic societies where respect for ascribed power and status is the "common sense," to treat an elder the same as a child, a woman the same as a man, or a friend the same as a blood relative, is nonsensical. What the modern may denigrate as nepotism, immorality, or corruption is common-sensical for the pre- and unperspectival worlds. Only via systatic comparison (relativization) do the value judgements inherent in the very structures of human lifeworlds become perceivable (through each other).

Modernity presumes, and through discursive means, establishes and maintains the consistency version of a fixed, measurable, and systematic universe. The modern world is unitized into discrete bits that are essentially identical and infinitely divisible. The modern value of synergy, as manifested in Buckminster Fuller's geodesic dome and the hologram, celebrates fragmentation and holistic identity (interchangeability). Each bit is identical with every other piece. Unitization enables manipulation. This fundamental way of looking at the world enables technology (reshaping, reconstituting, and making) on a grand scale. Technology is making, not describing. Unitization enables precision and efficiency (conformity), which heralds the awakening of temporal anxiety in the modern world. This metaphysic is central to modern pragmatism and utilitarianism. It is intolerant and totalitarian in that the perspective available to the modern individual is very often inflated to universal status (holism).

Scales

The domestication of space/time is the central problem of visiocentrism: to render all experience as visual/spatial (Kramer, 1992, 1994). The privileging of the eye-brain is visiocentrism. The more faith in the veracity of mediated information grows, the more the faithful become vulnerable to the power of the medium. Because seeing is "real," seeing is believing. Though scales are social constructs having power/value only so long as convention holds, scales are real. Scales orient the world spatially, including invisible phenomena like opinions, so they can be made visible and thereby "grasped." Scales are magical. They visually constitute (make) ratios in the mode of operation. They can transform anything into a spatial quantity, which is Real. For modern scientists, measurement *is* the thing. An electron *is identical with* the sum of information one has about it, and information *equals* measurements. As magic, ratios are seen as things-in-themselves, as if the numbers are independent of human agency. Measurement is ("by nature") the very essence of the object or relationship. If one admits that measurement is nothing more than a utilitarian contrivance, then one must question the validity of the entire project. An operational definition contains the essentially modern prejudice that the phenomenon defined is conceived *a priori* as being measurable (spatial and unitary). Operational definitions include *a priori*, the means of *creating the phenomenon as measurement*. The measures never existed before. By this operation, the world becomes a mathematical product. The world is thus reduced to a mathematical construct, an aggregate of unrelated units. Hence, the modern is concerned with fragmentation and reunification in wars, knowledge, families, cultures, everything. This is Pythagorean and Platonic mysticism.

Scales are mythical when their products are assumed to exist *before* human intervention and are *represented* (revealed) by measurement. Mythically, measurement is not seen as identical with what it measures, but the numerical values are not wholly arbitrary either. There is an emotional association between the two. The thing and its measurements are connected by a visceral reality. Money is a very good example. Though value exists only as exchange, and not as a thing-in-itself, and money merely represents that value, still humans have very strong emotional reactions to money. The magical aspect of money is expressed by its *mana*-like qualitative power to transform and convert. To ask how much something is worth is to identify its value in numerical terms, which is essentially the same process social scientists call operationalization. Money, or more properly capital, though an icon of materialistic modernity, is not at all a material thing. Value is realized only via exchange. In the form of an instrument of exchange, monetary magic can be stored up, as it were, in various forms. Its "liquidity" is expressed by the power of conversion. Money can be exchanged for almost anything including other "storage instruments." Wealth (power— *mana*) is practically the perfect example of morphological form-shifting. Like the ancient Greek mythological water creature, Proteus, wealth is liquid. That is its power/magic. While the form changes, the wealth remains not so much "transferable" as transformative, at least so long as the game exists, as long as people agree to agree. In a "bad" transformation or transaction, one can lose wealth as when one pays "too much" for an object, and cannot later trade it for at least what it originally cost. The wealth simply vanishes, as when a stock market "crashes." Under the sway of pecuniary logic, tribes become markets defined by demo- and psychographics.

Scales are mythical in that they make relationships visible (imaginal), which is what mythical stories do. Myth is a narrative that expresses values ("truth"), but does so in an oblique way by means of metaphor. As such, scalar phenomena are symbolic. Money is more straightforward, more "literal" than "figural," although these two designations merely present the difference between magical and mythical awaring.

According to Gebser (1985), Husserl (1962), and Gadamer (1981), such dissociating pretensions as when someone says "it's only money" expose the difference between reason and deficient rationalization (mindless operationalization). Rationalization is actually an emotional response to critique, as well as a strategy for legitimating wants and desires. Authentic reason is expressed by the concept *theoria*, which has two component parts, *praxis* and *phronesis*, or "prudence." Authentic reason involves conscious (reflexive) judgement about the rationality of an act, not automation. To be sure, automation is more efficient than deliberation, and can offer a moral alibi. Under the auspices of "headless" (meaning "deficient") rationalization, activity proceeds without the inconvenience of "senseless" prudence. This amounts to *techne*, which does not demand reflexive "reasons" for proceeding in the first place. Rationalization is the technical application of logic to random behavior. Behavior is thus transformed into operation. Its narrow interest is in how to maximize "output," and to function without consciousness, automatically, in accordance with preestablished criteria. Authentic reason logically integrates various relationships, including the complex of text and context. Reason expands the determination of whether or not the operation itself is worthy of pursuit, which requires a clarification of presupposed beliefs, interests, and values. This requires a systatic view "outside of" the rules of the system, or labyrinth, of technique.

Rationalization, by contrast, rejects context as irrelevant. Rationalization is a rhetorical effort to preempt, by *a priori* definition (internal criteria), unquantified discourse, which is deemed meaningless. According to positivistic existentialism, if a thing cannot be expressed as measurement, it does not exist (Popper, 1959). Karl Mannheim (1952) responded to this magical proclamation by claiming that, in such a world, a thing exists *because* it is measured (created). Thus definition replaces authentic discovery (openness) with incorporation. The hegemony of measurement and spatialization expands. Something new is recognizable only insofar as it conforms to the existential criteria of categorizing measurability. The "new" is transformed so that it will fit into a preestablished system of knowledge. Consequently, the new is seen as simply a variant of the old.

The closed system forces everything to conform to its criteria so that the new is denied existence except in terms of the old. This is essentially colonialism. Mannheim, rejecting Aristotelianism, insisted that a thing or relationship could exist and be meaningful, on its own terms, prior to categorization and unitization. Otherwise, all nonscientific cultures would be deemed senseless, by definition (as would science itself; see Chapter 2). Of course, some do hold this view, so that entire continents, species, and peoples must be discovered by Western scientists before they can enjoy the mantel of being really Real.

One of the best examples of the modern attitude is not only manifested by machine tooling and operation, but also the precise approach utilized by Nazis (including the instruments and measurements they yielded) to subdivide, identify, and categorize people whom they reduced to phenotypical (exclusively material) surface characteristics. Only these spatial characteristics were allowed to constitute the identities of the people they measured. The people were nothing more than the sum total of their measurements. Context was deemed, according to interest, irrelevant. The criteria chosen on which evaluation was to be *made*, of course, betrays the interests that were programmed into the very structure of the instruments/methods applied.

The product of the machine bears the unmistakable stamp of the interests articulated in its very structure. Hence, to tell me what someone's race is, is to tell me less about that person than about the instrument used to *make* the determination and the interests of those who conceived the instrument. Indeed, even the fact that the phenomenon is "instrumental" reveals the reckoning attitude of its creator.

Via systatic attention, one can see through (make transparent) the instrument to evaluate what it is "trying to get at." This is what Husserl, in *The Crisis of European Sciences and Transcendental Phenomenology* (written from 1934 to 1937; in English, 1970), meant by "archaeology," and Nietzsche meant by "genealogy" (systatic hermeneutics) in *Human, All-too-Human* (1878), and *On the Genealogy of Morals* (1887). No one generates data for the sole purpose of generating data. The very choice and structure of the method employed indicates a directional interest. What it yields is predetermined by the structure of the method, hence being mindlessly methodical (reliable regardless of who does the operation). The application of method always imposes the boundary of interest, excluding (ignoring) some information while consolidating other information. The relative achievement of that interest is the measure of "progress." However, most "breakthroughs" occur as violations of the boundaries prescribed by the method (or regional ontology otherwise known as "discipline") such as alogical free associations, accidents, and interdisciplinary "violations."[7]

When one (the kynic) asks what the method is "trying to get at" (actually generate), that then raises the question of what searchers and researchers intend to *do* with the data once generated. This is an *a priori* interest. Methods are selected on the bases of the kind of information one wants. Often, it is possible to surmise a plausible answer to the question "what are you trying to get at?" (the implicit motive of the researcher) by studying the inherent characteristics of the method and, by technological imperative, its product share. However, because human subjects, unlike dead molecules, often see through (interpret and anticipate) the procedure (react to it), researchers sometimes take great pains to fool them by employing confederate respondents, placebos, and other deceptive techniques (such as the fake shocks administered in the famous experiments conducted by Stanley Milgram at Yale from 1960 to 1963, which pretended to study learning but were really studying obedience and disobedience to authority).

Just as the machine of method creates, by definition, a product (data, for instance), so, too, the Nazis and other eugenicists methodically (objectively—mechanically) organized empirical differences, thus creating ever more carefully differentiated racial classifications. Their methods yielded, by operational definition, races and subraces.

The Nazis invented complex scales that would produce precise measures of skin, hair, and eye color. The interest was in defining race as a scalar phenomenon, and to do so mechanically ("objectively") and thus, "naturalistically."[8] No discussion of the moral value or ideological interest of such activity was permitted since statements of value were presumed to be meaningless. Like all methodical behavior, no matter who does the operation, if procedures are followed according to protocol, the results must be thus (replicable, reliable). All important objectivity and value-freedom are thus preserved. The machine runs smoothly, obliviously.

But the obsessive drive for ever more precise definition (subdivision and control) inevitably leads everywhere and nowhere, as in "pure" science and "pure" mathematics. By carefully discerning what percentage of Aryan each person is, for instance, we eventually lead to every individual manifesting a category of one. The process of purification progressively eliminates more and more people on the basis of less and less information (racial pollutant in this instance). Everyone is his or her own race. When this quantitative obsession with subdivision (precision) is imposed on humans, as in the case of ethnic cleansing in the interest of absolute purity, more and more people are "progressively" excluded until the system of reductional precision eventually and logically (automatically) eliminates practically everyone.

The modern fragmentation of knowledge into "disciplines" and modern sectarian conflicts is an example of this endless striving for the whole truth and nothing but the truth. The same compulsion is evident in the subdivision of space and time into smaller and smaller units until each dimension vanishes. Ironically, however, the more invisible a medium or method is, the more insidious becomes the fundamental ontological difference between a simulation and what is simulated (Heidegger, 1962; Baudrillard, 1983). Numeric scaling has the power to reduce everything to spatial extension, removing qualitative difference. As a consequence of magical operationalism, one can say that there may be a world "out there," but that that remains mere speculation, at least until the magic of operationalization is performed, transforming hypothesis into pure and real measurements. As pointed out, in the modern world, only measurements are really reliable; really Real. Thus, as this Galilean-style existential magic is performed on humans, they, too, fail the test of being real (knowable). The virtual human becomes more valuable, more meaningful, more real, surpassing the actual in metaphysical and instrumental status.

The One and Only Value: The Golden Mean

Gebser (1985) understood, perhaps better than any scholar since Nietzsche, that an overemphasis on individual freedom triggers a self-reflexive massification of society. In late modernity, reason has deteriorated into "deficient quantification." As the will-power-drive for control turned even upon itself in the form of positivism (self-improvement and self-monitoring), Western culture became obsessed with social engineering, cybernetics, and super-vision (Comte, 1865; Parsons, 1951; Ruesch and Bateson, 1968). This will-power-drive for control found a singular value to be most profitable or utilitarian, and therefore privileged. That value was the "golden mean."

The modern obsession with the ("golden") mean is based on the desire to control humanity *en masse*. The dissociated mathematical manifold, with its "purification" of the problematic world of direct personal experience (deviance), as in "pure mathematics" or "pure science," manifests a rationalized will-to-regiment, to control: to purge reality of troublesome complexity (difference) (Mumford, 1963).[9] As mentioned above, the enforcement of a uniformally consistent clock-time for everyone, regardless of class and the natural and constantly changing duration of daylight throughout seasonal variations, is the prerequisite for modern mass behavior, and industrial mass production (Mumford, 1963: 41).

The obsessive interest in the numerical average is the clearest statement of the rise of mass society. While fascination with the mean and "central tendency," "tendency toward it," "regression" from it, and "standard deviations" relative to it proved to be very powerful for control of material and biological environments, one must ask why statisticians began to apply this synthetic reasoning to human beings and to reject as irrelevant direct experience of idiosyncrasy (anti-synchrasy). This is precisely what several German scholars asked at the inception of quantified humanity. In 1837, rejoicing in "diversitarianism" (the celebration of the "branches" of the human race and the variety of histories), Friedrich Schleiermacher (1961: 224–225) asked:

Why, in the province of morals, does this pitiable uniformity prevail, which seeks to bring the highest human life within the compass of a single lifeless formula? How can this ever have come into vogue, except in consequence of a radical lack of feeling for the fundamental characteristic of living Nature, which everywhere aims at diversity and individuality.

Agreeing with Gottfried Leibniz, Schleiermacher challenged those who would make of humanity a thousand identical "copies." For him there was no excuse for enforcing uniformity.

What would the uniform repetition of even the highest ideal be? Mankind—time and external circumstances excepted—would be everywhere identical. They would be the same formula with a different coefficient. What would this be in comparison with the endless variety which humanity *does* manifest? (1961: 308)

With the rise of positive sociology and other massifying conceptualizations (especially modern mass consumption, mass production, and mass marketing), interest in modifying not simply the material substrate, but human behavior, led to behavioral science and its singular preoccupation with the average mass human. Although no one person may be empirically identical with the synthetic average, this dissociated mathematical ideal became the privileged (indeed exclusive) guide for behavior modification and mass conformity. Empirical, actual humans became subject to endless comparison with the virtual, mathematically derived human. Thus, mass conformity was promoted as a moral imperative called "normative behavior." Marketing research and mass advertising have been the major beneficiaries of this "science" of social engineering.

As Nietzsche, too, pondered the central obsession with this singular numerical value (the "tendency toward the mean"), he identified one of the essential characteristics of modernity to be a rationalized fixation on the technology of social engineering, which was clearly expressed in the beginning of social science by Saint-Simon and Comte in their call for a "positive religion" that would establish and maintain social order. What Schleiermacher decried as a push for only one religion. Modernity rationalizes (and promotes) herd behavior, which is quite premodern. Time, as change, erupted with the French Revolution (which even involved the establishment of an entirely new calendrical system and therefore history), and it was exactly this event to which ("value-free") *positive* social engineering reacted (Comte, 1865).

Since the "mean person" is completely different from actual people, given the parameters (interests) preprogrammed into the method which creates this virtual person, what is posited is an imaginal human being dissociated from the lifeworld. However, this mean person is imbued with more "reality" than actual people, who are deemed irrelevant. What is posited is an ideal "ought," and any difference is "deviance." When modification of behavior is the interest, then a utopia is being implied. Administration of an ideal order is facilitated by the application of statistical rationality. Order is the ideal-value. It is individuals who are modified even though large-number theory makes no claim to be able to address specific persons.

Under these cultural conditions, "deviation" implies more than mere difference. The call for monoculturalism is a consequence of this fundamentalistic reductionism. The empirical reality of multiculturalism is not conducive to the values of utility, efficiency, and profitability, which are held supreme by modern pragmatism. The goal is to manage behavior on a massive scale. Behavior modification is the means to achieve this goal. Hence the singular pinpoint focus on the mean; hypertrophic perspectivism inflated to virtual reality. Just as a map is distorted according to the choice of the source of its rays, what constitutes the mean is determined by what measures one chooses to compute. Mass communication is the most extreme form of vertical organization whereby a single source univocally speaks at everyone else.[10] The best social science is done by marketing firms and governments. Otherwise, fascination with the mean is scholastic voyeurism. In any case, arrogance is writ large, and the other is reduced to an object of study for ulterior motives.

Understanding humanity, too, is either denigrated as a field of study categorically, because it defies generalizability and utility; or is permitted existence as a weak sibling in the form of a pretender to the mantel of Newtonian mechanics, whereby one studies human bodies in motion (in space) but is not allowed to discuss meaning, motive, value, intent, or judgement. Consciousness (agency) is displaced by random stimulus/response. Absurdly, in order to maintain its apodictic status, the existence of statistical logic itself, which enables one to measure degrees of randomness, must be reduced to a random occurrence. Its solutions too, must be regarded as merely random accidents.

But the modification of human behavior on a mass scale possesses more serious questions which are typically not addressed because ethics, according to spatial metaphysics (empiricism), do not exist. People are presumed to be ontologically identical with dead, mindless dice. Ethical statements have no meaning, meaning that they are not measurable, or have no spatial extension, so that it makes no sense to ask how much "good" weighs or what color "bad" is. Thus, deficient modernity posits nihilistic dystopias. No course of action can be considered "better" than any other because valuative statements are, by definition, meaningless gibberish. Of course, the real concern is the power of prediction, which closes the future (creation) and thereby leads to nihilism. We are left in the hands of technocrats who avoid responsibility by incantating mechanical determinisms like modern history, market forces, and genetics. An example is financial markets constituted of virtual transactions such as junk bonds, residuals, and other instruments that no one understands.[11]

Disintegration and Alarm(ing) Clocks

The effort to spatialize and control time (as a false extension) backfires. Instead, clock-time controls the modern human, and hence the tragic abandonment of consciousness mentioned above. Perspectival thinking posits a *telos* or goal which presumes spatialization. It also posits a steady-state universe which began to disintegrate in the Renaissance. For instance, the heavenly vault was lifted revealing an ever-expanding space, against which the individual became decentered, and less and less secure as it shrank to a point-like monad. The culmination of this has been, in philosophical terms, the terror of modern existentialism or "*ex-sistere*" ("being exposed").

As space expanded, the individual, in equal and opposite proportion, shrank into nihilism. For a time Newton and Kepler rescued the steady-state cosmos with laws which explained the clockwork universe. But disintegration of permanence has continued especially in the aperspectival physics of quantum me-

chanics and relativity. The ground of matter itself has been refined to the point
of being a substanceless crypto-materialism. Then, an astronomer at Mt. Wilson
observatory discovered that the universe displays in all directions the Doppler
shift which Fred Hubble adduced to mean that the universe is on the move,
expanding. Likewise, in order to explain an expanding yet "steady-state" universe, Fred Hoyle, Hermann Boni, and Thomas Gold, put forth a cosmogony
which argued that the universe is a "continuous creation" of emergent "background matter" that "does not come from anywhere . . . [but] simply appears"
(Hoyle quoted in Hawking, 1992: 62).

APERSPECTIVITY: PROVISIONAL "CONSTANTS"

By comparison, temporal relationships are transparent to the aperspectival
world which is now emerging. With the realization that the planet Earth is a
sphere and is not the center of the universe, aperspectival awareness began to
emerge as a verition of radical relativity (along with the perspectival spatialization of temporal relativity into fragmented and systematized longitudinal
"time zones" according to degrees of arc and other coordinates, a la Ptolemy
and Descartes). As physical (irregular) edges and boundaries began to disappear,
they were replaced by ambiguous curved surfaces and multidimensional ge-
ometries. History became histories. Even the heavenly vault faded to reveal an
infinite depth-space. Within a period of only two or three generations, the mythical cosmic womb (represented by the church sanctuary as in "Notre Dame"),
with its secure interiority, vanished. A millennium of orientation disappeared.
This frightening "development" acted as a catalyst for the consolidation of the
"exposed" self into a dissociated individual articulated in philosophemes and
psychologies as monadology, and as an egological nexus where the perspectival
("pyramidal") lines converge.

By contrast, atemporicity is a despatialized, and therefore clock-free realization. Aperspectival "time" is a fluxing intensity, rather than a fixed extensity,
and as such it is not prone to being fragmented into identical and repetitive units
of measurement such as past, present, or future. Nor is it directional as expressed
in the deterministic teleology of religious thinking and the great "chain of causation" that mechanistic science and modern ideologies have adopted from religion and astrology. Rather, aperspectival time is a dimensional constituent of
the world. Time is not anywhere, nor is it going "anywhere." Nor is time a
"constant." Instead, it enables "going." It enables difference, constance (identity), and discontiguity. In the aperspectival universe of infinity and eternity, the
center is everywhere and the circumference nowhere. Every "place" and "person" is the/an *axis mundi*, the center of everything as well as an edge. Because
there is no single edge one is always the center and never the center.

Unperspectival mythic peoples express time as a harmonic atunement with
variable cosmic cycles such as the seasons and migration of sun, moon, stars,
and beasts. Mythic people rise when the sun comes up and retire when it goes

down, *regardless of the daily fluctuations of the length of daylight through the seasons.* Quite differently, temporal ordination (abstraction), as well as modern (as differentiated from aperspectival) science presumes a steady-state absolute God/Nature, which was fundamentally disrupted by geology, paleontology, and acausal physics. For instance, as people like R. Brookes Jean-Francois Robinet, Abbe Jacques-Francois Dicquemare, and Georges Cuvier began, around the beginning of the eighteenth century, to invest interest in fossils and geologic strata, despite their initial and profound misgivings, they began to realize that either (the Christian) God "makes mistakes" (because some creatures "fail" to survive), or God "changes His mind" which presumes the blasphemy that God is (in time) a temporal being.[12] Furthermore, the earth seemed to be much older than modern (quantifying) biblical scholars like James Ussher (1581–1656) had claimed. Such findings flew in the face of totalitarian absolution. Another example of the aperspectival disruption of a fixed universe, and materialism generally, is manifested by aperspectival physics:

Up to about 1910 it was thought that matter was made out of particles like billiard balls that had definite positions and speeds, and whose behavior could be predicted precisely by the laws of physics. However, evidence began to come from experiments that these precise so-called classical laws had to be replaced . . . by what were called quantum laws. According to these quantum laws, particles didn't have exactly defined positions or speeds but instead were smeared out with a probability distribution, or wave function, which measured the probability of finding the particle at different positions. The quantum laws implied that one couldn't measure both the position and speed of a particle. The more accurately one could measure the position, the less accurately one could measure the speed, and vice versa. (Thorne, 1992: 71)

What a thing is depends on how one looks at it. Matter cannot be measured as such, but instead is articulated as a wave function which integrates time to produce a non-Euclidean space-time fluxing (or warping). The famous Hartle-Hawking proposal even deconstructed the impermeability of the event horizon of singularity. Another boundary which fell in the twentieth century occurred with Kurt Godel's demonstration that mathematical consistency is *open to* inconsistency.

NOTES

1. This is very similar to the mythical efforts of what this author calls Derrida's salamander logic.

2. Interactive computer games present a false sense of "participation," by programming metatheatrical scenes, as when an actor turns to the camera/viewer and poses a set of options. This is not integrality, however. Instead the options, like an opinion survey, are preprogrammed and therefore present a systematized closed structure. The game is "fixed." "Participation" is *required* and preformulated into the structure of if/then branch logic. In the end, such "interaction" is only a simulation of genuine reciprocity.

To play, one must submit to the system. It will not change for you. One is communicating with a dead machine, which is essentially the same as playing solitaire. After a time the monotony defies being called communication. Even an "old" use of technology like call-in radio remains more open, spontaneous, and uncertain (interesting). Nevertheless, because humans are temporal (creative) creatures, even the pretension of choice is enough to drive a lucrative industry in computer "interaction" (more like inter-reaction).

3. The radial arrangement of roads leading into the central power of Rome also had a vertical organization. When the horizontal circular field of roads is combined with the vertical power structure centralized in Rome (with the divine kings of the Empire at the pinnacle) one has a cone, or in two dimensions a pyramidal arrangement. The three-dimensional cone is the shape of the modern perspectival sector yielded by vision. This pragmatic rationality was reasserted during the (also "eternal") French Revolution, with the hypertrophic perspectivism maximized, not only by the radial layout of the roads of Paris, but also when Napoleon crowned himself. According to Gebser (1985), the sphere is the "shape" of the aperspectival world.

4. Henry Ford, and other organizers of mass production, experienced constant "labor problems." Ford's anti-union and anti-Semitic writings, which embarrassed his son Edsel, even inspired Adolf Hitler. Taylor was so compulsive (some have said "neurotic") that he used to sleep sitting up in a chair while holding his ever-present vest watch so that he could, upon awakening, immediately reckon how long he had slept. The modern world has been shaped by obsessive-compulsive personalities, as celebrated in best sellers like *The One Minute Manager* by Kenneth Blanchard and Spencer Johnson (which promises on the cover to "increase productivity, profits, and your own prosperity," and to remind the manager via the digital one-second symbol that "the people we manage . . . are our most important resource"—so be "nice" to them for just one minute a day so that they will make you "prosper"), and *Power Shift* by Alvin Toffler (1990). This is a common-sense fact repeatedly pointed out by such corporate gurus as Malcolm Baldridge. Perhaps less sinister examples of the submission of the human body to massifying mechanization include exercising, marching, swimming, skating, sky diving, dancing, and practically everything else including sex (see Jean Luc Godard's *See You at Mao*) in formations like chorus lines and cheerleading. Such very Western modern behaviors stress conformity, unitization, and systematization (precision) even of jubilation. Perhaps the first regime of such structuring was the alignment (rows) of spectators in the stone amphitheaters of classical Greece. The prefix "amphi" means "on both sides" which indicates that the first theaters (that were, like Plato's dialogues, on the cusp between mythic and perspectival worlds) presented a space that was ambivalent concerning the distinction between subject and object, audience and stage. Marble tiers of seats may have signaled the massification of humanity and the organization of a singular perspective. Another example is the perspectival church which is recognizable by its "rational" (spatial) organization. Neat rows of parishioners both living and dead (i.e., graveyards organized into straight rows of deceased) are engaged by a speaker who preaches at them. This is a very different experience from either magical or mythical participatory ritual. The more perspectival the church, the less the parishioners merge into an emotional unity. Northern European Christian organizations have the unmistakable mark of perspectivity on them, even by such names as "method-ist," and "protest-ant." The more mythical and magical the church, the more parishioners "melt" into a single rhythmic movement where individualism gives way to the common sway of collective atunement exemplified by black, Latin American, and Filipino churches). As Edward T. Hall (1983)

has observed, polychronic, high-context people like Latin Americans and blacks invest more energy in interpersonal and emotional "involvement" than monochronic, low-context, Northern Europeans and Euro-Americans. Being embarrassed is a modality that afflicts the self-conscious perspectival human. For the circle of the collective "we," if shame exists, it pervades and permeates the whole.

5. Preperspectival magic peoples live an essentially spaceless and timeless existence. Timelessness, it must be understood, is not the same as aperspectival atemporality. "Eternity" for instance, is a temporic, not atemporic, phenomenon.

6. The advent of modernity is marked by two obsessions, one with time, the other with sight. This author has called this combined essence of Western culture visiocentrism (Kramer, 1988, 1993). In the year 1050, Prince Bhoja (1018–1060) wrote *Samarangana-sytradhara*, describing the construction of automata. Between 1070 and 1079, Abu Ishaq al-Zarqali constructed a series of complex water clocks at Toledo, Spain, some of which displayed the phases of the moon. Between 1088 and 1092, Su Sung in China constructed a giant water clock orrery (a mechanical representation of the heavens, somewhat like a planetarium), and mechanical armillary sphere thirty-five feet tall. It utilized a constant flow of water to turn its escapement wheels which were geared to power the clock and orrery. The armillary sphere was used to check the accuracy of both the clock and orrery by observing the sun and planets. In 1086, the Chinese thinker Shen Kua wrote a collection of essays called *Dream Pool*, which contained the first known references to the use of a magnetic compass for navigation. From 1280 to 1289, the first mechanical clocks begin to appear in Europe, largely as a response to stories of a time machine in China. In 1286, Allesandro della Spina is said to have made use of eyeglasses invented by his friend, Salvino degli Armati. They were intended to correct nearsightedness. In 1268, Roger Bacon wrote *Opus Majus* in which he discussed spectacles for correcting farsightedness. In 1288, one of the first mechanical clocks in Europe was installed at Westminster Abbey. It had only one hand to mark the hours. In 1292, a clock was installed in Canterbury Cathedral. Between 1300 and 1309, the hourglass was invented. During the same decade, eyeglasses became common, and as a consequence, Venice became a glassmaking center. In 1364, Giovanni de Dondi published the first description of a modern clock. It was weight-driven, escapement-regulated, and it had a balance wheel. This form of clock was invented either by Dondi or by members of his family. However, the key elements of the mechanism are no doubt borrowed from the Chinese. The major difference was that the Chinese used water to power their automatic time machines and the Europeans used weights.

7. Husserl (1962) noted that each discipline polices its boundaries according to metaphysical criteria so that, for instance, it is illegitimate to study poverty in a chemistry department (they will not support research in that region), or electron bonding in a sociology division. Meanwhile, such disciplines insist that they do not partake in metaphysics when, in fact, their very identities and projects presuppose dogmatic beliefs about the nature of "the Real." This fragmentation of knowledge itself is a hallmark of modernity and it led Husserl, in his antimetaphysical crusade, to formulate a method which begins by "bracketing" metaphysical dogmatism. He did this because metaphysical dogmatism leads to an intolerant (absurd) form of relativity whereby each discipline is mutually exclusive and knowledge becomes impossible. One solution has been the ideology of the hierarchy of sciences which posits as ultimate explanation a ground of physical laws. However, marriage counselors find it futile to apply Newtonian mechanics to interpersonal problems (though some have tried). Sociologists may argue that what chem-

istry "really is" is a materialistic ideology that is a relatively recent development in the history of knowledge, while chemists may argue that sociology "is really" chemical reactions. Each will argue that the other just doesn't know what they "really are." From a perspectival worldview, both cannot be correct. Neither accepts the validity of the other so that their attempts at mutual reductionism lead to contradiction. Systasis is an ability to appreciate, and thereby present a tolerant relativity that recognizes the relative validity of each ontology, thereby escaping blind allegiance to any one metaphysical system. Systasis also legitimizes interdisciplinary dialogue and open and free association.

8. The Holocaust Museum in Washington, D.C., has an extensive display of the instruments used to measure and categorize people.

9. This modern propensity toward pure abstraction is also manifested among Christians in the fundamental absolutism of intolerant "Puritanism." Fundamentalism of all sorts, such as the Islamic variety, takes principle to its logically (absolutist) violent conclusion. History advises that those who claim to know the "full Truth, the whole Truth, and nothing but the Truth" should be avoided. History teaches that compromise is far more dialogical, and far less deadly.

10. In the modern world, organizers displace leaders just as competence displaces passion. There is a fundamental difference in that organizers do so in their own interests, and typically serve the status quo which confers upon them status, while premodern leaders and heros typically served the needs of the clan and presented revolution. Hence, the hero almost always meets with a tragic end (sacrifice) and is dispersed, sometimes literally chopped up and scattered. As articulated by the stories of Jesus, Socrates, Gilgamesh, the Arthurian legends, and countless other tales, the preperspectival hero is self-effacing. By contrast, the modern celebrity manifests hypertrophic egocentrism where all things lead inward toward the focus (cult) of personality.

11. After several economic calamities, including the infamous bankruptcy of Orange County, California, and the collapse of Barons Bank of London in 1995, investigations proliferated with the conclusion that no two "experts" understood the operation of these instruments in the same way. The most quantitative of all "human sciences," and the only one recognized by the Nobel Committee, economics turns out to be as magical as voodoo.

12. Fossils were first described by Theophrastus of Lesbos (372–287 B.C.) as he observed that "The earth brings forth bones and . . . bone-like rocks." But it was not for nearly 2,000 years that an organized discipline about such phenomena emerged. Although the Oxford Professor Robert Plot is widely recognized for his description of the thighbone of Megalosaurus in his *Natural History of Oxford-shire* (1677), the idea of extinction did not even occur to him. Paleontology did not emerge as a full-blown discipline until the early 1800s with scholars like James Parkinson, who named "megalosaurus" ("giant lizard") in 1822. But it was not considered a "bonafide scientific entity" until William Buckland published a description of it in 1824 (Jean-Guy Michard, 1992: 27). Other notable pioneers in the field include Gideon and Mary Ann Mantell, and Richard Owen who, in 1841, concluded that the "rock-bones" were of a completely extinct group of animals he called "dinosaurs." It was not until 1859 that Charles Darwin published *The Origin of Species by Means of Natural Selection*, within which he asserted that the earth was far more ancient than theologians had claimed.

REFERENCES

Bales, R. (1970) *Personality and Interpersonal Behavior*. New York: Holt, Rinehart & Winston.

Baudrillard, J. (1983) *Simulations*. New York: Semiotext(e).

Bormann, E. (1985) *The Force of Fantasy: Restoring the American Dream*. Carbondale: Southern Illinois University Press.

Burke, K. (1962) *A Grammar of Motives and a Rhetoric of Motives*. Cleveland: World.

Campbell, J., and B. Moyers (1988) *The Power of Myth*. New York: Doubleday.

Cassirer, E. (1944) *Essay on Man*. New Haven, CT: Yale University Press.

Comte, A. (1865) *A General View of Positive Religion*. London: Trubner.

Derrida, J. (1973) *Speech and Phenomena*. Evanston, IL: Northwestern University Press.

———. (1974) *Of Grammatology*. Baltimore: Johns Hopkins University Press.

———. (1978) *Writing and Difference*. London: Routledge & Kegan Paul.

de Saussure, F. (1974) *Course in General Linguistics*. London: Fontana.

Fisher, W. (1987) *Human Communication as Narration: Toward a Philosophy of Reason, Value, and Action*. Columbia: University of South Carolina Press.

Fowles, J. (1992) *Why Viewers Watch*. Thousand Oaks, CA: Sage.

Frazer, J., ed. (1981) *The Voices of Time*. Amherst: University of Massachusetts Press.

Gadamer, H. G. (1981) *Reason in the Age of Science*. Boston: MIT Press.

Gebser, J. (1985) *The Ever-Present Origin*. Athens: Ohio University Press.

Geertz. C. (1973) *The Interpretation of Cultures*. New York: Basic Books.

Godard, J. L. (1970) *See You at Mao* (U.S. title) [British title: *British Sounds*]. Kestrel Productions for London Weekend Television, London.

Gurwitsch, A. (1974) *Phenomenology and the Theory of Science*. Evanston, IL: Northwestern University Press.

Hall, E. T. (1983) *The Dance of Life: The Other Dimension of Time*. New York: Doubleday.

Hawking, S. (1992) *A Brief History of Time*. New York: Bantam Books.

Heidegger, M. (1962) *Being and Time*. New York: Harper & Row.

———. (1971) *On the Way to Language*. New York: Harper & Row.

Heisenberg, W. (1970) *Natural Law and the Structure of Matter*. London: Rebel Press.

Husserl, E. (1962) *Ideas*. New York: Collier.

———. (1970) *The Crisis of European Sciences and Transcendental Phenomenology*. Evanston, IL: Northwestern University Press.

Janis, I. (1982) *Victims of Groupthink: A Psychological Study of Foreign Decisions and Fiascos*. Boston: Houghton Mifflin.

Katz, E. (1974) "Uses of Mass Communication by the Individual." In *Mass Communication Research: Major Issues and Future Directions*, edited by W. Davidson and F. Yu. New York: Praeger (pp. 11–35).

Kramer, E. M. (1988) *Television Criticism and the Problem of Ground*. 2 vols. Ann Arbor, MI: University Microfilms International, 8816770.

———. (1992) "Gebser and Culture." In *Consciousness and Culture: An Introduction to the Thought of Jean Gebser*, edited by E. Kramer. Westport, CT: Greenwood Press (pp. 1–60).

———. (1993) "The Origin of Television as Civilizational Expression." In *Semiotics*

1990: Sources in Semiotics, Vol. XI, edited by J. Deely et al. Lanham, MD: University Press of America.

―――. (1994) "Making Love Alone: Videocentrism and the Case of Modern Pornography." In *Ideals of Feminine Beauty,* by K. Callaghan. Westport, CT: Greenwood Press (pp. 79–98).

Kramer, E. M., and R. Ikeda. (1996) "Japanese Clocks: Semiotic Evidence of the Perspectival Mutation." In Press.

Mannheim, K. (1952) *Essays on the Sociology of Knowledge.* London: Routledge & Kegan Paul.

Merleau-Ponty, M. (1964) *The Primacy of Perception.* Evanston, IL: Northwestern University Press.

Michard, J. G. (1992) *The Reign of the Dinosaurs.* New York: Harry N. Abrams.

"More Personnel Information Available for Commanders." *Tinker Take Off* 54, no. 1 (1996): 14.

Mumford, L. (1963) *Techniques and Civilization.* New York: Harcourt, Brace & World.

Nietzsche, F. (1966) *Thus Spoke Zarathustra.* New York: Viking Penguin.

―――. (1967a) *On the Genealogy of Morals.* New York: Vintage.

―――. (1967b) *The Birth of Tragedy.* New York: Vintage.

―――. (1973) *Beyond Good and Evil.* New York: Penguin.

―――. (1974) *The Gay Science.* New York: Vintage.

―――. (1996) *Human, All-too-Human.* New York: Routledge.

Parsons, T. (1951) *The Social System.* Glencoe, IL: Free Press.

Peirce. C. S. (1940) *The Philosophy of Peirce: Selected Writings,* edited by J. Buchler. New York: Harcourt.

Plot, R. (1677) *The Natural History of Oxford-shire.* Oxford, England: The Theatre.

Popper, K. (1959) *Logic of Scientific Discovery.* New York: Basic Books.

Rorty, R. (1991) *Objectivity, Relativism, and Truth.* New York: Cambridge University Press.

Ruesch, J., and G. Bateson. (1968) *Communication: The Social Matrix of Psychiatry.* New York: W. W. Norton & Company.

Sagan, C. (1974) *Broca's Brain: Reflections on the Romance of Science.* New York: Random House.

Schliermacher, F. (1961) *Ueder die Religion: Reden an die gebildeten unter ihren verachtern.* Hamburg: F. Meiner.

Schramm, W. (1971) "The Nature of Communication Between Humans." In *The Process and Effects of Mass Communication,* edited by W. Schramm and D. Roberts. Chicago: University of Illinois Press.

Thorne, K. (1992) Essay in *Stephen Hawking's "A Brief History of Time": A Reader's Companion,* edited by S. Hawking. New York: Bantam Books (pp. 68–71).

Toffler, A. (1990) *Power Shift: Knowledge, Wealth, and Violence at the Edge of the 21st Century.* New York: Bantam.

von Humboldt, F. W. (1973) *The Theory and Practice of History: Collected Manuscripts from 1829–1880.* Indianapolis: Bobbs-Merrill.

von Weizacker, C. (1949) *The History of Nature.* Chicago: University of Chicago Press.

Weber, M. (1949) *The Method of the Social Sciences.* Glencoe, IL: The Free Press.

Whorf, B. (1956) *Language, Thought, and Reality.* Boston: MIT Press.

5

Aperspectival "Postmodernity"

APERSPECTIVITY

Although many "postmodern" writers (including Jacques Derrida) exhibit some aperspectival, non-Aristotelian tendencies, Gebser's (1985) neo-Nietzschean and neo-Husserlian writings are preferred by this author.[1] Gebser does not present a longing for the magical past, evident in Derrida's Talmudic style tracings. Instead, Gebser developed Nietzsche's incisive critique of a self-satisfied, Aristotelian rationality (monologic), and Husserl's investigations of time-consciousness and modern Galilean-style Platonism. Consequently, a "new" mode of (a)waring is referred to as "aperspectival," a term first introduced by Gebser in 1936. The Greek prefix "a" is used in conjunction with the Latin-derived word "perspectival" in order to articulate a sense of *alpha privativum* rather than *alpha negativum*. The prefix is used in its liberating connotation (*privativum* is derived from Latin *privare*, "to liberate") (see Gebser, 1985: 2).

Poststructuralism, postindustrialism, and postmodernism presume to "move on." But the age of messiahs, of salvific discourse no longer has the vitality it once did. To be sure, gurus are everywhere, but all are suspect in the paranoia of late modernity. Logicians are conservative. The prefix "post" connotes modern temporal anxiety and linearity. It also privileges whatever word that follows it, making of it the central concern. Thus, postmodernism must presume and centralize modernity as the source of its differentiation. Insofar as postmodernism means anything, it is as it differs from modernism. The act of "posting" modernity confers status on it as the source, the semantic place where the diacritical project begins. Postmodernism presupposes modernity as the founding premise of its project. Thus, postmodernism, via its two-valued, diacritical "play," is nothing without modernity. In this way, postmodernists privilege modernity. Aperspectivity does not obsess this way. There is no drive to "deconstruct" anything. Instead, appreciation of differences is promoted without any discursive engineering.

Aperspectivity is not post- anything, which has a strong tendency to be dualistically antimodern and to manifest a form of "minus-mutation." The aperspectival world can be identified only as it differs from the modern perspectival, magic preperspectival, and mythic unperspectival worlds (Gebser, 1985; Kramer, 1992). While the modern is manifested as the establishment and exploration of three-dimensional depth-space, the aperspectival is marked by freedom from the exclusivity of spatializing metaphysics (i.e., center versus margin).

Consequently, aperspectivity is not dualistic, and therefore not antisystem, antipatriarchal, anticategorical, antimathematical, or antianything. Dualistic thinking is recognized, but not as the only source of validity or sense. Neither is aperspectivity pro- or con- any typically modern option. Nor is it un-, or irrational. Rather, it is aspatial, which implicates all of the manifestations of spatialized, dualistic thinking. Hence, aperspectivity is a mode of perception that integrates oppositional tandems while escaping their exclusive claim to Reality. Aperspectivity is a mode of (a)waring that is acategorical and ahierarchical.

Aperspectivity is an (a)waring of the dynamic process of differential integration which identifies the unperspectival, preperspectival, and perspectival limitations, respectively. Each is appresentiated through the others. These world boundaries are manifested as mutually excluding forms of validity (metaphysical prejudices). They constitute regional ontologies that, as has been demonstrated above with many examples, can and do co-exist. Recognition of differential dynamics, and of the vitality (thus validity) of each standard, enables us to escape confinement to any singular system, such as materialism or mentalism.

"Confinement" entails being blindly adherent to, and constituted by, a singular legitimacy/reality. Nationalism is a good example, as it promotes blind patriotism ("my country right or wrong," meaning that it is always "right" even when it is wrong) while also giving the patriot a fixed identity.

Aperspectivity does not condemn, deny, or deconstructively verse, and reverse, modern dualities. Aperspectivity is an integrating awareness that the sense of modernity is recognizable only through the other modes of awaring. The very magics and mythologies which modernity seeks to exterminate are necessary conditions for its existence. For instance, the spatializing contribution of systematic thinking can be appreciated only as it differs from other modes of awaring. But at the same time, its contribution is not privileged over all the others because no metacriterial position is presumed that would enable such an excluding value judgement. By contrast, systematizers believe that knowledge does not exist until operational definition and unitizing coordination (ratio) are applied to phenomena. For instance, everyone already knows that some people talk much more than others and that that variance effects (causes) different kinds of relating. But systematizers do not believe that this is really knowledge until it is transformed into a scalar phenomenon.

From the perspectival worldview, nonscalar "knowledge" is discredited ignorance. The consequence is that there cannot, by definition, be any truth in art,
literature, drama, myth, and so forth. According to modernity, only moderns
can know when they know. Operationalization is a tautological metaphysic.
What is "IQ"? It is whatever my scale says it is. This attitude presents a very
powerful bias in favor of what Marshall McLuhan (1962) called "typographic"
reality, and Jacques Derrida (1976: 12) called "logocentrism," the idea that
truth does not exist until someone systematically presents it (once and for all);
"the determination of the being of the entity as presence." This is the "epoch
of the *logos*," of "ontotheology," of mental-rational existentialism, of which
science, in its obsession with substance and significance, is the prime example.
This world is established by the communication form Gebser (1985: 84, 309)
called the "philosopheme" (as compared to the "eteologeme").

Perhaps there is some truth in the novels of Sinclair Lewis, Thomas Mann,
Yukio Mishima, or Ernest Hemingway, but how could we know? It is not systematically logical. It is not replicable, except that it is a best seller. The "truth"
lies in between the audience and the text. So, the most powerful truth is the
knowledge that one knows, or as Karl Popper (1959) put it, to know that one
does not know (the principle of falsifiability). But this knowing about knowing
leads to a Zenoesque infinite regression. This is what Nietzsche calls the "new
infinite." According to Nietzsche (1974: 336, sec. 374),

Our new "infinite."—How far the perspective character of existence extends or indeed
whether existence has an other character than this; whether existence without interpretation, without "sense," does not become "nonsense"; whether, on the other hand, all
existence is not essentially actively engaged in *interpretation*—that cannot be decided
even by the most industrious and most scrupulously conscientious analysis and self-
examination of the intellect; for in the course of this analysis the human intellect cannot
avoid seeing itself in its own perspectives, and *only* in these. We cannot look around our
own corner: it is a hopeless curiosity that wants to know what other kinds of intellects
and perspectives there might be. . . . But I should think that today we are at least far from
the ridiculous immodesty that would be involved in decreeing from our corner that perspectives are permitted only from this corner. Rather has the world become "infinite"
for us all over again, inasmuch as we cannot reject the possibility that *it may include
infinite interpretations.*

This is also why Husserl refused to arbitrarily (just because my teacher was this
way or my society) privilege any one regional ontology (he refused to do spec-
ulative philosophy). Without a divine-like metacriterial position, the choice of
"ground" is arbitrary. The Nietzschean choice is to not choose, but instead to
appreciate different systems as seen through each other; to remain flexible and
marvel at diversity, the "new infinite" which leads to the unknown and "the
great shudder."

The bias of the West is in favor of a text-based recorded style of knowledge.

It is presumed that words can describe visual phenomena much better than tastes, smells, or even hearing. But words are just better at presenting and disseminating a truth to a public of others. The West spends a lot of time and energy describing and bisecting surfaces (topography and realism). This is because discourse is a spatial/perspectival phenomenon. This is also why many artists have claimed that writing about painting, for instance, is like critiquing music with a piece of architecture. Aperspectivally, we can appreciate the emphases and limitations of journal-based knowledge while acknowledging that other realities are shared by everyone, journal readers and nonreaders alike. These shared realities are not "verses," as in universe, but dimensions of (a)waring.

Aperspectivity appreciates the technology of systematization but also pre-, and unperspectival forms of truth/reality. For instance, taste and smell, though difficult to share "objectively" (meaning visually, in a spatially detached way) are shared nonetheless. Indeed, aperspectivity holds that such realities are presumed by the systematizers who must have something to systematically (re)present. Taste and smell are part of the world too, and if they are ignored or denied on the basis of metaphysical prejudice, then a less-than-complete sense of the world is availed. No matter how much one denies the existence of another reality, like myth for instance, in the very effort to demonize, distort, or deny it, emotion, value, and interest are manifested. Dogma, as Thomas Kuhn (1962) has demonstrated, is shared by archaic magic, mythological religion, *and* perspectival science. Ignoring something amounts to self-imposed ignorance. Also, to claim that other modes of knowledge are not generalizable or somehow not utilitarian, and therefore inferior, not only exposes a technological (instrumental) bias, but is not at all supported by the survivability of other worlds/realities. Both journals and storytellers have generalized audiences who share truths. Many aspects of the world are perhaps better established by novelists, dancers, and architects than analysts. It seems unlikely that any amount of analytical writing can match the truth of emotion conjured by Luciano Pavarotti singing "Che gelida manina" from Puccini's *La Bohème*, "Rondine al Nido" by de Crescenzo, "Nessun dorma" from Puccini's *Turandot*, and so on. There is no exclusively privileged perspective, and only the perspectival mentality is concerned with separating the what from the how, the content from the form. The most influential duality that forms the essence of modern/postmodern interests, permanence and flux, is recognized as an integral phenomenon, appresentiated with timeless magical, and cyclical mythic modalities.

Methodological Considerations: Structure, Event

Decades before either Derrida, Francois Lyotard, or Foucault wrote their respective "postmodernisms," Gebser articulated a morphological strategy based on Nietzsche's concept of "genealogy," put forth in *The Gay Science*. Not only did Gebser recognize the discontinuous nature of change, and the fragmenting tendency of a deficient rationality, he did so in a much more elegant style, and with far more evidentiary rigor than either Derrida or Foucault.

Gebser argued that a new form of statement was necessary. The philosophemes of the great Western systems theorists are exclusively categorical and spatial (causally dualistic). Consequently, they do not express the multidimensional and provisional quality of worlds. Based as they are on dialectics, they postulate a universe of binary oppositions that can be mentally synthesized, only to fragment again as synthesis perpetually, and subsequently, reverts to being a new thesis.

The modern concept of system (which reached its apex already with Hegel) postulates static abstractions of only momentary validity, like Ferdinand de Saussure's (1974) synchronic linguistics. Gebser's interest was in the "principle of transformation" which renders illusory all such "ideal quantities," thus destroying all "fixities." Structuralists, like Claude Levi-Strauss and Noam Chomsky, sought the universal rules of transformation (such as binary opposition), by following the conventional modernist hierarchy of knowledge put forth by Blaise Pascal, Baron Montesquieu, Auguste Comte, and Saint-Simon. Consequently, the structuralists reduced what they called the "unconscious structures" to materialism. However, while cultures present great variety, the brain does not appear to manifest great structural diversity. No correlation has been found between cultural differences and physical differences in the human species.[2] Furthermore, this Enlightenment faith in reductionistic metaphysics cannot escape detection as these authors, even in their attempt to explain transformation, do so in terms of universal, genetic grammars (inescapable structures), thus betraying their ambition to be seen as gods who think apodictic thoughts.

Gebser (1985) claimed that transformational processes are both differentiating and integrating. Transformational processes are neither eternal nor temporal, infinite nor localizable. Transformational processes are atemporal and aspatial. These dynamic processes enable one to recognize the various temporal and spatial manifolds that different cultures express.

Modern systems theory, which claims a temporally privileged status in the interest of control, is sectoral. Disregarding change, systems analysis recognizes only slices (or sectors) of reality as if the world freezes while relationships are measured. Such an abstracting method yields only momentary validity. In order to extend their contingent validity, modern systems, such as institutions, become increasingly preoccupied with self-perpetuation via intensified self-monitoring and "correction." Maintaining equilibrium (status quo) favors the "arrest" of troublesome elements, principally time, through an exclusively (intolerant) synchronic perspective. Diachronics (history, context, change) is not only resisted, but denied reality (as totally irrelevant, and/or inconvenient).

Modern knowledge and understanding takes the form of discrete, unrelated snapshots of currently visible reality. Implicate knowledge (or organic knowledge of synergistic interrelatings) was discredited by Descartes in 1637, with *Discours de la methode pour bien conduire fa raifon, & cherchet la verite dans les sciences* (*Discourse on the Method of Properly Guiding Reason in the Search for Truth in the Sciences*). Descartes believed that the best approach to truth was to split ''large difficulties'' into smaller ones, and to argue hierarchically from the simple to the complex. Thus, social scientists and linguists have tried to identify the social and linguistic ''atoms'' (the individual, demographic categories, the seme, the phoneme, the bit, etc.) so that they may progress to the ontological level of which they desire knowledge.

However, copying the natural sciences, social scientists have failed to realize that even in the dead reactive (not alive pro-active) world of matter, engineers do not build bridges by doing quantum mechanics. A simple linear progression from the subatomic to Newtonian mechanics is not evident. What is evident is discontinuity. The two ''worlds'' appear to function from different principles, to be *qualitatively* different. They have different rules. For instance, while the Aristotelian logic of binary mutual exclusivity (stated as ''q not q'') was translated by Newton into his mechanical notion of parity, an experiment conducted by Monroe et al. (1996) has demonstrated that a particle can occupy two places simultaneously. But, in the macro world of bowling balls and bridges, at least so far, Newton's law holds true. It depends on which ''uni'' verse one is concerned with at the moment.

Time has proven to be the enemy of structure, the disrupting threat to total order. The most fundamental dispute remains Plato versus Heraclitus. Ricoeur (1974: 83) reminds us that ''structure'' has come to be synonymous with system.

Of course, Saussure does not use the word ''structure'' but the word ''system.'' The word ''structure'' appeared only in 1928 at the First International Congress of Linguists at the Hague, in the form ''structure of a system.'' The word ''structure'' would appear then as a specification of the system and would designate the restrictive combinations, highlighted against the whole field of possibilities of articulation and combination, which create the individual configuration of a language. But in the form of the adjective ''structural,'' the word has become synonymous with system.

Gebser (1985) believed that back-and-forth motion restricted to fixed parameters (a binary and oppositional conceptualization of the world) was not a very accurate rendering of experience. The hallmark of perspectival ordination originated in the medieval church. Control (resistance to change) was enhanced by a bureaucratic structure inherited from the ''eternal'' Roman Empire, which was inspired by Plato's grandstudent Alexander. The medieval church, with its ''orders'' of monks (most notably the Benedictines), initiated a strict devotion to a monochronic world of schedules that now dominates the modern industrialized world (Mumford, 1963; Gebser, 1985; Hall, 1966). This strange obsession with conformity and synchronization of bodily functions and behaviors practiced by a handful of clerics has now become normative, the very essence of modernity.

Community

At least forty years before Francis Fukuyama's work The *End of History and the Last Man* (1992), Gebser recognized the growing irrelevance of the modern individual, linear (spatial) history, and also the end of philosophy as spatialized systems theory (1985: 309). Egology, which emerged as classical Greece and again as the Renaissance, is an expressed concern with the increasingly isolated monad, which was correlated with the sudden and rapid expansion (awareness) of depth-space. With perspectival painting, architecture, writing (including science, history, and the novel), jurisprudence (individual rights), government (democracy), religion (having a personal relationship with God), romanticism, and so on, the modern individual asserts its will, and is localized. The needs of the group are subordinated to the needs of the individual. But this power arrangement has become overdetermined (hypertrophic), and increasingly untenable. Extreme individualism threatens community.

For instance, the total fragmentation and decentralization of power, so popular among right-wing politicos, who appeal to unfettered competition, greed, and fear, and see no legitimate limit to individualism, undermines the ability of the electorate to exercise democratic tendencies because of information overload. Community means sharing, including the redistribution of wealth in the *interest of group viability*. If individuals are no longer willing to share according to their abilities, or have time to identify those in need and administer to them, then community ceases to exist and aggregation predominates. An aggregate of individuals is qualitatively different from a community. The former is marked by reciprocity and accommodation, the latter by might and enforced conformity (Buber, 1970). Rational redistribution of wealth requires some degree of centralization and systematization.

The rhizomatic world described by Gilles Deluze and Felix Guattari (1983) would be one where the average citizen would have to spend inordinate amounts of time keeping track of innumerable local officials. So long as the citizenry has the power of election and impeachment, "classes" are permeable, and there exists a fairly honest and free press; one strength of modern centralization is that policy debates and public finance can be kept in sharp focus, enabling better oversight of just a few (officials) by the many. Granted, the few must concede to live in a "fish bowl" in exchange for policy leadership (ego satisfaction). Almost nothing is so difficult to watch as an incumbent politician who must publicly concede defeat. The public ego can be kept in check. Master narratives, master plans, master races, master truths, master logics, and other "masters" can be made to serve. Nothing is eternal.

Leaders, messiahs, and salvific discourses can be debated. For instance, very much second-guessing of the press occurred after it had investigated whether or not Jeremy "Mike" Boorda, the United States Navy's top admiral, had illegitimately worn a "V Device," which is a decorative pin signifying valor during direct participation in combat. The second-guessing concerned the inquisitorial nature of the news media, but only after Admiral Boorda had committed suicide. It is quite likely that if an individual of lesser rank and status had been suspected of doing the same thing, an inquiry would have been made, and possibly disciplinary action taken, perhaps by Admiral Boorda's office itself.

Most Americans have no idea who their city council members, their state legislators, or any number of other local officials are, or what they are doing. In a complex society, very few have time to become ''political junkies'' or ''policy wonks.'' As a consequence, corruption is much more difficult to recognize and avoid at the local level. Unless we abandon the most basic aspect of civil and communal life altogether, the division of labor, it must be that power can become too disseminated; so fragmented as to be of no use to the group, as such. As President Abraham Lincoln said, government does for the individual what he or she cannot do alone.

Gebser's concept of integral aperspectivity enables one to appreciate the contributions of each consciousness structure, *including the mental-rational perspectival*, so that it is not antimodern anymore than it is antimythical. Aperspectival integrating consciousness opens up the consolidated spatial world to noncategorical elements, thus enabling one to perceive and presentiate the integrity or integrality of the never complete ''whole,'' including mental-rationality (measurement). Systematization and individuation have both proven viable. For all its weaknesses, modernity has accomplished great advances in technology and human rights. It is only when moderns claim to manifest the only (universal and exclusively) valid reality that their proclamations become logocentrically ''deficient'' (Gebser, 1985: 3). Antimodernists rely on modernity not only for physical sustenance but also as a target for their critical reflections. But modernity does not need the postmodern. Aperspectivity appreciates the reciprocity between the modern, postmodern, magic, and mythic worlds.

As population and societal complexity increase, centralization must exist in order to take care of things such as water and air quality, which are group phenomena. Modernization has its own imperatives which cannot be ignored. There is no viable ''going back'' to exclusively mythical or magical validity. We cannot erase the modern. Life is made possible because we can trust each other to do our jobs. We can presume each other's labors. But, by also recognizing the mythical and magical contributions to the world, we escape the specter of being reduced to pure functionalism.

What had dominated modern history as a global opposition between two intensely centralized and hierarchical systems of ordination is dissolving. They were the left Hegelians (communists), and the right Hegelians (fascists), both of which deployed highly coordinated feedback mechanisms (various channels of internal surveillance) in the interest of self-maintenance and perpetuation. This efficiency in the pursuit of a system's interests threatens to transform humans into cyborgs. Since the advent of modern systems thinking, this threat is constant. But so, too, are the ''irrational'' magical and mythical modes of being. So, as nondemocratic systems are waning, an obsession with territorial and ideological "integrity" is reemerging along ethnic lines. For example, after the Dayton Peace Accords were signed in December 1995, to stop the aggression in the Balkans among the Bosnians, Serbians, and Croats, peoples from all the warring factions had to move into their assigned territories. The ethnic hatred and distrust was so great that during the implementation of the peace plan (spring of 1996), thousands dug up their dead relatives to take them with them.

However, despite such strong evidence of the tenacious endurance of ethnic intolerance, there is also evidence that such magical (blood defined) and mythical ("traditional") demarcations are being superseded by aperspectival consciousness. This is evinced in many ways, including the burgeoning worldwide Internet, which was designed to survive nuclear destruction of "power-centers."[3] The key to an open future is to keep talking.

A "NEW" ARTICULATION

The Eteologeme

Gebser argued that, just as philosophy had replaced myth, so "eteology" would replace dualistic, two-valued conceptualization. The aperspectival world does not establish orders as such. The validity of the group, the individual, and their relatedness, is recognized, but not as the one and only viable structure. According to Gebser, what replaces the great logical systems that were articulated in the form of philosophemes and synchronic structures (ideological rationalisms) is a new form called the "eteologeme."

An eteologeme is a "verition" free of dualities such as subject and object, permanence and flux. It "has nothing to do with representation; only in philosophical thought [including Galilean-style science] can the world be represented; according to integral perception, the world is pure statement, and thus 'verition' " (Gebser, 1985: 309).

The word "eteologeme" is derived from the Greek *eteos*, which means "true, real." The adverbial form is *eteon*, meaning "in accord with truth, truly, really." *Eteon* comes from the root *se:es*, meaning "to be." Just as Ludwig Wittgenstein (1969) and Husserl (1962) argued for absolute positivity (not in the ideological sense of justifying power relations or in generative quantification, but in experience), the analytics of modern method/mediation are rendered contingent.

For instance, a postcard of Crater Lake is not the same as the bodily experience of Crater Lake. One can work very hard to generate a simulation, and it is a real simulation. But neither the simulation nor that which is simulated takes ontological precedence over the other. In other words, there are no fixed meta-criteria that deny one the right to marvel at Michelangelo's *David* just as much as marveling at the "real" David. The ontological reversal and prioritization imposed on experience by the modern Galilean style of truth is evident by the fact that the "actual" David is reduced to the status of being a mere "model" that does not endure like the virtual sculpture. The sculpture becomes a part of history and a thing more highly valued than the model ''upon which it is based.''

Modern metaphysical squabbles such as between empiricism, idealism, rationalism, and other such philosophical dogmas are bracketed by Gebser. Gebser avoids such quagmires because the world simply ''is the case.'' No method or representation need render it because no Cartesian metaphysical split, or canon of veiled direct experience, makes operation necessary (although operationalization is convenient when the interest of technological utility is presumed). Sense and meaning are given as experience. What something ''really'' means does not have to be reckoned by an expert, whose version is exclusively and absolutely privileged.

Systasis

The way to make the new form of discourse is ''systasis.'' Systasis stresses process, while system stresses statics. Statics is a quality of being taken from Newton's first law of motion which states that matter has a tendency to maintain its state, whether in motion or rest. An object does not change unless an outside force acts upon it. Instead of this physical, causal line of thinking, systasis is nonspatial, and as such, allows the efficacy of acategorical intensities, like time. ''Systasis'' is Greek, meaning ''putting together,'' ''connecting'' so that partials merge. Relating emerges with static relationships. Systasis is a fitting together into four-dimensional integrality. It is an (a)waring of temporalization. It is an (a)waring of, and therefore a supersession of, isolated (mutually excluding) self-contained systems. The monadology of Leibniz's systematics is integrated into the communicative (temporal) field of a shared world that presents differentiation, the *aporia* of continual discontinuity—flux). Solipsism is recognized as only one solution to the self-identity of mathematical, and other ideational truths. The modern, three-dimensional mode of perception (exemplified by dialectics), leads to various kinds of partitioning. Systasis is *not* an ordering scheme like system. Systasis is both process and effect. It builds on Husserl's (1962) realization of an immanent transcendence.

Language is a good example of an ideational process that is contingent. This is so for at least two reasons. First, language is in a ''*constant* state of *change*.'' Second, when I say ''a car is going by,'' others in my linguistic community understand that ''c-a-r'' is a categorical statement. ''C-a-r'' can be used to describe many different cases of vehicles with engines and four wheels. Language is essentially a shortcut way to interact. I do not need a different word for every ''car'' that goes by. Language is ideational. And yet not everything is adequately expressed by just one word ''thing.'' Language is transcendental in that it identifies contingencies in a transcending way. Meaning can be translated, while language itself is contingent and utterly flexible. You can *say* one thing, but *mean* something quite different. There are paralinguistic aspects to communication such as the way (the volume and tone one uses) to say something. You may answer a question about how you are with "FINE! Just FINE," which indicates that nothing is "fine."

Another example of a systatic realization is Hans-Georg Gadamer's (1975) notion of historically effective historical consciousness. Gadamer uses the phrase "*das Wirkungsgeschichtliche Bewusstein*," which, according to David Hoy (1978: 63), means "the consciousness of standing within a still operant history (*Wirkungsgeschichte*)." The world is a process that is self-referential, both affect (process) and effect. In other words, what and how a historian writes is affected by history (which he and others are part of).[4] What and how a social scientist writes is affected by his social position, and, his social position is affected by his writing. Experience changes how we see the world. Experience affects our future experiences. However, the world is not a closed system, which is why Gebser rejected the universal theory of lingualism promoted by Heideggerians, including Gadamer (what Fredric Jameson, many decades after Gebser rejected lingualism, called the "prison-house of language," 1972). Heidegger himself invented words because none existed to express his new realizations. Words establish, at least as much as they refer and indicate. The magical dimension of language is incantatory. The mythical dimension is metaphorical, and the mental-rational perspectival dimension is discretely and arbitrarily signalic.

The past is perpetually created in the future. Past and future are continually differentiated and integrated. Expectations affect the interpretation of past and present behavior. The past, present, and future are integrally (mutually) appresentiated (but without any hierarchical distinction between "direct" and "indirect" status of being). The "whole" is never given. There is no final and permanent integration, but instead an awareness of the permanence of integrating. Insofar as the world is, it is as Husserl (1962: 91) said, "*for me simply there*." *We* are continually exposed to a world of "*indeterminate reality*," prior to any theorizing (Husserl, 1962: 92). According to Husserl, "It is then to this world, *the world in which I find myself and which is also my world-about-me*, that the complex of forms of my manifold and shifting *spontaneities* of consciousness stand related" (Husserl, 1962: 93).

Like truth, history, too, is not a fixed empirical object, because subjects are constantly creating it, and vice versa. But it is not just history that is variable. The human condition is one of differencing. The world is always there but always different. Fixed "reality" and fixed (external) "facts" are myths. They are never "the same." When data are reevaluated, "breakthroughs" occur. I travel to another country, and this affords me an ability to starkly compare. This difference enables me to reevaluate everything. I return "home" to a different country, one "lacking" in some ways and noticeably "better" in others. My values, my dogmatic slumber has been interrupted. I see with different eyes, taste with a different tongue, hear with different ears. I not only see home differently, but I become aware of difference itself, the possibility of the world, its perpetual pregnancy with potential.

What is a fact? What are principles? What is maturation or growth? Even the most "concrete" things, like my house, have changed. My Tokyo apartment that always satisfied me before, after my stay in the United States, seems "small," "cramped," "overpriced." One need not go to another country to have this shift in values, this reevaluation of the world. The passage of time brings with it continual difference/meaning. Nothing is absolutely redundant. If it were, it would be invisible. Even the boring is painfully apparent. I go to my childhood house and everything and nothing has changed. It is "smaller," every surface, shadow, and view is saturated with emotion. This is so because it is the same, but, of course, I never saw it before like this because it is also very different. The same is true of a novel read two or more times or a face, my aging face reflected in the mirror. "It," the phenomenon of the "text," is never quite the same. In fact, if years separate my readings/viewings/tastings (etc.), it may be profoundly different. And the text need not be mediated by my senses. A memory, dream, fantasy, or idea may pass upon me again but seem utterly silly "now." I may wish to locate the change inside of myself, but no such metaphysical speculation is necessary or sufficient to explore relativity. Since "I" am never the same, such a claim is inadequate to the point of being self-evident anyway.

The more one is interested in order and permanence, the more the world (time—spontaneity) presents itself as a problem to be conquered. Time becomes a criminal in need of arrest, or to be escaped. Anxiety in the face of uncertainty is a characteristic of the modern "organizational man." Systematization is an attempt to fix and organize time (relationships). It is a response to the modern preoccupation with speed and efficiency of change.

Mythical and magical peoples do not worry about time. For instance, for many magical and mythical peoples such as the traditional Navajo, the future is unreal and therefore they are not motivated by it. Aging is acceptable. As Nietzsche (1974) demonstrated in his phenomenology of causality, for the modern causalist, the cause of current behavior is actually concern about a projected future. Like the Navajo, the Hopi have no verb tenses to designate past, present, or future. Closure is not a value for them. It is not really important to finish what one begins. To posit a deadline, or to suggest that a dam, for instance, must be finished by a certain time, as if it has an inherent and natural proclivity like ripening fruit, is absurd to the Hopi (see Hall, 1983).

Time, for magical and mythical people, is not a thing, a constant, but a quality (Gebser, 1985). Recalling the work of Benjamin Lee Whorf, Edward T. Hall concurs that summer for the Hopi is not a thing but the quality hot (Hall, 1983: 37). Summer is a mood. Neither the Hopi nor the Navajo have a word (noun) for time. Time, as a consequence, is not a harsh taskmaster. Likewise, in Hindi, one does not say that this is a "fist," but rather that one is "fisting." Chinese and Japanese also emphasize process over product, relationships over individuals. Such cultural differences, which inevitably lead to moral judgements (i.e., Native Americans are lazy, whites are anal retentives always trying to get us "in line"), constitute a major source of interethnic conflict.

Because of the presumption of progress (linear positivism), the tendency of the modern Western subject (whenever and whoever it is) is to defend the "system" which *creates* progress. Thus, one has the oxymoron of "progressive structure." The present (whenever that may be) always sees itself perspectivally as the latest, most "developed" "cutting edge." As discussed in Chapter 3, Kronos (time) cut Uranus (sky) to pieces with his sickle. Time is a cleaver, a piercing arrow on the tip of which the whole world sits. As the now, which includes everything, moves, in its wake histories accumulate, but they are also in the now, or nowhere. Despite this paradox of linear time, the present thus privileges itself with being more true and having greater understanding than any and all "past" presents. Time is a process of continual reevaluation of the stuff at hand. Memory is ever-present. Thus, to deny the existence of values is to attempt to ignore the very essence of being. Only a linear perspectival person has a "present" as such, because "present" presumes "past" and/or "future."

However, through integral appresentiation, the past is written in the future and the future presumes the past. This explains how two historians in different times can have different interpretations, but neither be wrong, because they are not fixed subjects confronting a historical "object" (singularity). Neither truth (even the "empirical" kind) nor history is a fixed object somewhere. The world is a complex of mutually integrating differences. The world is dynamic, not frozen in a dead structure of permanent relationships. History writing is constantly changing, because it is affected by history. What the history writer writes, which in the future will constitute the past, will integrate with prior and future histories. History writing, like science writing, is sedimented in the lifeworld, which is temporal. The linear concept of time is thus not merely reversed ("deconstructed"), because linearity has no simple opposite. Rather, linear time is integrally appresentiated with other "times."[5]

Even materialism cannot escape time. A strictly empirical metaphysic either rejects history because it is not a thing, or conceives of it as a line of discrete "points" that alternate as cause and effect, depending on one's perspective. The identity of any phenomenon is thus in constant flux, and the points have no relationship between each other so that the idea, the image, of a line becomes senseless. What is a cause and what is an effect is determined by when/wherever the researcher decides to establish the "initial state," and the scope of the frame of observation. Continuity, which is presupposed by all law, is not at all empirical. For the idea of law (natural or otherwise) to make sense, it must presume knowledge of the initial state of a system, and a systematic, deterministic process that never changes. While both Maxwell's classical laws of electromagnetism and quantum laws are written in the language of differential equations so that predictions require that the initial data be specified, Heisenberg's uncertainty principle states that the initial data cannot be specified with sufficient precision to enable the application of classical laws. When classical laws are applied to quantum phenomena they lead to incorrect results. So it seems that this logic of method is limited to the macro world. But Newtonian mechanics has also failed to enable scientists to predict human behavior even on the most gross levels such as the price of futures, stocks, and the likelihood of war. Perhaps initial data cannot be collected with certainty. And/or perhaps the freedom expressed by a human being confounds the assumptions that bodies, once set in motion, do not change, thus making initial measurements irrelevant.

In physical sciences, constants like the inherent nature of matter are presumed. What constitutes human nature, however, remains indeterminate. Time, for Newton, is a constant; otherwise his universe becomes unpredictable. However, because the "initial" state is arbitrary, even in the physical science, laws have two surprising properties: They are all unproven and unprovable. Science is based on observation and experimentation, both of which depend on individual, direct, personal experience. Even physical laws are assumed valid only so long as there are no observed violations of them. Consequently, history (memory) becomes vital to the maintenance of law! It is called precedent. Thus, physical (and all other types of) law depends on the nonphysical phenomenon known as memory. Justice is consistency across contingencies. Law itself is not at all an empirical thing but a transcendental phenomenon. Naive natural and social scientists who strive to discover the "laws of nature" are absurd. The very phenomenon they seek is, according to their own metaphysical prejudice, nonexistent. And without the consciousness of continuity, there can be no sense of law or prediction. The history of science demonstrates that it is a memorial process. A "breakthrough" or "discovery" can exist only against the background of a known (past tense) reality. Empirical science is not an empirical thing.

Consequently, it is not surprising that the most archaic of peoples with little or no history, or individuals with extreme cases of amnesia or Alzheimer's, behave in the most empirical of fashions. If something or someone is out of sight for a moment, when they return, because there is no retention, they are not recognized. Likewise, without the unempirical phenomena of protension and projection, very little planning occurs. In extreme cases as with "Schneider" (one of Merleau-Ponty's patients, 1962), he could hear and understand what a doorbell meant, but he could no longer synthesize or associate the empirical sensation with getting up (in the immediate future) and answering the door. The line of time, which is synthetic, was gone. All Schneider knew was what was immediately, empirically, present. Likewise, noise is qualitatively different from flowing music. Cultures are identifiable because, and insofar as, they synthesize time and space differently. Thus, the culture on a factory floor can be different, and as such recognizable, from the culture in the executive suite. In the same way, children live in a different, parallel universe from adults.

Systasis is *not* causally determined. Systasis is *neither* a modern mental-rational concept (like Heraclitus's *panta rhei*, "all things in flux"), *nor* a mythical image (like a flowchart), *nor* a magic presumption that all things are interchangeably identical. Systasis is not integral, but integrating. While systems are static abstractions, systasis is a recognition of the dynamic dimension within the world of contingent systems. Becoming aware of the "principle of transformation'' enables one to recognize the effectuality of acategorical systasis, thus becoming aware, not merely of mental synthesis, but of integral "synairesis.''

Synairesis

"Synairesis'' comes from the Greek *synaireo*, meaning "to synthesize, collect,'' notably in the sense of "everything being seized or grasped on all sides'' (Gebser, 1985: 312). While synthesis, however, reaches a logical conclusion, synairesis opens up the consolidated spatial world (including the ordination and spatialization of time as "clock-time,'' which dominates modernity) that is rigidified and breaking apart. As soon as one measures an intensity, like time, it is categorically fragmented; unitized. Synairesis dissolves the spatial circumference of the isolated and self-enclosed, self-monitoring cybernetic system. Synairesis is a creative perception that is an aspatial and atemporal potential whereby "the'' center is everywhere and so too is "the'' circumference.

Synairesis "fulfills'' the aperspectival, integrative perception of systasis and system. The goal is diaphany, or a transparency of awareness, which enables one to appreciate the relational "connections between'' and among various systems of awareness (the archaic, magic, mythic, and perspectival) as they form an integrating, dynamic world. If the spatial mode of thinking expressed by "connection'' and "between'' is dropped, then it is possible to realize that each system contains, and is contained by, the others. What this means is that each system co-constitutes the identity and difference of each other system. Unlike the classical logic that presumes that no two things can exist in the same space/ time at once, synairesis suggests that one thing can never be given alone. Nothing, no meaning, can exist alone. Even monotheistic gods create others. Two or more phenomena are always given together so that the distinction that enables awareness is possible.

Gebser (1985) rejected the universal applicability of the distinctly modern notion of progress, which would have us believe that as we become systematically rational, for instance, we totally abandon so-called "previous,'' and no longer effectual, modes of being such as magic and myth. Magic remains, but is reintegrated by the imperatives of the perspectival structure as falsehood, superstition, and emotion. Synairetic diaphany is achieved when modern, arbitrary signality (and codes), mythic symbolism, and magic symbiotic idolatry are appresentiated with equal efficacy.

For example, all levels of consciousness/meaning are present in "race,'' and to ignore one or more on the basis of a metaphysical/methodological prejudice or ideological arrogance would be to have (at best) only a partial understanding of this phenomenon. To ignore one of the differences affects the identity of all the others.

Synairetic (integrating) consciousness enables one to perceive and appresentiate the integrality of the process of "racing'' (which is not a fixed unity).

Synairetic perception allows the efficacy of noncategorical elements into the sphere of experience. No systematization (with its own inherent interests in rational ordination and hierarchical perspective) can express the mutability of a phenomenon as it presents symbolic, signalic, and idolic meanings simultaneously. Synairesis, which systasis makes possible, enables the recognition of the integrative process that phenomena are, thus revealing acategorical values (or elements). Systasis is neither irrational nor prerational, but rather, arational.

According to Gebser (1985: 312), the new form of statement based on systasis and synairesis, which retains the efficient validities of symbiosis, symbol, and system, is a form of expression that renders perceptible the content and principal motif of aperspectival awareness. The modern world of spatial extension inadequately limits our perception of the phenomenon.

This is why calls for philosophemes articulating a unifying Afrocentrism, pan-Africanism, and monadic self-actualization establish yet more versions of Westernizing modernity (either/orism) (Asante, 1987). Such perspectival ways of thinking may be why Molefi Asante finds "continental" Africans rejecting African Americans and also why Kwame Ture is so repulsed by African leaders that he calls them the "scum of our race." Despite all of the presumed coherence and identification with a single racial group, their works belie not only strong Eurocentric, modern values (in organization for instance), but also a strong shock (judgementalism) when confronted with the realities of undemocratic African cultural norms. Fighting fire with fire just leads to more fire. Mohandas Gandhi presented a truly postmodern alternative path, first made famous by Christ; patently irrational, unconditional love. It is important to note that Gebser spent a good bit of time living in India and studying its languages and literatures. Rather than hypertrophic perspectivism, integrality allows evil to become irrelevant. This is Tony Brown's (1995) insight about communal cooperation. Forget confrontation and grow money. From a position of wealth, confidence renders inferiorization impotent. Community is based on mutual respect, not competing centrisms seeking to dominate each other.

PLUS MUTATION

Gebser clearly stated (1985: 40–41) that the application of the idea of "incremental *growth*" (implying maturation or sophistication) in dimensionality, as a judgement, was not warranted. According to Gebser, the emergence of each dimension appears to be a mutational, nonlinear (meaning discontinuous), and indeterminate process that reveals no uniformity in overall purpose or design, nor any extrinsic superiority favoring one world over another.

As the histories of religion, philosophy, and science demonstrate, suprasystemic "laws" and "rules" keep changing (including the canons of history-writing itself). However, there seems to be a basic faith that the more permanent a discourse is, the more reliable and therefore "true" it is. The political phenomena of persistence and conservation win in the war of paradigms (Kuhn,

1962). Gebser did not ascribe to a neo-Hegelian "reason" to and for history ("entelechy"). Insofar as their much less rigorous efforts extend, scholars such as H. Innis, W. Ong, L. Mumford, T. Kuhn, E. T. Hall, M. McLuhan, J. Campbell, M. Eliade, and M. Foucault exhibit an almost total unanimity with the conclusions Gebser came to in the 1930s and 1940s.

Gebser did not presume a continuous, or coherent notion of history (1985: 40–43). He critiqued the spatialized progressivistic conceptualization of history which (the value free!) *positivistic* ideologues had established as the *non plus ultra* of human development. Such a discursive formation is obviously a typical perspectivistic conceptualization positing two opposing camps, those loudly proclaiming the utopia of "positivism," and by implication, the unnamed negativists. Gebser demonstrated that the world presents itself quite differently. Hence, the magical, mythical, mental-rational, seen through each other (aperspectival [a]waring), are not mutually exclusive "stages," or "phases" in a teleological purpose-and-goal orientation. Instead they enable each other to exist as such. Nor are they fixed "mentalities." Neo-Hegelian systematics, divine or otherwise, is neither presumed by synairesis nor thus far evinced, except within the perspectival world that creates systems that scholars then "discover" and describe as "naturally" occurring phenomena.

Outside the sphere of theological belief (including Marxism), there seems to be no evidence to support the existence of a transcendental rhyme or reason to history. No "naturally occurring" system, no ultimate metacriteria. And since scales are utterly arbitrary constructs which are essential to operational definitions, they, too, fall short of having a legitimate right to usurp absolutism. Unless one can demonstrate a metacriterion or metanarrative such as God, things are whatever we say they are. Each language-game (for it is definition, communication, and convention that we are about here) has its own rules, and the game exists only so long as two or more people are playing (Wittgenstein, 1971). Hence, cultures and even civilizations can be "lost." The human world is a cultural world including retention and protention.

The idea that life systematically adapts to changing environments, as if life, *sui generis*, has a "mind of its own," and reasons out a reaction to new stimuli (a la nineteenth-century German vitalistic and anthropomorphic philosophy) is not what is observed, with but one exception; human agency.[6] Rather, when the environment changes, as with the sudden introduction of a new pesticide, some individual members of a species and some species in the biosphere accidentally, randomly, survive while others die out. The dead individuals obviously fail to reproduce while the survivors, who had the good fortune to be different (*before the environment changed*) do have offspring, thus passing on the characteristic(s) that made them viable ("successful" in ideological terms), enabling them to repopulate the "niche."

Likewise, "niches" do not exist before they are established by so-called "occupants." As far as we know, God does not have a prefabricated flowchart somewhere else, with empty slots awaiting fulfillment. The universe does not present itself as a finished thing with preestablished options. Instead of system only, the world presents itself as openness. A single environment spawns innumerable varieties (''solutions'' in ideological terms). The spatializing limitations inherent to modern systems thinking is recognizable by aperspectival systatic and synairetic (a)waring. Despite internal, intrasystemic surveillance (feedback as in fascist regimes), systems ''fail'' (change). Change is ''failure'' only when permanence enhancement (status quo) is the singular goal and value.

Gebser (1985: 38), being keenly aware of the modern proclivity toward spatializing hierarchy, argued for a notion he called ''plus-mutation,'' which is different from Newtonian ''minus-mutation'' and presumes that no two ''things'' can occupy the same space at the same time. Minus-mutation presents a concept of evolutionary progress whereby the past is surpassed, extinct, and no longer effectual.

According to Gebser, ''plus-mutation,'' by contrast, means that the ''past'' is never totally abandoned, but that the present formation, whatever that may be, is *dependent upon the ever-present origin* (the past that is present) (1985: 38). For instance, all living cells on earth manifest the ability to produce protein. No matter how ''high up'' (in ''orders of organizational complexity'') one goes on the evolutionary ''ladder,'' this potential is presupposed. Without it, no ''higher structure'' can survive. For this reason, genetic engineers can splice a segment of genetic material from a virus into a human (so long as there are ''stem cells'' available) in order to complete the sequence the person lacks to make protein, and thereby ''cure'' that person. This is possible because every living thing (on earth), from the amoeba to the dandelion to the blue whale, has the identical sequence for protein production, plus more.

Not unlike medieval builders, who quarried classical ruins for stone, engineering knowledge, and styles, genetic engineers are able to create (and even patent) ''new'' species only by presupposing ''old'' genetic material/code. Thus, the past is impossible to abandon, although it may be unconsciously presumed (forgotten), which leads to the ignorant arrogance of the present (what Derrida and Foucault have called ''logocentrism,'' the privileging of the ''now'' as ''metaphysics of presence'') (Derrida, 1976: 12; Kramer, 1988: 241–295, 343–367).

Even before Francis Crick, James Watson, and Maurice Wilkins expounded the double-helical structure of DNA, Gebser articulated this principle of addition. He argued that this is the case not only in biological structures, but also in the constitutional structure of human consciousness/world. Thus, the aperspectival is defined as (a)waring that can consciously recognize the continual effectuality of all the so-called ''previous,'' ''extinct'' modes of awaring as they differ from (not necessarily oppose) each other, and *actively co-constitute each other. They are present, or ''present''* each other through absence (difference).

Some of the qualities that mark one world as unique are ''presented'' as unique, because they are absent in the others. Other qualities are shared. ''Present'' is in quotation marks because the past, present, and future are also appresentiated (co-constitute each other through difference). In other words, you cannot perceive the "present," *as such*, without a sense of past and/or future. For instance, some perspectival writers claim that the Hopi in North America live in a "perpetual now" (Whorf, 1956). But this is impossible without a past and/or future. In this case, "now" is a modern temporal concept, which presumes linearity, applied to a timeless magical world, thus imposing an alien perspectival formation onto the Hopis.

The process of synairesis is vital to the identification (perception) of the different modes of being. Once so perceived, one is liberated from being bound by any one system. In fact, limitations that define singularity as such become evident only when one runs into them, tests them, and ruptures them. A person does not know that he or she is in a glass cage until he or she walks into the wall, thus enabling two things to occur. The revelation that one is in a cage, and the opening of the option for staying "in," or going "beyond."

Systasis involves an "opening" into other systems and structures (the same thing) which accomplishes two things: An awareness of the limitation of self as defined by one's "home system," and an awareness of relativity as such. The self need not be lost, but it does "open up." Systasis is (a)waring of the integral process of aperspectivity.

For example, we "still" behave magically and mythically even as we generate new material technologies, as when we emotionally christen a fighter bomber and use it to defend the "vital interests" of our tribe; refrain from putting floor 13 into skyscrapers; or hoist a tree to the top of modern high-rise construction. Likewise, once a year, engineers all over Japan perform a ritual giving thanks to the electronics components that they have disassembled ("killed") in the interest of quality control. In one of the most pragmatic and capitalistically hard-nosed societies on earth, real estate prices in Hong Kong are largely controlled by Taoist priests who determine the auspicious quality of housing and office space. Some office space that has been divined to be very unlucky, although it exists within a state-of-the-art skyscraper in a territory desperate for space, may very well remain entirely unoccupied or used for storage by "rational" bankers, engineers, and business persons. The same is true in the case of intense "superstition" exhibited by pragmatic (to the point of pure physicality) athletes.[7]

CHANGE

Gebser's approach undermines the arrogance of modern historical thinking which suggests that the present (whenever that is) is always sitting atop of all "previous" discursive formations (on the tip of time's arrow as it were) with a uniquely informed purview, so that the "best truth" (the truest truth) is always, and only, in the present. The problem is that the present is always slipping into absence. In the absurd modernist way, truth is supposedly permanent but yet progressively getting better and better, moving in Hegelian fashion, inexorably toward the Absolute Truth (self-evident actualization). Instead, the world offers no evidence of "background" continuity or teleological (final, dead or deceased) destination. "Past," relatively latent structures can (and do) reemerge at any time into a dominant relationship with other modalities. Despite its proud history in the sciences, arts, and humanities, the eruption of magical and mythical behaviors in Nazi Germany is yet another example (see Kenneth Burke's 1941 work on *Mein Kampf* as the "well of Nazi magic," in his essay "The Rhetoric of Hitler's 'Battle' ").

The belief that humans cannot act in a certain way "again," or change unpredictably, is refuted by the world. Most "prediction" has the benefit of hindsight as in historical narratives that, after the fact, explain how something occurred, making it appear completely linear-logical. History is continually rewritten in the future. This is why the world is dramatic (worth living), why despite all the data and the rules, we still have to play the athletic event to see who will win. If social science ever even approximated predictability, it would negate itself because humans, unlike dead matter, react to the future which is not present. If an astrologer says I will die in a car crash in a certain place, and at a certain time, I will avoid those coordinates. Most "predictions" presume freedom, and are integrated into *making* plans (the future). The best athletes are the ones that live in the future *while making it happen.*

Predictions are rhetorical devices. For instance, the greatest efforts at future modeling have been sponsored by the Club of Rome. Initially, using the "modified Delphi-Approach" computer model for systems analysis in order to predict the future world scenario, the Club attempted to predict the future world system. Even with presuming no change in the system's structural rules, this proved to be too simple an instrument to render a convincing representation of the world. So they approached Jay Forrester at the Massachusetts Institute of Technology, to use his "Industrial Dynamic" model. Forrester's (1961, 1968, 1971) predictions from his "World 2" model were published by the Club of Rome in 1972, under the title *The Limits to Growth: A Report for The Club of Rome's Project on the Predicament of Mankind.* Dennis Meadows, Forrester's assistant, then created an even more complex systems model called "World 3." His predictions were published in 1974, by Mihajlo Mesarovic and Eduard Pestel under the title *Mankind at the Turning Point.* More recent publications in this genre include J. E. Lovelock's *Gaia* (1979), Pestel's *Beyond the Limits to Growth* (1989), Dennis Meadows et al.'s *Beyond the Limits* (1992), and Lester Brown et al.'s *State of the World: A Worldwatch Institute Report on Progress Toward a Sustainable Society* (which appears annually).

These computer simulations constitute the most advanced efforts at quantifiable prediction. They illustrate the morphological principle of integral transformation Gebser expounds, and the fact that humans are time makers and time thinkers. Each new program was more "powerful" than the last, and each new instrument rendered a different world. But beyond this mundane sort of relativism, these modelers made their predictions in order to become false prophets in the tradition of the Latin proverb *utinam vates falsus sim* (that I were a false prophet). Because their predictions of impending world system collapse are judged catastrophic (due to overpopulation, food shortages, pollution, and many other variables), the modelers want people to react to their predictions in order to make them *not* come true (Kramer, 1995).

As far as we know, dead matter and other life forms do not constitute future horizons of anything near the complexity of humans. Humans project (imagine) future scenarios and then react to those (empirically unreal) scenarios either to make them come true (changing investments to make more money) or to make them not come true (changing one's diet to avoid cancer).

Theories (predictions) about the future, which are generated in the present, are continually reintegrated into future deliberation which also affects behavior, including theorizing itself. Humans are creative and free (conscious), which is evident with the aperspectival awareness of time as a constituent of lifeworld.

While systems offer only momentary validity based on always-fixed data and already existing relationships, synairesis attends to the principles of potential and transformation, which appear to be not law-like, but in flux. There is no universal, fixed "transformational grammar" (to quote Chomsky's modernist terminology) for the world. Rather, the world seems to be more like Heidegger's (1962) concept of the temporalization of temporality. *Relativity is a contingent theory.* People, unlike elephants and molecules, can and do change their minds, adapting to the environment (not just accidentally surviving it) and adapting the environment to their interests.

Politics is precisely the struggle over the future, which is not causally determined, but open and "up-for-grabs." Insofar as we do not flee from our own consciousness into systematized automation (and even then), we are responsible. As Jean-Paul Sartre (1956) argued, the world does indeed resist, but that resistance is evident only because humans push for change toward a vision, want, and/or felt need.

Even quantitative models reintegrate back into the dynamic world-horizon only to be actualized or avoided. Choice remains viable, even though modern efforts to maintain a closed system (cybernetics) and causal "chains" can persuade us otherwise.

NOTES

1. It is acknowledged here that neither Martin Heidegger (especially after editing Husserl's *Phenomenology of Internal Time-Consciousness* while also writing *Being and Time*), Jean-Paul Sartre, Michel Foucault, Jacques Derrida, Jean Baudrillard, Thomas Kuhn (following Alexandre Koyre, who was powerfully influenced by Husserl's reflections on Galilean-style science), or a myriad of other writers would have had much to say without Husserl's radical work. This includes Jean Gebser, who readily acknowledged his debt to Husserl. Some were not so candid, perhaps revealing an anxiety of influence. For instance, it is not until his posthumously published work with Bruce Powers, *The Global Village* (1989), that Marshal McLuhan reveals what was already obvious

to those familiar with phenomenology, that he drew much of his understanding of the world from them, and even called himself a phenomenologist. In this same book, however, it is also painfully clear that he did not have a powerful understanding of the profound differences between Husserl, for instance, and Hegel. The same lack of candor, or perhaps rigor (since this author informed Professor Hall of Gebser's contributions to cultural studies at a conference in Philadelphia at Temple University, October 1989) regarding the influence of Gebser's foundational studies seems evident. For instance, the popular writer Edward T. Hall (a former colleague of McLuhan's at Toronto at the time each was formulating his approach to human communication) obviously owes very much to Siegfried Giedion, whom he dutifully referenced in his *The Hidden Dimension*). Giedion was a student of Gebser, as were many European artists, poets, and architects, especially in Germany, Switzerland, Austria, Italy, and Spain (for instance, Gebser was a personal friend to Gropius, Piccaso, and Lorca). Giedion's honesty is evident in his dedication to Gebser's influence, as he titled his two-volume work *The Eternal Present: The Beginnings of Architecture* (which, like Gebser's *Ever-Present Origin*, was funded by the Bollingen Foundation), which is an obvious acknowledgment of Gebser's own *magnum opus Ursprung und Gegenwort (The Ever-Present Origin)*. Even in Hall's more recent work, *The Dance of Life* (1983), Gebser's contribution is not acknowledged.

2. Recently, yet another study demonstrated the lack of explanatory power reductionism offers. Niels Waller and Phillip R. Shaver surveyed and interviewed 107 male and 338 female adult twin pairs. They found that genetics (even among identical pairs) could not explain the great varieties of love exhibited by the participants. According to Waller and Shaver (1994) "This flies in the face of what we expected." Genes play virtually no role in "style of love" (i.e., monogamously or polygamously, impetuously or pragmatically). Instead, the environment and life experiences were cited as explanatory factors (in typically Cartesian style, as if these people do not constitute the "environment"). Romanticism is an important factor in the modern perspectival mutation.

3. The virtual frontier presents an opportunity for the lawless eruption of libidinal energy. Already (in January 1996) the German government has moved to tame this wilderness by managerial "over-sight" and control (censorship).

4. An excellent example of continual reintegration of reference and referred in modern style is American professional football. In professional American football, video representation is used *during the game* to manipulate the game. It is a new tool for coaching which is an integral process (because it is "live"). This new tool works by using several video cameras (some high-up in the coaching booth above the spectators and others down on the "sideline") and computers to print out "fixed framed" pictures from the "real-time" video. These "snapshoots" of the unfolding action are then faxed to the coaches on the sidelines for immediate evaluation to aid in strategic and tactical adjustments during the play. American football is a modernized version of soccer, whereby the field is subdivided into units drawn like a ruler; there is a "line of scrimmage," and measurements are constantly being taken with regard to territorial gains and time. Those who possess the ball have a set number of times to move it a set number of yards; scoring occurs in "end zones," and "plays" are "called" in meetings (huddles) that frequently stop the action.

5. Martin Heidegger expressed a similar realization as the "temporalization of time," in *Being and Time*, which he wrote while editing Edmund Husserl's work *Phenomenol-*

ogy of Internal Time-Consciousness, a work to which Heidegger owes many insights that also appear in *The History of the Concept of Time*.

6. The one exception is human agency and imagination, which can project future scenarios and react to the future. Human beings do not adapt to, but create and continually reintegrate the "old" with the "new" and "not yet."

7. It is interesting that in the most physical of behaviors, athletics, one finds the most intense expressions of mythical and magical tendencies, as in the "momentum" of a game, the visualization process elite athletes practice, and the sheer dramatism of brute physical competition. The most highly paid athlete in the world by far (if one brackets endorsements) is the heavyweight boxing champion of the world, which is testimony to the relationship between physicality and emotional interest. People go crazy at soccer matches for instance, when they never do so at work or at their religious activities.

REFERENCES

Asante, M. K. (1987) *The Afrocentric Idea*. Philadelphia: Temple University Press.

Brown, L. et al. (1995) *State of the World: A Worldwatch Institute Report on Progress Toward a Sustainable Society*. Annual. New York: W. W. Norton.

Buber, M. (1970) *I and Thou*. New York: Charles Scribner's Sons.

Burke, K. (1941) *The Philosophy of Literary Form: Studies in Symbolic Action*. Baton Rouge: Louisiana State University Press.

Deluze, G., and F. Guattari. (1983) *On the Line*. New York: Semiotext(e).

Derrida, J. (1976) *Of Grammatology*. Baltimore: Johns Hopkins University Press.

de Saussure, F. (1974) *Course in General Linguistics*. London: Fontana.

Forrester, J. (1961) *Industrial Dynamics*. Cambridge, MA: Wright-Allen Press.

———. (1968) *Principles of Systems*. Cambridge, MA: Wright-Allen Press.

———. (1971) *World Dynamics*. Cambridge, MA: Wright-Allen Press.

Fukuyama, F. (1992) *The End of History and the Last Man*. New York: Free Press.

Gadamer, H. G. (1975) *Truth and Method*. New York: Seabury Press.

Gebser, J. (1985) *The Ever-Present Origin*. Athens: Ohio University Press.

Hall, E. T. (1966) *The Hidden Dimension*. New York: Anchor Books.

———. (1983) *The Dance of Life: The Other Dimension of Time*. New York: Doubleday.

Heidegger, M. (1962) *Being and Time*. London: SCM Press.

Hoy, D. C. (1978) *The Critical Circle*. Berkeley: University of California Press.

Husserl, E. (1962) *Ideas*. New York: Collier.

Jameson, F. (1972) *The Prison-House of Language*. Princeton, NJ: Princeton University Press.

Kramer, E. M. (1988) *Television Criticism and the Problem of Ground*, 2 Vols. Ann Arbor, MI: University Microfilms International, 8816770.

———. (1995) "A Brief Hermeneutic of the Co-Constitution of Nature and Culture in the West Including Some Contemporary Consequences." *History of European Ideas*, vol. 20, nos. 1–3 (pp. 649–659).

Kramer, E. M., ed. (1992) *Consciousness and Culture*. Westport, CT: Greenwood Press.

Kuhn, T. (1962) *The Structure of Scientific Revolutions*. Chicago: University of Chicago Press.

Lovelock, J. E. (1979) *Gaia*. New York: Oxford University Press.

McLuhan, M. (1962) *The Gutenberg Galaxy: The Making of Typographic Man*. Toronto: University of Toronto Press.

McLuhan, M., and B. Powers. (1989) *Global Village.* New York: Oxford University Press.

Meadows, D. H., D. L. Meadows, and J. Randers. (1992) *Beyond the Limits.* Post Mills, VT: Chelsea Green Publishing.

Merleau-Ponty, M. (1962) *Phenomenology of Perception.* London: Routledge and Kegan Paul.

Mesarovic, M., and E. Pestel. (1974) *Mankind at the Turning Point.* New York: Signet.

Monroe, C., D. Meekhof, B. King, and D. Wineland. (1996) "A 'Schrodinger Cat' Superposition State of an Atom." *Science* 272, May 24 (pp. 1131–1133).

Mumford, L. (1963) *Techniques and Civilization.* New York: Harcourt, Brace and World.

Nietzsche, F. (1974) *The Gay Science.* New York: Vintage.

Pestel, E. (1989) *Beyond the Limits to Growth.* New York: Universe Books.

Popper, K. (1959) *Logic of Scientific Discovery.* New York: Basic Books.

Ricoeur, P. (1974) *The Conflict of Interpretations.* Evanston, IL: Northwestern University Press.

Sartre, J. P. (1956) *Being and Nothing.* New York: Simon and Schuster.

Waller, N., and P. Shaver. (1994) "The Importance of Nongenetic Influences on Romantic Love Styles: A Twin-Family Study." *Psychogical Science* 5, no. 5, September (pp. 268–274).

Whorf, B. L. (1956) *Language Thought and Reality.* Cambridge, MA: MIT Press.

Wittgenstein, L. (1969) *On Certainty.* Oxford, England: Basil Blackwell.

———. (1971) *Prototractatus.* London: Routledge & Kegan Paul.

6

(In)Evitabilities

Legitimate power (such as "expertise") is manifested as the act of granting voice or agency to a particular person, literature, or institution. One might well argue that the "real power" is in those who do the granting of voice. But Francois Lyotard (1984) has argued that in the narrative process of defining what is real (knowledge), the very act of narration is self-legitimating. Story-tellers are "legitimated by the simple fact that they do what they do" (Lyotard, 1984: 23). As author(ity) they define what is said and done.

The "research game" of scientific discourse might seem to offer a refuge from self-legitimation. And, in fact, the subjection of truth claims to dialectical interrogation by others of equal or greater ability leads to consensual validation. Objectivity is thus intersubjective agreement. Scientific laws are all unproven and fundamentally unprovable. Their validity is only as good as the next ob-servation. Science falsely claims that unlike the narrative production of truth, no social bond is necessary. However, hermeneutics is presumed, for a scientific community must share a language in order to be able to debate and agree. More specifically, as Edmund Husserl (1962) and the late Ludwig Wittgenstein (1958) noted, what is necessary for science (and all other community projects) is a shared "language-*game*," which is not the same as a board game, for one makes up the doing of language along the way. "Here the term 'language-game' is meant to bring into prominence the fact that the *speaking* of language is part of an activity, or of a form of life" (Wittgenstein, 1958: 11).

Therefore, necessary conditions for the existence of scientific truth are com-munication (hermeneutics) and life, neither of which is scientifically derived. Rather, science is a derivative of the everyday lifeworld (Husserl, 1962). Lan-guage is creative, not merely referential. Language is much more than com-mands, reports, descriptions, nouns. Neither life nor language (nor the self) is fixed. Empirical "knowledge" is based on direct, personal, *subjective* perception. Therefore, science is based on a "ground" that is fluid, which is narrative, and not "knowledge" as such, but verition (Gebser, 1985). However, narrative knowledge formation is condemned by science for being barbaric and primitive.

Scientific knowledge cannot know and make known that it is the true knowledge without resorting to the other, narrative, kind of knowledge, which from its point of view is no knowledge at all. Without such recourse it would be in the position of presupposing its own validity and would be stooping to what it condemns: begging the question, proceeding on prejudice. (Lyotard, 1984: 29)

But what motivated Husserl's entire project of phenomenology was his realization that either science, too, is self-legitimating (is validated by its own internal processes) and therefore no better than narrative discourse, or it must rely on a transcendental ground or "first philosophy" of indubitable principles such as the Cartesian *cogito ergo sum.* Since science is not a naturally occurring phenomenon (Bacon did not discover the scientific method lying in a forest), and since scientific claims are contingent upon additional information and judgement, Husserl believed that phenomenology would save science by grounding it apodictically.

Empirical science is not an empirical thing. Its power of generalizability is dependent on memory and association, neither of which is an empirical thing. Of course, "generalizability" is not an empirical thing either, but rather an ideational phenomenon. Generalizability is essentially an eidetic process of transcendentalism. The epistemic force of a scientific (or any other) claim is measured by the scope of generalizability of the claim. This is done by comparing the claim with various examples about which it is supposed to refer. The examples are recognized as "appropriate" because a categorical logic already exists and is applied, which enables one to identify cases of which the claim is supposed to be about. The comparative process between the cases and the generalized claim being made about them presupposes an interest, a motive, and a judgement that making generalized claims about these particular cases is worthwhile (interesting, valuable). The equation $E = mc^2$ is great because it holds for all times and places (so far). It is transcendental, not contingent, not empirical.

Science is a set of contingent explanations of states of affairs. So science cannot validate science by its own criteria. In fact, it violates its own empirical criteria of existence. This, among other absurdities, indicates that science is merely a cultural artifact, a mode of discourse, defining, categorizing, arranging, organizing, inventing. Science, like philosophy and religion, is about "being systematic." To question the arbitrariness of which system to presume is almost always perceived by those who have faith in the system to be heresy. What is normative is "systematic," repetitive, reliable. As Thomas Kuhn (1962) noted, "normal" science, by definition, is not creative but archival. What makes science and art interesting is not itself scientific but nonconformist and apolitical. As an institution, the power of science is derived from defining what is and is not real (normal). Power is derived from systematic conformity. To be conventional is to be "normal." The phrase "libido over credo," which Joseph Campbell (Campbell and Moyers, 1988: 187) uses to express the precedence of experience over dogma can be applied to all of life, including science and religion. But this hierarchy is difficult to demonstrate because life is dogmatic. As Nietzsche (1974: 336, *The Gay Science*, sec. 374) pointed out, we cannot "look around our own corner" (see Chapter 5). It seems senseless to wonder of an existence without interpretation, or to escape ourselves so that we are confronted by a new infinity, the infinity of interpretations. In order to expose the limitations of perspective, we must take a perspective. How can I know that my perception is fallible unless I have some immaculate, infallible access to Reality for comparison? We are told by Cartesians that the books are not the same as what they are about. Systematization of life is not the same as what was previously nonsystematic about living. Systematization makes those who wish the power of prediction comfortable, but they must constantly struggle to keep everybody and everything "in line." Feedback mechanisms serve the interest of permanence, the same, and equilibrium.

On the surface (literally), this may seem to be a simple task, albeit totally arbitrary, and this is an important issue because assimilation (or amalgamation) of perspectives (including ethnic and racial ones for instance) depends largely on identity. Nevertheless, it is not so easy. For example, well over 90 percent of all "blacks" born in the United States have at least one white ancestor and 23 percent of "whites" have at least one "black" ancestor (Brown, 1995). The major racial categories used to measure America are both ethnocentric and socially contrived (constructed linguistically and through interaction). These categories say more about those who constructed the instruments than about America's racial reality. Africans did not come to America as "Africans," "Negroes," "African Americans," or "blacks," but as Akan, Yoruba, Ibo, and Wolof (McDaniel, 1995: 181). Likewise, Europeans did not come as "whites," but as Scots, Irish, Poles, and so on. The same is the case for "Hispanics," and "Latinos," and "Asians." These classifications are ethnocentrically applied to people in the interest of instrumental reason manifested as bureaucratic control, reducing them to color, but stopping short of the precision of measurement the Nazis attempted.

Race in Africa is not a simple matter either. Every "race" categorized by Western science (except the aboriginal Australians and their relatives) is at home on the African continent. By the time the first Europeans arrived in Africa in the fifteenth century, Asians, blacks, Khoisan, Pygmies, and whites were already long established. And competition among racial groups had been occurring there long before Europeans "officially" arrived. "Black" farmers displaced and fragmented the Pygmy hunters who had lived throughout the equatorial forest region. "Today there are just 200,000 Pygmies scattered amid 120 million blacks" (Diamond, 1994: 75).

Meanwhile, Madagascar is peopled by a mixture of blacks and Southeast Asians, specifically Indonesians. The language of the Malagasy is very close to the Ma'anyan language spoken on the island of Borneo, over 4,000 miles away. According to Diamond, "this is the single most astonishing fact of human geography in the whole world" (1994: 76). Years earlier in 1963, the linguist Joseph Greenberg noted that Africa's 1,500 languages could be divided into just four families and that these language families corresponded to anatomically distinct human groups. Thus, the Nilo-Saharan and Niger-Congo speakers are black, the Khoisan speakers are Khoisan, the Afro-Asiatic languages are spoken by a wide variety of both whites and blacks, and a non-African category of language, Austronesian, is spoken in Madagascar. The Pygmies tend to speak whatever their black neighbors speak which tends to indicate that the "black invasion," which pushed the Khoisan southward and fragmented Pygmies into isolated pockets, devastated their linguistic identity. Today, only traces of the Pygmies' original language survive as a few words and sounds.

SHORTHAND AND SHORT MIND

But it must be realized that each of these groups is very diverse. Lumping different groups like the Zulu, Masai, and Ibo under the single heading "blacks" is a sort of institutionalization of ignorance (ignoring differences as "unimportant" or "inconvenient"). Likewise, combining Berbers and Egyptians with Europeans is scientifically legitimized stereotyping (which exist "by definition"). As Diamond notes, "the divisions between blacks, whites, and the other major groups are arbitrary anyway because each group shades into the others. All the human groups on Earth have mated with humans of every other group they've encountered" (Diamond, 1994: 74).

So then why do we continue to live by the metaphor "race"? Diamond argues that "recognizing these major groups and calling them by these inexact names is a shorthand that makes it easier to understand history" (Diamond, 1994: 74). But these "Africans" never recognized these categories. Such stereotypes are not part of *their* history. It seems to be an easier way to misunderstand the complexity of poliversal "reality." "Shorthand" is a mode of discourse, a type of language-use, that serves the interest of the Western writer more than the subject matter being investigated. For this reason, the phenomenologist Herbert Spiegelberg (1982) argued that serious investigators should reject the principle of parsimony for a generosity of effort. One should dedicate as much time and effort as the *subject matter* (not the convention of a community of writers) requires. But perhaps more metaphors bring one no "closer" to "reality" (as a referent) than fewer.

Such categorization disregards how people identify themselves and literally institutes a new identity for them, forcing them to transform their very concept of skin color (racializing it), and thus of themselves. Such stereotyping forces quite different peoples to accept a myth of ethnic and historic similarity imposed on them by the dominant "host" or scientific (defining) culture. Thus, Europe has "Western," "white" culture. The definitive high ground taken out of colonial arrogance has invented broad categories to "cover" the rest, including the invention of "Africa" and "Asia" (Mudimbe, 1988). "Shorthand" privileges parsimony over other discursive values and needs. The prejudice reflects modernity's anxiety in the face of emergent time-consciousness (Gebser, 1985; Husserl, 1964). It also reflects the modern economic structure such that since one realizes profit with each unit sold, it behooves the profiteer to move as many units as fast as possible. These may include "souls" so that the "mass" began in the church and colonized the rest of life leading to global quantification and the "cult of efficiency" (Ellul, 1964). Operational definitions manifest the instrumental interest of manipulation on a grand scale (hypertrophic perspectivism); control for a single purpose. The information that such measures manifest is hardly "disinterested."

The communicative (hermeneutic and semiotic) basis of the designation "race," and the obsession with measurement are further complicated by the fact that people from around the world have very different conceptions of racial identity. For instance, Mexicans have a racial continuum that runs from white to red, while Puerto Ricans have a continuum that runs from white to black (McDaniel, 1995: 187). Furthermore, the Puerto Rican continuum is not so perspectively bipolar as in the United States. In Puerto Rico, culture has more to do with "racial" distinction than skin color. Likewise, racial identification for Asians is not based on a color continuum. The complexities of racial self-classification have rendered the category nearly useless. Many Hispanics classify themselves as "white" in their countries of origin and continue to do so after immigrating to the United States. In the 1960 and 1970 censuses, 95 percent of the immigrants from Latin America (with Latin surnames) were classified white. In 1980, the U.S. Census Bureau broadened its racial classifications to compel Hispanics to indicate their "Spanish" origin. But aren't Spaniards "white"? In 1990, the "Spanish" category was dropped (McDaniel, 1995: 189). Short of lining everyone up for racial measurement (as the Nazis did), determining the racial composition of the United States is fraught with problems.

Despite the arbitrariness of the measure, because of the import still ascribed to "race" as an essential aspect of identity, it remains a salient issue. For instance, quotas have been, and still are, instituted on the basis of this measure. The Asiatic Barred Zone Act excluded Asian immigration to the United States until 1952. Conservatives, such as Sir Jeffrey Howe (the Governor of Hong Kong), like quotas so long as they are used to exclude. In 1994, Sir Howe justified the refusal to allow Chinese (who hold British passports and are citizens of the Crown) living in Hong Kong to immigrate to England, after the communist regime in Peking takes over the colony on June 13, 1997, by claiming that such an influx of Chinese would upset the "racial balance" of Great Britain, as if this "balance" were a natural thing (beyond question) (quoted in *China: The Wild East*, Turner Broadcasting System, 1995).

In the United States, the Hart-Celler Immigration Act of 1965 attempted to eliminate "race" as a condition for immigration. But the heated debates about affirmative action remain very salient, and have helped to fuel the "white male" anger manifested in a historic change in the composition and agenda of the United States Congress in 1994. Race and culture intermix in discussions about standards of "appropriate behavior," incarceration rates, parenting, unemployment rates, and "culture wars." Conformism is rewarded along racial lines, as "Asians" are regarded by conservatives as the "ideal minority," while blacks present resistance to assimilation—an "American dilemma."

WHO WANTS TO BELONG TO WHAT: DIRECTIONAL POLITICS OF SELF

The idea that minorities are clamoring to become "enculturated," "mainstreamed," "melted," "assimilated" presumes that they want and/or must "deculturize" themselves in order to become "American" (Gudykunst and Kim, 1992: 215–217). The typical Aristotelian logic is presupposed so that the more one "deculturizes," or forgets one's home culture, the more "adapted" to the new culture one will become. The presupposition is that there exists a parity between these two concepts and that an inverse and proportional relationship exists between only two ends of a single spectrum. As one approaches absolute adaptation (enculturation) one moves away from alienation with equal and opposite degree and rate of change. The whole experience of moving into another culture is reduced to a single-line variable with only two ends. This conceptualization of assimilation is false for two reasons. First, America has never presented a monolithic and finished cultural narrative. Even extreme efforts, which have proclaimed divine (eternal) absolutism to present and maintain a system such as the Egypt of the pharaohs, the Rome of the Caesars, or the China of the dynasties (and Mao), change. The idea that there exists a unified, coherent, and changeless American culture is delusional. Both the left and right Hegelians are wrong. There is no end to history.

Even if we insisted on perpetually recycling cultural products like *The Donna Reed Show*, *Leave it to Beaver*, and *Father Knows Best* (etc.), and removed all the music, films, art, television, everything that has appeared since 1965, the past would not be "the same." Such television shows are viewed through different eyes, as nostalgia, foolish silliness, hypocritical versions of fiction, quaint kitsch, and so forth. In short, if the goal is assimilation, then one is shooting at a complex and ever-moving target.

Second, most people come to America to realize a dream of freedom to fulfill a lifestyle they *already* want and associate with America before coming here. Furthermore, the lifestyles they seek to fulfill are not all the same. They come from many different cultural backgrounds. What they seek, as did the Puritans, is the right to be *different* without persecution. Regarding the Cartesian notions of exclusion and inclusion, Anthony Lemelle points out that

It is never demonstrated that the masses of black Americans wished for inclusion in U.S. political institutions, though some did. . . . The logical support for the bias of inclusion is that more inclusion is synonymous with more progress. . . . In the end, there is only an apology for the fact that the election of more blacks has been accompanied by deterioration in the quality of African-American life. (Lemelle, 1993: 63)

Joining the country club can mean co-optation, which is very different from starting a different kind of club altogether. Lemelle's defense of difference, of the subculture, is not a new idea. Ralph Ellison (1966), James Baldwin (Baldwin and Mead, 1971), Oscar Handlin (1966), and others have argued that it was the projection of white America, their utopian ideal, that everyone wants to become like them. Ellison put it this way, ''I wish that we would dispense with this idea that we are begging to get *in* somewhere'' (1966: 437). Handlin (1966) believed that ''Desegregation will not solve any of the important economic, social, and political problems of American life'' (Handlin, 1966: 284). Ellison, Baldwin, Dubois don't want to integrate, if that means being ''deculturized,'' or putting one's self under erasure in the futile search for another, white, identity. They don't want to become American if that means becoming white and only white.

   For many, being designated ''white'' is an option, which, within a racist society, carries with it privilege. But for others, being ''white'' is not optional. Hence, the limits of racial assimilation can be measured by such indices as rates of intermarriage, residential integration, and racial classification of children. As many writers have noted, black blood is potent (Morrison, 1970; West, 1994; Russell, Wilson, and Hall, 1992). One drop changes one's race from white to black. Other kinds of racial mixing reveal Asian, Native American, and Hispanic blood to be far weaker. The offspring of mixed race marriages evince this as well as confound the issue of homogamy in counting race. This is the case around the world, as with ''mixed-blood'' children (*Konketsuji*), or ''*hafu*'' (also *Ainoko*), which is one of several derogatory terms used in Japan to describe ''mixed'' people) (Hayashida, 1976).

   In marriages between white and African Americans, the children are routinely classified as African American (Waters, 1994). Native Americans and Asians in mixed marriages with whites classify their children as white almost twice as often (McDaniel, 1995). With regard to rates of intermarriage, about 40 percent of Japanese American women, and 50 percent of Native American women are interracially married. By contrast, only 3 percent of African-American women and 1 percent of African-American men are interracially married. While Native Americans and Asians are largely assimilated culturally and physically, African Americans remain largely segregated culturally, residentially, and physically (McDaniel, 1995).

Ironically, perhaps the most ferocious "racism," and or "ethnic cleansing" occurs where people are, for all intents and purposes, genetically identical. For instance, the word "Balkanize" was taken from a region of the world which likes to see itself as a crossroads, where East meets West in commerce, war, and intellectual/cultural exchange. But, when the communist government in Bulgaria decided, in 1988, to forcibly rename and then expel (what the communists euphemistically called the "regeneration process" and "exodus") those of "Turkish" descent, the government had to rely on a census by surnames in order to do so. They had to proceed in this fashion because, due to the intense intermingling (especially during the 500-year Ottoman domination of the region now comprising Greece, Bulgaria, Romania, Yugoslavia, Macedonia, and Albania), people are physically indistinguishable. Keep in mind that Bulgaria is about the size of the state of Ohio, and over its 4,000-year history borders have shifted many times. In the 1988 "cleansing operation" (which anticipated and may have been a catalyst for the ethnic cleansing that followed in neighboring Yugoslavia), "Bulgarians" had difficulty identifying the despised "Turks." That did not stop them, however, from driving several hundred thousand people across the border into Turkey, a geographic convenience the Muslims in the former Yugoslavia did not have (Kramer 1993: 125).

Language differences, religious differences, economic differences, and so on, have also served as signs of identity. Without disagreeing with W.E.B. Du Bois's (1989: 3) famous observation that "the problem of the twentieth century is the problem of the color line," it must be recognized that race is a "line" that may have been the start of civilization. We only need to recall Socrates' choice of suicide over living among the "barbaric" non-Greek speakers, beyond the walls of Athens, and the Great Wall of China, and the fact that Aristotle had been a slaveholder. Certainly, the dividing flesh of race predates 1900. The fact that the line can now be seen as such, and that it has come to be seen as "problematic," is a testament to an increased awareness of the ethical dimension of inequality. It has to do with a rise in humanism, the realization that anything that has to do with human desires and behavior necessarily involves ethics. This post-Enlightenment attitude sees inequality as not simply "the case," as in dogmatic and deterministic caste systems. Rather, inequality based on color difference is seen as ideological, as created and sustained by certain modes of discourse, power interests, and manifested in the ways people interact (praxis), and by how they *interpret* racial difference. These ways of interacting are neither natural nor permanent. The revelation of the contingency of the line is in large measure a consequence of late and postmodern thinking which reduced color to an arbitrary phenomenon. The ancient postmodern thinker Democritus claimed that "A thing merely appears to have color, it merely appears to be sweet or bitter. Only atoms and empty space have a real existence" (quoted in Heisenberg, 1958: 67). However, much of the world is not modern (let alone aperspectival or "postmodern"), and much variable analytics is actually used as a rhetoric to rationalize convention. Color still has meaning.

As long as one is interested in playing the games of races, then the rules must be conventionally ''observed.'' The magic game of race sees it as an identity that flows through semen and blood, binding the flesh of the group. The mythical game disrupts the identity somewhat, suggesting that the meaning (of) and the flesh may slip or shift a bit so that the flesh and its meaning may not be totally identical, one with the other. The modern (nihilistic) game sees race as a totally arbitrary sign, having no particular ''import.'' Meaning is dissociated from what is meant (the skin). Meaning is contingent upon the interests that seek invisible correlations between it (color) and other measurements like IQ, or wealth. The flesh is material so that it is immaterial unless it repeatedly matches (correlates) with something else, and it is the in-between of the matching (the invisible relation revealed by high-speed automated sorting) that really ''counts.''

Regardless of which game one is interested in, one cannot change the rules without abandoning the game. Hence, the rules are not wholly arbitrary. But neither are they absolute. As Nietzsche and Ludwig Wittgenstein understood, if one has the interest and courage, any of the games (which are really the sum totals of their respective rules) can be abandoned.

Interest in race games waxes and wanes. The importance of race, and what it means, rises and falls in our world. What is important is not the color of someone's skin, but what that color means. And as Edmund Husserl (1962) demonstrated, the meaning is the thing, and meanings change. We find ourselves in a temporal world. Likewise, Husserl's critique of metaphysics, and his refusal to privilege any one regional ontology (reductionistic discipline like historicism, psychologism, scientism, etc.), elevating it to the divine status of master narrative or metacriterial power, requires that we continually question the presuppositions of our lives. Racism can be relativized, bumped from its pedestal of central and defining power, thus deflating racial stereotyping. If an African-American doctor is saving a white man's life, the white man may very well find his skin color to be far less significant than his medical skills. Likewise, a small business owner, who otherwise despises ''colored people,'' may be quite happy to receive their money. Dead presidents all come in green.

The *praxis* (which, unlike *techne*, includes a moral dimension) of doing takes precedence over ''being.'' Perhaps one day we all will become bored with color games, and they will fade into irrelevance, only to be reborn another day or to be gone forever. If this happens, then this book will be perhaps only a curiosity, a figment of a time when mythical e-motionalism, magical identity, and rationalized motionalism based on color, was rampant; a time of lines and privilege.

For now, this book does not enter a curious little discursive space isolated by time, but instead it enters a world thoroughly inflected with race; a highly raced world. And this book is part of the world. So what kind of world is this? It is a world of lines and walls of skin, which block our views and which we sometimes reinforce out of fear and sometimes wish to climb out of. It is a world where hope and hate spring eternal, and since one does not hope for what one already has, then there must always be something missing, and since something is always missing then there is always anger and frustration. I don't believe in utter hopelessness. Nihilism is an impossibility. But suffering is very real. Hope can only be replaced by satisfaction and contentment, not nihilism.

A CHRONICLE OF HOPES

To Make a History, to Tell a Story

Several times African Americans have anticipated fundamental change which failed to materialize. As many, such as the Swedish scholar Gunnar Myrdal (1944) observed, America presents a reality that is very often in complete opposition to the principles of its founding. When the United States declared its independence from England, the Constitution, Bill of Rights, and Declaration of Independence missed the blacks. Patrick Henry, who is famous for saying "Give me liberty, or give me death," owned 65 slaves at the time of his death. But blacks in America did not become extinct. When they were converted to Christianity, it was hoped that one Christian could not enslave another, but a 1667 Act in Virginia declared that baptism did not alter the condition of bondage. This was not wholly inconsistent with tradition, since Saint Thomas Aquinas, Martin Luther, and John Calvin had all been slave owners. The same is the case for Islam (Willis, 1985).

Again, despite disappointment, like the often-persecuted Jews, the American blacks did not become extinct. Instead, several revolts occurred, including the Prosser and Bowler revolt of 1800, the Denmark Vesey-led revolt of 1822, and Nat Turner's revolt in 1831.

In 1820, the Missouri Compromise sanctioned slavery in the southern states. Then in 1857, the Supreme Court of the United States ruled in *Dred Scott v. Sandford* (actually "Sanford" since it was misspelled in the legal documents) that states' rights (regarding treatment of slaves) took precedence over the federal Constitution. Slaves were declared noncitizens and therefore unable to own property, sit on juries, or have any redress through the courts. In essence, there was no law for slaves except their masters' whims.

As the Civil War unfolded, hope rose again. But President Lincoln *supported* federal protection *for* slavery in the southern states. During the early part of the war, he even ordered that slaves that escaped into the Union lines be returned by federal troops. For a time Ulysses S. Grant, leader of the Union armies, owned four slaves, one having been given to his wife as a wedding present. As support for the abolitionist movement grew, however, Lincoln shifted his position, and put forth the Emancipation Proclamation, which declared slaves to be free *if the areas in which they were held still revolted against the Union.* Compliant states could keep slavery! At its inception, the proclamation was basically war propaganda, expedient politicking, and punishment for rebellious states. The real goal was to preserve the Union by any means. Slaves were declared free only in the states where no real authority existed. Where federal authority did exist, no action to free them was taken.

In 1862, blacks were enlisted into the Union army as racially segregated units. Unlike other Union troops who were captured, black soldiers were not allowed to surrender. Instead, they were shot by the Confederates. A famous example is the fall of Fort Pillow to the Confederate general Nathan B. Forrest (later a founder of the Ku Klux Klan). All the black Union soldiers were massacred. Overall, during the Civil War, 68,178 black soldiers died in battle or as a result of wounds. Black soldiers were paid less than the white Union soldiers, but yet the desertion rate among blacks was more than 50 percent lower than for the rest of the Union army.

With victory, hopes were high. In 1865, abolition became law as the 13th Amendment to the Constitution. It abolished slavery and involuntary servitude, including peonage. Many blacks, and poor whites, hoped that land reform would accompany reconstruction, but it did not. Hence, many freed slaves remained dependent on former slave owners. Nevertheless, the 14th (1868) and 15th (1870) Amendments were passed proclaiming all those born in America to be citizens, and extending suffrage to black males. However, by 1877, interest in the North to protect blacks waned and all federal troops were withdrawn from the South. In the wake of withdrawal, white terrorists burned black churches, attacked residences, and between 1882 and 1938, lynched 3,402 people. Several attempts to pass an antilynching bill at the federal level failed. Jim Crow laws saturated southern states so that both *de jure* (by law) and *de facto* (by custom) racism was practically the same as before the war. Poll taxes, literacy tests, and grandfather clauses were instituted to stop blacks from voting. In Alabama, black voter registration declined from 181,471 in 1900, to 3,000 in 1901, and in Louisiana from 130,334 in 1896, to 1,342 in 1904.

From 1870 to 1900, the so-called "Gilded Age" presented an intense and exploitative form of dualism in the form of massifying collectivism on one hand, and extreme individualism (concentration of wealth and power) on the other. While industrial workers, southern sharecroppers, and displaced American natives suffered, a mood of optimism possessed the privileged in America. Happy positivism was embraced, and Charles Darwin's work was used to legitimize policies that instituted "survival of the fittest." Competition became naturalized so that insects, plants, birds, all of life "competes." Modern Westerners cannot imagine that people elsewhere could actually be satisfied—satisfaction is the bane of consumer culture and the industrialist. The weak were not, indeed *should* not be aided by the strong. One should survive according to one's own abilities. Rational means of organizing labor, such as Fredrick Winslow Taylor's "scientific management" techniques, maximized worker exploitation. Productivity increased enormously as wealth was concentrated. Powerful interests favored a laissez-faire world which freed the robber barons to amass immense fortunes by mercilessly exploiting all resources available (including people who had been reduced to "hands"). The numeric bottom line was used to inoculate the system from critique because it was deemed objective and, according to the laws of market forces, manifest "natural selection." But of course, neither nature nor another master narrative has ever selected out "the weak." If "it" did, then there would be only the "strong" left, which means that there would be no "strong." Everything would be equally fit and starving.

Those in weak positions were most vulnerable to this thinly legitimized Hobbesian war of all against all (isolationist ideology). For instance, Chinese workers found it necessary, in the hostile environment ("hostile" because it explicitly, by law, did not allow/want them to integrate or adapt, but only wanted their obedient and cheap labor), to congregate in "Chinatown" ghettos. Today, new arrivals from Asia stepping off jet airplanes and heading for American universities have encountered a very different America. Those who have been here "all along," who have toiled, fought, and suffered, who have been put into internment camps, onto reservations, and segregated by housing, those who could not "blend in" like European workers, continue to lag behind the new-comers that have no taste of bitterness toward the American system. But many newcomers, too, have discovered a "glass ceiling" that blocks promotion into the managerial ranks of power.

In the South after reconstruction, those who were supposed to enforce the new laws very often hated blacks. According to the 1896 *Plessy v. Ferguson* decision, the Supreme Court of the United States echoed the pre–Civil War *Dred Scott* decision upholding states' rights. According to *Plessy v. Ferguson*, seg-regated railroads were legal in Louisiana. "Intermingling" of the races was not deemed good. This 1896 ruling legitimized the system of Jim Crow throughout the South. In the North, mob attacks against black enclaves in cities occurred as early as the eighteenth century. During the Civil War, white workers who feared competition from freed blacks attacked them. In 1863, white working-class "draft rioters" in New York City, who were subject to the new conscrip-tion law, vented their hostilities on blacks, murdering many. As freed blacks migrated north for industrial jobs, white reaction often took a deadly form of expression.

The First World War raised hopes again. One of the greatest migrations in U.S. history began. The black press carried want-ads encouraging southern blacks to move to northern cities. Restrictions in immigration and industrial expansion created a labor shortage which southern blacks could fill. Blacks became much more urbanized, and although their population actually dropped from 19.3 percent of the total U.S. population in 1790, to 9.7 percent in 1930, their visibility increased. Many blacks believed the war propaganda that America was fighting to "make the world safe for democracy."

To counter the new hope, segregationists increased lynchings and antiblack violence. For instance, in 1917, in East Saint Louis, Illinois, violence erupted over the employment of blacks in a factory that held government contracts. Blacks began to respond, not as adaptive "Uncle Toms," but as proactive lead-ers like Marcus Garvey and W.E.B. Du Bois.

Not since reconstruction (and until The New Deal) had poor minorities had any assistance from the federal government. President Franklin Roosevelt's policies encouraged many blacks, so that despite the largely racist Democrats that ran the southern states, blacks began to align with that political party. As expected, the southern white electorate did not share the same political agenda as blacks. Consequently, southern white Democrats became increasingly uncomfortable with the federal Democratic reforms. In the 1960s, the independent presidential candidate Governor George Wallace of Alabama offered an intermediate step for southern whites away from the Democratic Party. By 1968, the northeastern "establishment" (including intellectuals) was shunned by the Republicans who were, paradoxically, strongly supported by northeastern industrialists and capitalists. Today, the South and West, where many Confederate soldiers had gone after defeat, have become strongholds of Republican support.

World War II raised hopes once again. The concentration of large numbers of blacks in northern and western cities increased the potential for political influence. Anti-Nazi propaganda also exposed the gap between American idealism and American reality, but at the same time it represented a strident antiracist message. Although 891,000 blacks joined the armed services, many were never trained in the use of basic weapons.

In response to a threat of black unions striking, and a need for trained minority labor, President Franklin Roosevelt established a national Fair Employment Practices Committee which attempted to end discrimination in defense plants. In 1942, the Congress of Racial Equality (CORE) was founded. However, the war ended with no major changes in hiring practices. Not since the mid-1880s had the federal government done anything to combat discrimination. In 1947, the Fair Employment Practices Act was passed. It forbade discrimination on the basis of color or national origin. Then, in 1948, President Harry Truman desegregated the armed forces. Still, some school districts in the South did not offer twelve years of education to black children.

Following World War II, blacks began to attack racism in the courts. Several suits were brought against universities that offered separate, but clearly unequal graduate and professional education. In 1954, in the case *Brown v. Board of Education of Topeka, Kansas*, the U.S. Supreme Court reversed *Plessy v. Ferguson*, finding that separate facilities were inherently unequal. Contrary to conventional reasoning, however, segregation in public schools *increased* after 1954.

In 1955, a young Ph.D. from Boston University had been pastor of the Dexter Avenue Baptist Church in Montgomery, Alabama for less than a year when (on December 1, 1955) Rosa Parks defied the local ordinance segregating seating on city buses on December 1, 1955. Along with the Reverend Ralph Abernathy and Edward Nixon, that young Baptist preacher, named Martin Luther King, Jr., organized a year-long boycott of the Montgomery public transportation system. The boycott had about a 98 percent success rate among blacks. The ordinance was rescinded. Two years later King and Abernathy founded the Southern Christian Leadership Conference (SCLC). White terrorists dynamited Abernathy's home and church. They also bombed King's home, narrowly missing his wife and children.

Beginning in 1957, a series of civil rights acts were passed in an effort to guarantee voting rights, access to housing, and equal opportunity in employment. In 1957, the first true civil rights law since 1875, was drafted by the Commission on Civil Rights, and enacted. In 1960, a second enactment that provided for federal referees to aid blacks in voting in federal elections was passed. King helped to organize the Student Nonviolent Coordinating Committee (SNCC) after a lunch-counter sit-in at a Woolworth Store in Greensboro, North Carolina. The next year, blacks (the so-called "freedom riders") from the Congress of Racial Equality rode interstate buses from the North into the deep South, where they were denied accommodation and finally attacked. In 1962, President John Kennedy dispatched federal troops to the University of Mississippi and to the University of Alabama to enforce desegregation. The governor of Alabama, George Wallace, and the police chief of Birmingham, T. Eugene ("Bull") Connor tried to enforce segregation through intimidation and state-sponsored terror. Meanwhile, A. Philip Randolph, Roy Wilkins, and Whitney Young joined King in leading a march on Washington, D.C. On August 28, 1963, King gave his "I Have a Dream" speech and "subpoenaed the conscience of the nation before the judgment seat of morality." President Lyndon Johnson responded to the march on Washington by prodding the Congress into passing the 1964 Civil Rights Act, which undermined the Jim Crow laws.

In 1965, in Selma, Alabama, Sheriff James G. Clark and state troopers attacked and killed several protestors. In the same year, the Voting Rights Act was passed in order to end interference from local governments and individuals who sought to block blacks from voter registration and electoral participation. In just one year the proportion of registered black voters jumped from less than 30, to over 53 percent.

Throughout the early 1960s, dozens of black churches were burned, people attempting to help blacks register for the vote were murdered, the FBI attempted to undermine King's credibility while at the same time trying to enforce the right to vote, and other obstacles emerged. Against Governor Ross Barnett's resistance, in 1962, James Meredith became the first black to attend Ole Miss University. He would later organize voter drives in Mississippi. In 1963, the murder of Medgar Evers, the leader of the National Association for the Advancement of Colored People in Mississippi by Byron de La Beckwith, prompted President Kennedy to put before Congress the most sweeping civil rights legislation in the history of the United States.[1] As antiblack violence increased, resistance to King's nonviolent approach to civil disobedience began to rise. Stokely Carmichael (presently Kwame Ture) and H. Rap Brown succeeded King as chairmen of SNCC. Their call (along with Meredith) for "Black Power" sounded a new militancy. The Black Panther party (led by Bobby Seale and Huey Newton), the Organization of Afro-American Unity, and the Black

Muslims became more visible. Malcolm X, Imamu Amiri Baraka, Ron Karenga, and Huey Newton preached black pride, group unity, and a renewed calling for postcolonial blacks around the world to rise up and help determine world destiny (a dream promoted earlier by Du Bois). From 1964 to 1968, more than one hundred U.S. cities experienced race riots. According to a report to President Johnson by the National Advisory Commission on Civil Disorders (the ''Kerner Commission,'' so-called after the first chairperson, Otto Kerner), in 1967, 83 people were killed and 1,800 injured in such disturbances.

Political enfranchisement in the absence of economic mobility began to ring hollow. Anger over low wages, social exclusion, the Vietnam War, and high unemployment was erupting. Rumors that blacks were in the front lines in disproportional numbers in Vietnam added fuel to the fire. As King toured northern cities he came to realize what Randolph had been fighting for all along, that economic discrimination, poverty, and racism were deeply related. In early 1968, he began to shift the strategy of the SCLC, and to plan a multiracial poor people's march on Washington, D.C. to protest against all forms of discrimination, and for an ''Economic Bill of Rights.'' He was calling for a ''second reconstruction'' that had far-reaching, transracial implications for the American system. While in Memphis, supporting a strike by sanitation workers, he was assassinated on April 4, 1968. Rioting erupted in over 150 cities. The Kerner Commission concurred with many black leaders, linking the unrest with chronic high unemployment in black neighborhoods.

White Backlash

Once Kennedy and Johnson signed civil rights legislation into law, the Democratic Party lost the South. The violent explosion of black rage caused whites to quickly recoil from its reformist stance. The country moved to the right politically, electing President Richard Nixon, who did not support government assistance to the disadvantaged as much as he promoted individual achievement through individual effort.[2] The promise of a second reconstruction turned into a second Gilded Age. This effectively ended the activist phase of the civil rights movement. But the success of the black movement encouraged other liberation movements, including the women's movement.

President Nixon occupied the White House from 1968 until his resignation on August 9, 1974. The massacre of 300 peasant farmers at My Lai in 1970, the Watergate scandal, images of a frantic evacuation from the roof of the United States Embassy in Saigon, Vietnam in April 1975, and in that same month the advent of the Khmer Rouge's two-year reign of terror in Cambodia all conspired to deepen a sense of malaise in the American spirit. During President Jimmy Carter's term, the Organization of Petroleum Exporting Countries, which induced gas lines and double digit inflation, the taking of the embassy by students in Tehran, Iran, and the subsequent debacle of a rescue mission, only deepened the funk. The ''white backlash,'' which is a misnomer because it is too race-specific to fully appreciate the class warfare that is ongoing, and which King was just beginning to recognize when he was killed, recommenced under President Ronald Reagan.

President Reagan took office in 1981. During his presidency the number of people below the poverty line increased by 8.4 million, which amounted to a 40 percent increase in the poor. Over half were children, and most minorities. Cuts of nearly $50 million in federal social-welfare programs exacerbated the condition for the poorest of the poor. Reductions in subsidized housing from $30 billion in 1981, to $7 billion in 1988, made "homelessness" a common term. The number of Americans without any health insurance rose to 37 million. By borrowing rather than taxing to rearm, for the first time since 1914, the United States became a debtor nation. While increasing defense spending 35 percent over 1980 levels, in 1986 he also secured congressional approval of a major income tax reform that further reduced taxes on corporations and wealthy individuals. Although high interest rates helped to restrain inflation, lowering it from 12 percent in 1980 to less than 7 percent in 1982, unemployment soared from 7 percent to 11 percent, which was the highest rate since 1940. The annual federal budget deficit nearly doubled, the highest it had ever been. The United States suffered its worst recession since the Great Depression Era. Conservatives were most pleased with his defense of "family values," his attack on "welfare Queens," and his staunch patriotism. This scapegoating continues, as the former governor of Texas Ann Richards pointed out in a March 1996 address to the National Press Club. She noted that if a woman stays home to raise her babies she is considered unliberated and lazy, and if she goes out into the work force she is considered a bad mother. Either way, women lose.

Corporate welfare, deregulation, mergers and acquisitions, and domestic restructuring of the economy have led to a dissociation between corporate profits and capital gains, and workers' prosperity. As the stock markets boom, wages remain stagnant and large numbers of American workers live in constant fear of layoff. Most live one paycheck and one illness from economic disaster. Forty percent of the economic expansion under President Reagan's "revolution" went to the top 5 percent wealthiest Americans. Not much "trickled down." Cynicism and fear have been masterfully promoted and manipulated as those lowest on the socioeconomic ladder increasingly feel left behind (Frank and Cook, 1995). The strident cries for "states' rights," led in the 104th Congress by House Speaker Newt Gengrich (Representative from Georgia) echoes the sentiments of the segregationist South.

The Myrdal Journal (Where Are We Now)

Under such conditions, color, as Ralph Ellison noted, forms an "easy and reliable gauge for determining to what extent one [is or is not] American." Cornel West has argued that the 1992 Los Angeles riots indicate a "lethal linkage" between a continual and prolonged economic decline for most Americans with "cultural decay," and "political lethargy" (West, 1993: 4). White supremacist feeling, legitimated by presidential messages like President Bush's Willie Horton campaign ads, and talk radio ideologues like G. Gordon Liddy, Pat Buchanan, and Rush Limbaugh, are increasingly resentful of the entire situation. Blacks, like those who nearly killed Reginald Denny, the truck driver caught in the 1992 Los Angeles riot, also feel justified in their violence. Scapegoating is predictable, and indeed the numbers of black churches being burned in the South has risen sharply during 1995 and early 1996. Conservatives are also railing at a new pitch, against illegal immigrants.

It is predictable that black reaction should take the form of increased nationalism (literally defensiveness), manifested in the person of Louis Farrakhan who, in January of 1996, visited Libyan President Mohmar Quadafi, in search of financial support for the Nation of Islam's projects. Also predictable is the racial divide evinced by the reactions to the verdict of O. J. Simpson's 1995 murder trial.

THREE RESPONSES TO A HOSTILE ENVIRONMENT

Theories of adaptation and accommodation are usually propagated by people who know nothing about being utterly rejected by those they desperately wish to join. Until very recently (if even now), Native Americans, Latinos, Chicanos, and African Americans have struggled to fit into an environment which is not disinterested or mute, but an environment which consciously and maliciously rejects them. For years, southern whites created "accommodations" for "colored" people. Accommodation meant a separate world. Trying to join a club that openly hates you gets old pretty quick. But some internalize this duality, and suffer from what Du Bois called "double-consciousness," meaning to always see yourself through the eyes of the Other, dominant culture. The social fabric of minority groups has taken a terrible beating. "Adaptation" has amounted to what West (1994: 137) calls, "a pervasive self-loathing" and a financially impoverished and spiritually decimated family institution.

The quagmire of adaptation is this: the more I share the dominant white values and perspective (see through their eyes), the more I see my own face as inferior, ugly, distasteful, and incompetent. When tested by the standards of the Other, I am proven substandard. The more I adapt, the more faith I put in the standards of the Other, the more the evidence of my inferiority becomes stronger in my own mind. The more one adapts to a racist culture, the more one becomes racist. And if that culture is racially prejudiced against my phenotype or culture, the more I will seek to separate from myself, my own culture, and even physical appearance. I will try to hide from myself. The inevitable failure of this attempt results in suffering from an internal antagonism among fragmented selves. Dreams become pathetically naive "wishful thinking." The result is the alienation (alien nation) of inferiority complexes. Such alienation defeats the self-confidence that is necessary for dreams and ambition, dreams which are defeated by the terrible inertia of "Reality." "Reality" expresses the politics of metaphysics, the insidiousness of hegemonic self-definition. For the inferiorized, becoming an "adult," "getting real," means being defeated. Dreams evaporate, goals become increasingly unthinkable. This causes the dissolution of institutions that traditionally sheltered the young and their dreams. Once this process starts, it spirals into a self-fulfilling prophecy of defeatism that can take generations to reverse. Self-doubt is a deep hole with slippery walls.

In such an environment of widespread racial distrust, traditionally three responses by the underclass have dominated social action. One, expressed by Booker T. Washington and Du Bois, is assimilation. As president of the Tuskeegee Institute, and advisor to presidents, Washington promoted industrial training and economic assimilation, while remaining relatively silent on the issues of social and political equality. Du Bois also argued for assimilation, but he believed that an educated black elite should lead blacks to liberation. In 1905, Du Bois started the Niagara Movement, which was a forerunner of the National Association for the Advancement of Colored People, which he also helped to organize. Because Du Bois (like the actor/singer Paul Robeson) made no secret of his admiration for the USSR, he ran afoul of the anticommunism hysteria (especially during the 1950s). Finally, he renounced his American citizenship and moved to Africa.

Another response to the hostile environment blacks found themselves in has been Black Nationalism as promoted by Marcus Garvey, for instance. To this end, Garvey founded the Universal Negro Improvement Association in 1914.

A third way, which inspired King, is Mahatma Gandhi's doctrine of *Satyagraha* ("holding to the truth") and nonviolent disobedience. Holding to the truth or verition of "what is," however, is not intolerance manifested as violent action. It is more creative and fluid. This path has been explored as an aperspectival verition in Chapter 5 ("Aperspectival 'Postmodernity' ").

NOTES

1. Mr. Beckwith was confident that no Mississippi jury would convict him. In fact, he was acquitted of the murder of Mr. Evers. He eluded justice for over two decades, when witnesses finally came forward. He was later convicted of the murder. Strangely, in 1975, Mr. Beckwith, an avowed racist, was sentenced to prison for five years for carrying a time bomb *without a permit*. Apparently, the state of Mississippi (at least in 1975) issued permits for time bombs!

2. However, compared to subsequent Republican presidents Ronald Reagan and George Bush, President Nixon's social agenda was practically liberal.

REFERENCES

Baldwin, J., and M. Mead. (1971) *Rap on Race*. New York: J. B. Lippincott.
Brown, T. (1995) *Black Lies/White Lies: The Truth According to Tony Brown*. New York: W. Morrow and Co.

Campbell, J., and B. Moyers. (1988) *The Power of Myth*. New York: Doubleday.

Diamond, J. (1994) ''How Africa Became Black.'' *Discover* 15, no. 2 (February): 72–81.

Du Bois, W.E.B. (1989) *The Souls of Black Folk*. New York: Bantam.

Ellison. R. (1952) *Invisible Man*. New York: Random House.

———. (1966) ''Transcript of the American Academy Conference on the Negro American—May 14–15, 1965.'' *Daedalus* 95, no. 1 (Winter): 433–444.

Ellul, J. (1964) *The Technological Society*: New York: Vintage.

Frank, R., and P. Cook. (1995) *The Winner-Take-All Society: How More and More Americans Compete for Ever Fewer and Bigger Prizes, Encouraging Economic Waste, Income Inequality, and an Impoverished Cultural Life*. New York: Free Press.

Gebser, J. (1985) *The Ever-Present Origin*. Athens: Ohio University Press.

Gudykunst, W., and Y. Kim. (1992) *Communicating with Strangers: An Approach to Intercultural Communication*. New York: McGraw-Hill.

Handlin, O. (1966) ''The Goals of Integration.'' *Daedalus* 95, no. 1 (Winter): 279–290.

Hayashida, C. T. (1976) *Identity, Race, and the Blood Ideology of Japan*. Dissertation for the University of Washington. AAC 7625413.

Heisenberg, W. (1958) *Physics and Philosophy: The Revolution in Modern Science*. New York: Harper & Row.

Husserl, E. (1962) *Ideas: General Introduction to Pure Phenomenology*. New York: Collier.

———. (1964) *The Phenomenology of Internal Time-Consciousness*. Bloomington: Indiana University Press.

Kramer, E. M. (1993) ''Investigative Journalism in Bulgaria: A Postponed Renaissance.'' In *Creating a Free Press in Eastern Europe*, edited by A. Hester and K. White. Athens: University of Georgia, The James M. Cox, Jr., Center for International Mass Communication Training & Research.

Kuhn, T. (1962) *The Structure of Scientific Revolutions*. Chicago: University of Chicago Press.

Lemelle, A. L. (1993) ''Review of Ralph C. Gomes and Linda Faye Williams, *From Exclusion to Inclusion: The Long Struggle for African-American Political Power*.'' *Contemporary Sociology* 22, no. 1 (January): 60–63.

Lyotard, F. (1984) *The Postmodern Condition*. Minneapolis: University of Minnesota Press.

McDaniel, A. (1995) ''The Dynamic Racial Composition of the United States.'' *Daedalus* 124, no. 1 (Winter): 179–198.

Morrison, T. (1970) *The Bluest Eye: A Novel*. New York: Holt, Rinehart and Winston.

Mudimbe, V. Y. (1988) *The Invention of Africa: Gnosis, Philosophy, and the Order of Knowledge*. Bloomington: Indiana University Press.

Myrdal, G. (1944) *The American Dilemma: The Negro Problem and Modern Democracy*. New York: Harper & Brothers Publishers.

Nietzsche, F. (1974) *The Gay Science*. New York: Vintage.

Russell, K., M. Wilson, and R. Hall. (1992) *The Color Complex: The Politics of Skin Color Among African Americans*. New York: Anchor Books, Doubleday.

Sollors, W. (1989) *The Invention of Ethnicity*. New York: Oxford University Press.

Spiegelberg, H. (1982) *The Phenomenological Movement*. The Hague: Martinus Nijhoff.

Turner Broadcasting. (1995) *China: The Wild East*. Turner Broadcasting System.

Waters, M. (1994) "The Social Construction of Race and Ethnicity: Some Examples from Demography." Proceedings from the Albany Conference, "American Diversity: A Demographic Challenge for the Twenty-First Century." April 15–16.

West, C. (1993) *Prophetic Reflections*. Monroe, ME: Common Courage Press.

———. (1994) *Race Matters*. New York: Vintage.

Willis, J., ed. (1985) *Slaves and Slavery in Muslim Africa*, 2 Vols. London: Frank Cass & Co.

Wittgenstein, L. (1958) *Philosophical Investigations*. Oxford, England: Basil Blackwell.

7

Integrum

What if all ponds were shallow?
Would it not react on the minds of men?
I am thankful that this pond was made pure and deep for a symbol.
While men believe in the infinite some ponds will be thought to be
bottomless.

—Henry David Thoreau

DON'T COUNT ON MATERIALISM

"Integrum" is an awareness yielded not by systematic arrangement, as in syllogisms and synchronic diagrams (with fixed relationships illustrated by arrows) that contrive only momentary validity.[1] Rather, integrum is the articulation of synairesis. As stated in Chapter 5, synairesis is not a mental synthesis (a la dialectics of "left" and "right") but an aspatial, acategorical realization of the constitutive viability of systemic signality, magic symbiotic idolatry, and mythic symbolism.

Aperspectivity is not merely an awareness that there are several different perspectives on any given phenomenon, but it is also an awareness of the field of nondistinction which all distinctions presume. Aperspectivity is not only an awareness and appreciation of relationships. Ancient mathematics is a good example of a systematic organization exclusively concerned with logical relationships. The difference between conventional systematics and systatic (aperspectival) (a)waring (which is the verition of integrum), is that in mathematics, for instance, relationships such as the law of noncontradiction are postulated as fixed and intolerant. Synairesis is (a)waring of the provisional validity of such rules as artifactual phenomena in flux. For example, aperspectival physics violates the so-called "inviolable law of noncontradiction."

Irrationality and rationality have been overdetermined in logic by C. S. Peirce (1940), in mathematics by Kurt Godel (1953), in anthropology by Arnold Gehlen (1980), and in physics by Hans Reichenbach (1944). While Peirce added "abduction" to deduction and induction, Reichenbach's "three-valued logic" posited a value called "indeterminacy" along with "true" and "false." Reichenbach articulated the "non-Aristotelian" and "non-Euclidian" logic that Janos Bolyai (1955), Nikolai Lobachevski (1892), Carl Friedrich Gauss (1902), Bernhard Riemann (1923), Werner Heisenberg (1958), Max Planck (1949), and Niels Bohr (1987) had "established." Likewise, George David Birkhoff (1923), John von Neumann (1955), Carl Friedrich von Weizsacker (1975–1977), and Wolfgang Pauli (1994) analyzed matrix mechanics (or quantum logic). They found it impossible to visualize. Quantum logic is beyond spatial dimensions. Unlike the Newtonian description of motion, matrix mechanics is concerned with transformational states *between* matrices.

Pauli (1994) articulated the indeterminacy of knowledge, which is not limited only to physics, when he discovered that he could choose to observe one experimental set-up, A, and ruin B, or choose to observe B and ruin A. But he could not choose to not ruin one of them. More fundamentally, he could not choose to not choose, or as Jean-Paul Sartre (1960) put it, we are condemned to freedom. Thus, the principle of complementarity limits knowledge and the classical law of the excluded middle (either A or not A) is superseded. Likewise, Godel (1953) demonstrated that mathematics, like quantum, can never, formally, reach rock bottom (complete systematization).

The optimistic *Zeitgeist*, that "positivism" in the seventeenth and eighteenth centuries manifested, was a form of neoclassicism (neo-Aristotelianism) which promoted the "principle of continuity" and the "principle of sufficient reason." Positivistic continuity, as formulated by Immanuel Kant (1929), presumed a universal reason by which all humans are uniformly guided, and participate in, as well as a closed system of perception. This was the motive force legitimating European colonialism. By the eighteenth and nineteenth centuries however, German romantics, notably Goethe, Novalis, August Wilhelm Schlegel (as well as Friedrich von Schlegel), and Friedrich Schleiermacher had established what came to be known as "diversitarianism."

While the young John Stuart Mill feared that "all the possible modes and combinations in, for example, music had already been realized, that there could be nothing really new," another distinguished Englishman publicly announced that Newton had written the final word on physics and that only "mopping up" remained (Lovejoy, 1936: 306; Kuhn, 1962). Meanwhile, many German scholars were celebrating a kind of integral openness to every mode of human experience. Their notion of universalism was not unitarian (seeking uniformity of norms and sameness among human-units) but rather, conceived of as a vast embracing of difference. In his condemnation of self-imposed ignorance (ignoring differ-ence), A. W. Schlegel (1960: 15) argued that

One cannot become a connoisseur without universality of mind, that is, without the flexibility which enables us, through the renunciation of personal likings and blind pref-erence for what we are accustomed to, to transpose ourselves into that which is peculiar to other peoples and times, and, so to say, to feel this from its centre outwards. Thus the despotism of good taste, by which some seek to enforce certain perhaps wholly arbitrary rules which they have set up, is always an unwarranted presumption.

Schlegel was following Friedrich Schiller's temporalized principle of plenitude (Schiller, 1910). Schiller attacked the "dictators of life" which amounted to the imposition of Kantian-style immutable rules of formal perfection (the idealiza-tions of a man who spent entirely too much time alone in his study). According to Schiller (1910: 51), "Since the world is spread out in time, since it is change, the complete realization of that *potentiality* [my emphasis] which relates man to the world must consist in the greatest possible variability and extension." Thus, universalism meant the appreciation of every mode of human experience, not a colonizing system or global architectonic.

Integral appreciation (see Chapter 5), as a continental attitude, confronted British systematics in physics. Toward the end of the nineteenth century, it was believed by not a few Newtonians and Saint-Simonians, that the relatively minor "mopping up" job necessary to conclude physics was at hand. The loose ends, however, included two (at that time) inconclusive problems: Neils Bohr's work on black body radiation, and the 1887 Michelson-Morley experiment concerning the speed of light. According to many arrogant scientists, once these were re-solved, the book could be closed on physical science. It was also presumed by many that Charles Darwin's work had nearly done the same service for biolog-ical and social sciences. However, instead of Newton being the final word on physics, the Michelson-Morley experiment led to Einstein's 1905 work, which revived interest in Max Planck's concept of discrete states (rather than linear continuity). Subsequently, when Bohr's work was combined with Planck's ideas, it led to a revolution in physics (quantum mechanics). Thus, just when the work of rendering the apodictic laws of nature was within sight, relativity theory and quantum mechanics broke the system wide open.

Werner Heisenberg (1958: 93) noted that "Newton begins his *Principia* with a group of definitions and axioms which are interconnected in such a way that they form what one may call a 'closed system.' . . . The mathematical image of the system ensures that contradictions cannot occur in the system." Self-assuredness is tautologically blind to anything beyond its own perspective. It is utterly prejudiced in the sense that it cannot even occur to one that reality may be questionable. Such certainty and security however, are chimera. A closed system is elegant while reality escapes its domesticating confines. Newton's game was "fixed." Filmer S. C. Northrop reminds us that this is so because such security exists only for an *isolated* (closed) system, which exists only in theory (Northrop, 1958: 24). It exists by operational definition only. Thus, reality hinges on one's definition of "state."

In the 1930s, arguments over the "wave-picture" and the "particle picture" *languages* became heated. Bohr's "Copenhagen interpretation" suggested a rather paradoxical nonresolution. He argued that the particle *and* the wave narratives should be accepted as "complementary." At least two other interpretations emerged in opposition to the Copenhagen one. Opponents included Albert Einstein and Erwin Schrodinger.

Thus, the new continental physics departed radically from the older Newtonian version. According to Heisenberg (1958: 147), "Matter is in itself not a reality but only a possibility, a 'potentia'; it exists only by means of form." Bertrand Russell and Alfred North Whitehead (1967), and Rudolf Carnap (1959) have gone so far as to suggest that science no longer has any need for the concepts "substance" and "matter." Substance became displaced by operational definition. According to Blochinzev and Alexandrov (quoted in Heisenberg, 1958: 138), "In quantum mechanics we describe not a state of the particle in itself but the fact that the particle belongs to this or that statistical assembly. This belonging is completely objective and does not depend on statements made by the observer." This state of affairs led Einstein (1949: 45) to complain that "It was as if the ground had been pulled out from under one, with no firm foundation to be seen anywhere, upon which one could have built." Likewise, Pauli wrote in 1921, "At the moment physics is again terribly confused. In any case, it is too difficult for me, and I wish I had been a movie comedian or something of the sort and had never heard of physics" (quoted by Ralph Kronig [1960: 22] in a memorial volume dedicated to Pauli).

Thomas Kuhn (1962: 84) has noted that such conscious and explicit recognitions of breakdown are "extremely rare" in the history of science, which is usually quite conservative (even dogmatic). Instead, communities of scholars usually defend their turf even if they must use extraneous power such as hiring and rejecting disagreeable submissions to journals. At any rate, the realization that perception is affected by the language one uses to describe it, that operational definitions guide the design of experiments thus leading to certain contrived results, greatly disturbed these thinkers.

Heisenberg too, believed that this "tissue of ideas," as Edmund Husserl (1970: 346) called it (see Chapter 3), had gone too far. Virtually every great physicist, including Heisenberg (1958), George Gamow (1966), and Stephen Hawking (1988), has written extensively on the language of science and how physicists have struggled with an old language which speaks of fixed reality rather than the world as "potentia" (Heisenberg, 1958: 180).

They all agree that classical logic, which prejudices thinking by positing axioms and theorems that restrict the world to an either/or closed systematics must be abandoned or fundamentally "modified" (Heisenberg, 1958: 181). It may "feel good" and dispel uncertainty, but it is false. Traditional Western (Aristotelian) thinking (like many imperialisms) has generated what this author calls a "noun culture" as differentiated from a "verb culture." For instance, in English, one says "fist" for a clenched hand, while in Hindi one says "fisting." A noun culture sees the world as an assemblage of fixed things in constant space and time. Verb culture sees the world as indeterminate and temporalized. A third way is integral (Gebser, 1985).

In classical Aristotelian thinking the principle of *tertium non datur* states that no third possibility may exist. But according to Heisenberg (1958: 181), "In quantum theory this law 'tertium non datur' is to be modified," and, because this mode of thinking is manifested in "natural language," "we have to speak at least about our eventual modification of logic in the natural language." Heisenberg noted that for Darwin and his followers, the only concept which need be added to physics in order to understand life was history. But historical time is still linear, directional (evolution), and constant.

But the temporalization of time, which had been occurring across disciplines in the German academy for at least a century (since Friedrich Nietzsche), goes beyond linear historicism. "The decisive step, however, was taken in the paper by Einstein in 1905 in which he established the 'apparent' time of the Lorentz transformation as the 'real' time and abolished what had been called 'real' time by Lorentz" (Heisenberg, 1958: 114).

Richard Rorty (1991) has distinguished between "edifying" and pragmatically systematic thinkers. Edifying thinkers have a tendency to saw off the branch (consensual truth) upon which they sit. But they do not fear falling because they suspect that there is no "ground" to hit, no "closure" of discussion, no "last word," but instead an endless play of metaphors which reveal as they conceal. Like changing the focus on a long lens, things come into definition as others go out, and vice versa. Aperspectival cubism collapses time such that the time it takes to turn the lens happens all at once. The result is a kind of diaphaneity, a seeing through time and space.

Russell and Whitehead's (1967) grand effort to establish a pure (nonfigural) metalanguage which the dirty hands of contingency (interpretive and temporal consciousness) could not soil, and with which to write pure metanarratives, failed utterly. When someone says "get real," they are saying conform. But conform to what? Which history? Which science? Which religion? Which reality should be exclusively privileged?

A great edifying thinker was Henry David Thoreau (1929) who told of the "vain attempt" of his neighbors to find the bottom of Walden Pond, to "fathom their truly immeasurable capacity for marvelousness" (*Walden Pond*, ch. 16). Observing the modern obsession with certainty, Thoreau suggested that we

settle ourselves, and work and wedge our feet downward through the mud and slush of opinion, and prejudice, and tradition, and delusion, and appearance, the alluvion which covers the globe . . . through church and state, through poetry and philosophy and religion, till we come to a hard bottom and rocks in place, which we can call *reality*, and say, This is, and no mistake; and then begin, having a *point d'appui*, below freshet and frost and fire, a place where you might found a wall or a state, or set a lamp-post safely, or perhaps a gauge, not a Nilometer, but a Realometer, that future ages might know how deep a freshet of shams and appearances had gathered from time to time. (*Walden Pond*, ch. 2)

No better description has been given for what would later be called "archaeology" by Husserl (1970), and "genealogy" by Nietzsche (1967). However, the "shipwreck" (as Ludwig Landgrebe [1981] called it) of Husserl's early essentialism, and Nietzsche's wanderer, are manifested in the realization that "it's turtles all the way down."[2]

The "exclusion principle" is present as an absence. Quantum action is not of substance but of indeterminate, acausal, and discontinuous relationships, or "implications" (to quote David Bohem [1980]). This aperspectival science has been called, by Arthur March (1962) and Pacual Jordan (1944), the study of a "dematerialized" and "desubstantivated" reality.[3] But it was Nietzsche who established this new space- and time-free "openness" by the end of the nineteenth century.

Dynamic Identity

While synairesis is (a)waring of the comparative validity of each modality (magic symbiotic idolatry, mythic symbolism, and perspectival signality), it is not determined, or entrapped, by the exclusive dominance of any one categorical reality. While they exhibit systematic and mutual exclusivity, synairesis recognizes that each mode of expression requires the others for its respective identities. "Identity" is pluralized because each structure (magic, mythic, and perspectival) has a fluid uniqueness dependent upon which comparisons one chooses to emphasize; mythic to magic, mythic to perspectival, and so on. What mythic means depends on what you are comparing it to. Synairetic (a)waring is awareness of the morphological (temporal) nature of identification.

Unlike the *popular* conceptualizations of spatial "interdependencies," or integration, which negates differences with the nihilistic consequence of a "melting pot," assimilation, or total adaptation (senseless, monotonous monoculturalism), synairesis recognizes the validity of each structure *as seen through* the others (the transparency of mutable difference/identity). For instance, identity is recognized via magic, to be an inherent part of a thing, and via mental-rationalism, to be a relational phenomenon between "things" (an ancient insight given new currency by Nicholas Cusanus, 1401–1464). In the *predominantly* magic world, identity is inherently self-evident while in the *predominantly* modern/perspectival world, it is conventional (keep in mind that they are co-present, not sequentially historical). In the magic world, one's essence is presumed regardless of the presence or absence of difference. In the mythic world, the gods represent aspects of the human psyche. For the perspectival world, identity is a linguistic difference such that, for instance, there would be no "whites" in America if there were no "colored."

By contrast, aperspectivity is a recognition that even the so-called "most obvious" of measurable ("empirical") categorical differences such as those between "life" and "death," "self-evident" and "other-evident," "criminal" and "innocent," and "significance" and "insignificance," are "matters" of civilizational semantics. Since humans are "fallible" (in the perspectival world change is "error"), and since definitions are human artifacts, then definitions are mutable. What may be self-evident by the criteria of one world may not be by the criteria of another world-structure.

Synairesis is the recognition that different types of identity are "valid" within their respective modes of awaring. And no one mode is transcendentally more real or correct or true than any other. Instead, we make value judgements based on our values; what is convenient, powerful, beautiful, and so on, to our current mode of awaring. Awaring shifts, and the shift is experienced via synairetic (a)waring. We change and so does everything we perceive. But these judgements themselves are made from the perspective of a consciousness structure. Judgements reveal more about the judge than the judged. Even though they are mutually excluding, there is no superordinate reality which can "finally" falsify any of them. As Ludwig Wittgenstein (1958) stated, the world is constituted of communicative games. Games are neither true nor false, but are simply the convention, and convention is perceived as contingent only in the company of other games (rules).

Synairesis avoids the existential logic of determining the absolute existence or nonexistence of a thing as being the basis of falsifiability. Nor does it recognize the exclusive validity of perspectival conventionalism. For instance, existentialists may be concerned to ask, does a tree exist or not exist in this yard, or does a virus exist in this blood. This is not a logical question but an existential one, which is the same as an "empirical" one for the perspectival world. Likewise, there is no logic to asking does that thing have to be designated by "t-r-e-e." Either it is designated that way, or it is not, according to current prejudice and/or interest. Forgoing any superordinate Reality, such as nature or divinity, this is all that can be said (see Chapter 1). There is no authority other than the sharing of a common sense—the social "bonds" which are dialogically maintained.

APERSPECTIVAL VALIDITIES

Synairesis is a recognition of the temporalization, or provisional (revealed via difference) validity of systems so that one day "whites" and "colored" may no longer be meaningful (perceivable) as such. One day it may seem senseless that people owned each other or could not attend the same schools. The fact that people concern themselves with racial distinctions tells us about their thinking (the structure of their mode of consciousness at the time of iteration), and nothing about race, *sui generis*, because race, as such, is synairetically manifested only as a contingent articulation.

Synairetically, valid means discernible within the parameters of a particular way of thinking. Thus, validity and reliability exist "by definition." They are creations. For instance, in the perspectival world, media and method (essentially the same thing) *yield* valid and/or reliable data according to *established* criteria. Despite the "naive natural attitude" of some practitioners, the scientific method is neither divine nor natural (Husserl, 1962: 102). Sir Francis Bacon did not discover his method lying in the forest somewhere, nor was he a god (although this may come as a surprise to the faithful). So long as a large number of people agree, or are intimidated into conformity, then the game (science or something else like magic) works, just as religious dogma has for thousands of years. What is meant by "works" is that the system proves vital, survivable (it is the case). It presents a meaningful cosmos that yields identity.

Studies in comparative civilizations demonstrate the arbitrary nature of cosmology. What is evinced by such work (Gebser, 1985; Durant, 1954; Lingis, 1983; Hall, 1983, 1976, 1966; Geertz, 1973; Spengler, 1926–1928; Mickunas, 1994) is a "background" of nondistinction which is segmented or "marked," creating difference and meaning. Paleohistorians like Helmut de Terra (1939) note that this nondistinction "appears" as an absence of human culture (artifactual or civilizational expression). The earliest artifacts are the expressed effort to make a difference, to mean. Expression or fabrication seems to manifest a need and/or want (to say), a not necessarily rational "reason," that does not necessarily lead beyond itself to a goal. The "goal" can be to iterate itself. Expression can be the "means" to its own "end," like art for its own sake.

Without perspectival dissociation, magic and mythic worlds exhibit an emphasis on being, rather than having. One cannot "have" something unless it is possible to not have it. Even the languages of magic and mythic cultures emphasize process rather than fixed things (see Chapter 5's discussion of the Hopi and Navajo; Sapir, 1990, 1949; Whorf, 1956; Hall, 1983). Most cultures are verb cultures while the modern West is essentially a noun culture. The modern West is individualistic and proprietary.

INDIVIDUATION

A parable, or "thought experiment," may help to clarify the relationship between segmenting expressivity and identity. Imagine that you are "floating in" "a" zero-dimensional archaic "spacelessness" of total nondistinction, a "void" before the distinction nothing/something, with no orientation, no hot or cold, wet or dry, loud or silent, light or dark, near or far. Then (for the sake of this story I must exploit a "line" which is already complex) a rope appears to hand. "You" grab the rope. As you look in one "direction," the rope stretches off without end. When you look the "other way," again there is no end. The endless rope is a metaphor for aspatial and atemporal infinity and eternity. While holding on to the rope you announce, "I am here." But this phrase is an utterly meaningless burst of noise because "here" is meaningless without at least one "there."

Now let us imagine that this nihilistic condition is, for some unknown reason, disturbing to you. So you begin to establish points along the line, thus making space and time (among many other "things" including self). A category cannot exist without a case. So too, a "dimension," as such, cannot be perceived without fragmentation, segmentation, differentiation. The curious thing about communication, which has propelled hermeneutics since Aristotle's exploration of metaphor in the *Poetics*, and his work *Peri hermeneias* (*On Interpretation*, 1938), is that messages both conceal and reveal at the same time. The same empirical text has multiple meanings. For instance, a child makes a drawing of his cat "Pickles." By perspectival standards, it is a very poor rendition. But we love it anyway, *because* it is not perfect. Despite the empirical evidence, we believe that we know what he meant, what he was trying to do. What does this crayon drawing tell us? It is a contingent example of many things; love, effort, failure, immaturity. What is evident is humanity. We love it because it is fallible. But how do we think that we know what fallible is without access to the infallible? Since nothing is perfect, nothing is imperfect. The duality is spurious. But then how do we know what spurious means? We see in the crayon drawing ourselves. A person tries to fix a wonderful dinner for us. Empirically it is a disaster. But seeing through the burnt chicken and collapsed souffle, we also know what they meant, what they had intended. What we appreciate is the effort *and* their disappointment. Just as we can see in the ruins of a civilization the splendor that once must have been, we see through the empirically given to more that is the absent. We see in a person "potential." We also see our own limitations and our own efforts to be accepted and loved. It is not personal. I may be looking at a child in a firefighter's arms from the Oklahoma City bombing or a child in the dust of Somalia. I don't know *that* child, but I am moved by this contingent case to a transcending emotion of sympathy. The transcendental is given through the contingent. Justice, fairness, love, hate, judgement is made of cases. Standards exist only as applied.

Emmanuel Levinas (1987) wrote of the countenance of the Other. It, the Other, is not a simple binary opposition, or Cartesian dualism, or classical dialectic. The Other matters to me because we share many things including life, hope, and suffering. The message (a drawing or a face) speaks as much about what is absent as what is present. The difference between the two is spurious. They both mean. Behaviorism, with its materialistic, metaphysical obsession, concerns itself exclusively with what people physically do. But often, what they fail to do is just as, if not more, important.

The case has meaning insofar as it presents a transcendental phenomenon, and there cannot be a category with no cases. Like the high school biology teacher who, while watching with her students a butterfly emerge from a chrysalis, says, "You guys are seeing metamorphosis in action." She means *this* metamorphosis *and* metamorphosis *generally*. The wonder is both immanent and transcendent, given in this singular space-time event. The reason existentialists like Jean-Paul Sartre, Martin Heidegger, and Maurice Merleau-Ponty were inspired by Edmund Husserl's writings is because he demonstrated that the boundary between the immanent and the transcendent is false. Case and category are always given together.

As you set out to establish your place, your identity, you establish ends to the rope; the big bang, genesis, the primal "singularity," the Prime Mover, the apocalypse, pure communism, final utopia, and so on. These establish you as being "in between" (because my metaphor is a modern line) nonbeing.

But the ends alone are too indeterminate, too imprecise for your want and need. You wish to establish yourself more specifically, "sharply," and to do so, you must establish more "points" along the rope. So you create complex stories in between the ends; elaborate magical systems that define discrete powers, mythologies that "locate" you spiritually, and perspectival sciences that define you as a localized spatio-temporal being, as "historic" and territorially attached. Sacred tribal stories establish the sacrality of your self-identity (Durkheim, 1965). "Sacred" dates are established, pseudo-sacred political traditions are marked and remarked (recorded), deferential rankings are established along an increasing number of variables. You are *your* marks; *your* colors, flags, songs, scares, and rituals, and they are you. Each distinction creates meaning (difference), and further defines the self, progressively localizing and shrinking or consolidating it into a fixed entity.

The definition of "definition" is to clarify. In optics definition is measured by how well adjacent objects can be perceived as such, as *separate* objec*ts*. Thus, as variance multiplies, the self becomes "clearer," it becomes identifiable, more isolated, individuated, fixed, and definite. Who and what you are becomes more and more established along the axes of multiple categories. Those who lived in the time of B.C. did not know that they were living in B.C. But once the distinctions "before Christ" and "*Anno Domini*" were established, everyone privy to this knowledge was compelled to be or not to be a Christian. This discrimination identifies everyone as a particular kind of spiritual and historical being. It is very difficult, if not impossible, to choose to not choose. And even then, the system has forced a decision; hence the totalitarian nature of systematic thinking.

Systems *force* one to choose. "Freedom" is imposed. For instance, which insurance or political candidate, or automobile . . . should I select? I am forced into a need to research and judge. Likewise, technological systems do not solve problems but create choices. Do I want an abortion or not? Should I unplug my dying parent or not? Should we use tactical nuclear weapons or not?, so on and so forth. Before such powerful technologies, these choices, these problems that beg for solution, did not exist.

The essential nature of perspectival distinction is its imperative (oppositional) logic. One *must* choose between the alternatives. But aperspectival agnosticism is a reaction that posits a third value of indeterminacy. It is a mode of deference. Of course, in the perspectival modern world, those that cannot make up their minds, those who hesitate are judged weak-minded (''women drivers''). Perspectival choice, which is forced upon everyone by the discursive imperative of the system has, according to several cosmologies, dire spiritual consequences. For the perspectival systems thinker, neutrality is the same as opposition. Most religious systems are mutually excluding, so it is a no-win situation for the well-informed.

Calendars are maps of time, and maps are clocks of space. Both are modern perspectival articulations, scales. But the felt need to know where and who I/we/they are predates and intermingles with the modern emphasis on material space/time coordination. Both calendars and maps manifest a mental-rational veneer added to this apparently universal desire to establish identity and a home (culture), a habitat, ''one's place'' relative to others and things, even if it is to one's camel and tent and kin as for nomadic Bedouin. When one's cosmological system is threatened, the self is threatened. This is so because the self is constituted by the cosmological system that one lives. They are co-constituting phenomena. World and self appresentiate each other. This is why metaphysical battles are nearly always deeply political and personal (not ''merely academic''). Even the perspectival modern, who claims that everything is arbitrary, and claims to be ''detached'' and ''disinterested,'' can become ferociously defensive when his or her ''arbitrary'' cosmos is challenged by one that proclaims pre-ordination. Many scientists literally hate religious (''superstitious'') missionaries, while missionaries expect atheistic scientists to go to hell.

APPRECIATING VALIDITIES

As an example of comparative validity, consider mythical European medieval painting, Tibetan mandalas (both of which express the importance of spiritual, rather than physical, relationships), and Renaissance art. One cannot adequately understand such human creations (behavior) if one insists on validity being restricted solely to spatial propositions such as proportional (ratio-nal) measurements, descriptions of texture and color, and so forth. Since spiritual relationships are not spatial, mythological painting not only has a content that is spiritual in nature, such as spirit beings and deeds like angelic visitations, but even its form expresses practically no concern for the rules of three-dimensional perspective. Regardless of physical (visual) perspective, people and objects that are important are painted bigger and higher up in the scene (toward heaven or in the center), than other, less important phenomena.[4]

By contrast, modern Renaissance painting expresses an earnest need to depict relationships between physical objects ''accurately.'' The relationship itself, the ''in-between'' is not a physical object, but an imperative, a logic. The relationship can be measured because, for the modern, the in-between, space itself is a constant, a thing that can be subdivided and quantified. With each system comes structural imperatives that enable error to exist. Someone can be "wrong." However, each modality is qualitatively different, with different "rights" and "wrongs."

"Accuracy" presumes referentiality, which need not be spatial. Each mode of painting, the medieval and the Renaissance, establishes its own criteria so that criteria do not exist *a priori*, in an exclusive "nature," or spatially "out there" or "in here."[5] *Validity ("accuracy") is achieved in both Renaissance and medieval modes of painting*. The medieval European artist and the Tibetan are just as careful and responsible about "depicting" the world as the Renaissance artist. (S)he was also just as "intelligent" and "innately talented." The difference is that depiction of spiritual relationships is very different from rendering relationships between physical objects. They express different metaphysical values and interests. For the medieval, physical relationships are irrelevant. Each may not even be aware of the "prejudice inherent in" their respective cosmologies. For those not exposed to difference, there is nothing "other" inherent "within" their artifacts.

Monoculturalism, via unilinear adaptation or extermination, is practically no culturalism, because one needs the other in order to perceive the home culture as such. However, when they confront each other, they may (and often do) simply see each other as "wrong." But this enables one to be "right." Pride and prejudice go hand-in-hand. Reality *sui generis* includes "fiction," and vice versa. To speak of the "real," one must presume the "unreal." Nietzsche, Husserl, and Gebser tired of such metaphysical nonsense, which forms the basis of knowledge. They "bracket," or set aside metaphysically derived arguments to attend to awareness of . . . prior to judgement. As Georg Lukacs (1963) reminds, "realism" is a form of "fiction." Reality and dreams are integral. Aperspectivity is a way of appreciation rather than oppositional egoism. The Other enables me to appreciate not only difference, but also my own plans, values, and accomplishments. Without the Other, I could never be "better" (or "worse"). My identity depends on Others, not necessarily in a binary oppositional way, which is the dominant mode of modern thinking, but in a very complex and fluid, variable fusion of horizons. And the Other need not be empirically present. It may be a dead parent, a figure from history, a god, or a tiger-spirit. How I am related to, and related with Others gives me value/identity. Am I tiger-like? Am I a success, compared to grandmother? Would she approve? Inspiration and potential are ever-present. The world gives these to us and constantly unfolds from them.

Appreciated synairetically, neither mode of expression (the modern Renaissance or mythical medieval or Tibetan) is exclusively "correct." Furthermore, so long as the works exist in some form, including as imitation and inspiration, each painting manifests a tradition that is not past (or inferiorized by being obsolete or out-of-date). Neither is invalidated ("demythologized" or "deculturized") by the other. The world is open so that there is no superordinate "need," or self-legitimating imperative, to make an either/or segregation that invalidates one or the other. Normalizing imperatives give way to the abnormal "outliers," whose necessity for the existence of the central tendency becomes transparent. The world is not a zero-sum closed system, nor is it totally controllable. The claim to innate superiority is thus limited so that it cannot be used to justify what are contingent decisions, or stagnation. Superman, the absolute, has nowhere to go. Perfection is changeless. Perfection is dead.

Those who make decisions (everyone) remain responsible. Innateness (universal naturalism) offers sanctuary from responsibility only when it is not thought about (critically reflected upon, which presumes a spatial worldview). For instance, in the mythic world of commercial mass media, advertising works best when it is prior to reflection. Reflection can be short-circuited by evoking "naturalism." A case in point is when Japanese advertising executives justify using Caucasian models even to sell cosmetics to Asians, because Caucasians are "naturally" more beautiful. In short, the Japanese executive may take credit for boosting sales by promoting the exoticism of Caucasians (an exoticism transferred via semiosis to the product). But, critically, he or she must also take responsibility for promoting an inferiority complex among Asian women regarding their own bodies and faces. This may also affect how Asian men look at Asian women as inferior to the Caucasian phenotype. The ad man is making a contingent decision to use Caucasians as models. He expects consequences and should be prepared to explain them.

"Accuracy" only has meaning if referentiality is presumed. And referentiality presumes a spatial reality that allows for a gap that is not universally shared. This realization is expressed in the aperspectival works of Chagall, Picasso, Tamayo, Braque, and others who painted emotional, spatial, and temporal "relationships" (and the relationships between these modalities) together. These artists generated integral, aperspectival paintings, that presentiated the "transparency" of each dimension by juxtaposing them, and by not privileging any one of them (Gebser, 1985: 6, 7). Consequently, each modality can be "seen through" the others, not via binary opposition and negation, but as *integrum* (the integral appreciation of the wealth of achievement). The verition of the world cannot be right or wrong, it is simply given, and to doubt it, or to privilege only one aspect, as Descartes did, is to promote a single metaphysical dogma. Without modern metaphysical distance, inaccuracy is impossible. If the modern dissociating metaphysics is set aside for a moment ("bracketed," in Husserlian terms, which is different from Cartesian doubting), then paintings can be appreciated as expressions that *establish* capacities and interests, rather then simulate some "external reality." They are expressed potential, openings. They establish new relationships.

So too, because it is pure verition (total positivity), an artifact cannot lie or hide from itself. I may not know its context and therefore, what "it" is, or means (the same thing), but it hides nothing. Even a secret code book speaks loudly about secrets, suspicion, enemies, deceit, and so on. Put in another way, what Peter says about Paul tells me very much about *Peter*. Peter's representation of Paul may or may not be accurate, and this may be impossible to determine. But Peter's description of Paul directly presentiates Peter's interests, capacities, valuations, and choices (whether he intends it or not). In any case, it is the systatic (meaning the integration of time with static system) nature of relationships, as they are given, that opens to several validities without any one imposing, exclusive dominion by claiming to be more "natural" or "real" than the other structures. Choosing one validity over others is contingent upon fluid, metadiscursive values and interests which amount to what is "important" at that time, and whose "importance" has power (Rorty, 1991).

THE APORIA OF SENSATIONAL KNOWLEDGE

There are many worlds, and they all appear to be human artifacts ("discursive formations" because agreement is sustained via communication which presumes a shared hermeneutic horizon). Otherwise, one must presume an order "outside" of all human epistemic systems, a superordination, which would mean that (a) one's knowledge is provisional, except that (b) one knows absolutely that one's knowledge is provisional, which (c) is evident only by immaculate access to the superordinate truth for comparison, which returns us to (a), that one cannot know the superordinate because one's knowledge is provisional. Short of super-special beings like divine prophets and messenger/interpreter gods, we are stuck with time.

Put another way, Bacon (1937) argued in "Advancement of Learning" that the only knowledge that there is is direct personal knowledge, which is sensory-based and limited by upbringing and innate intelligence (the "idols" of the cave, marketplace, tribe, and theater). But, in *New Atlantis*, he argued that, according to the "great instauration," Man would be the controller of all nature and society. Even though the senses are fallible (different, variable, temporal), and thus yield only provisional knowledge, Man has the right to produce Truth. For Bacon, partiality is defined as erroneous.

There are two absurdities at work here. First, Bacon is absolutely sure that he is not sure. And second, in order to know that one's knowledge is fallible or only "partial," one must know the whole Truth (be infallible) in order to make the comparison that reveals "partiality" as such. Maybe Bacon was too optimistic, but perhaps he is not wrong. Maybe the human condition is absurd but not meaningless. Instead there is an endless proliferation of meanings, systems, Others.

For some, more "problems" follow. First, the source of truth and distortion is the same manifold of sense organs, sociocultural prejudice, ontolinguistic prejudice, and limited ability. Second, Bacon claimed to know for sure that he could not know for sure. Third, to be able to recognize that knowledge is distorted, presumes that one knows The (whole) Truth somehow (despite the distorting lens of cognition), so that one can make a comparative judgement.

Immanuel Kant (1929) fell into the same set of absurdities in his duality between the noumenal and the phenomenal worlds (Kramer, 1992: 16–18).

Unlike Jacques Derrida's neo-Heideggerian "postmodernism," which fails to recognize the validity of spatial system, myth, and identity, synairesis offers a relative relativism. Integrum is not a utopian "ought," with an ontopolitical ambition to erase dissociation or perpetuate a Talmudic-style obsession with law, but rather openness to the verition of the world which shows itself to be magical, mythical, and perspectival, with each mode demonstrating a vitality and "success," or validity.

Despite whatever "deconstruction" may claim to be or not be, or be doing as a tactical reading (of the marginal voice), it expresses a frustration with power inequality, metaphysical domination, and the hypocrisy of those who acknowledge that their scales are purely arbitrary ("objectively" accidental), but yet insist that the reality these fabrications constitute is the only valid one. Deconstruction, like most Enlightenment-inspired pluralism, resists the closure of discourse, the end of interpretation, the final, total(itarian) Truth and normalization of colonial power. Like many before them, there is a suspicion that the entities operational definitions "describe" are actually the product of the operational process, that the "data" are not independent of the instruments used to "generate" them, and are therefore banal tautologies, which is total control (see Chapter 1). The world is "by definition," and whoever does the defining has the power, and everyone else must conform as the rules are "applied" to them. What is IQ? Whatever my definition says it is. Tautology masquerading as objectivism is seen synairetically to be a slick ideological apparatus that bolsters centralized power in the form of "experts." Feedback control is essential, because if people venture to disagree, the tissue of (whisper "conventional") reality comes apart. The players scatter and the game ceases to be. In this way whole civilizations are "lost" and others "founded."

Integrum, like utopia (*ou topos*, which means "nowhere," "no place"), is not physically localizable. Like "history" and "science," integrum is not a thing. Integrum supersedes the modern duality of virtual and actual existentialism.

Integrum is not "post-" anything, but rather appreciation of polyversality: multiple manifolds and cosmological orientations as they manifest through relative differences that are *not necessarily opposing* (like center/margin; speech/writing; present/absent) or necessarily sequential, but instead, mutually given. Awareness of difference never gives one *and then* the other in sequence, but all (as such) simultaneously.

No privileged knowledge is assumed. Only the mental-rational perspectival person "sees" systems everywhere. Comparative civilizational studies indicate that modes of awaring (consciousness) are not singularly consistent or uniform. By insisting that other worlds be expressed in flowcharts, path analytic designs, or numbers; that these are the only valid way of articulation, is very ethnocentric. Such operations confuse powerful prejudices with "objectivity." Many (if not most) worlds posit extra-worldly orders or "reasons" to which they (always in a self-serving manner) claim to correspond. Religions and sciences are good examples of this sort of referential legitimation. Everybody is a "chosen people." The totalitarian nature of mutual exclusivity often ends in conflict. Metaphysics is power. Those who deny metaphysics are either delusional or cynically attempting to avoid their own responsibility.

NOTES

1. Despite their momentary validity, "flowcharts" are quite useful. However, many scholars mistake such artifacts as spontaneously or "naturally occurring," and reify them. Some social scientists expend great energy creating descriptions of organizational systems which are already well understood by those, like military leaders (with their chains of command) and the followers of Henry Ford, who created them. We all know, for instance, that we usually "take turns" while talking to each other. Thus, nothing new is discovered. This is why (as a vice president of Kodak told me) many corporate managers see such grant-getting efforts as "merely academic." The "findings" are very often self-evidently trivial like the "discovery" that a major U.S. airline responds to messages in the order of their receipt, or that management and labor negotiations have a dialectical structure, or that television noise disrupts concentration when a person is trying to read. The managers of industry and other institutionalized rational systems are not blind. They understand that systems are products that are imposed in the interest of control. Gregory Bateson's great breakthrough was to "discover" spying (surveillance) in the interest of status quo; an institution as old as communication (tropism). Thus, the managers that scholars study often feel like indigenous peoples who are "discovered." Neither have a tendency to celebrate finally being designated "real" (statistically significant) by the master narrative of curiosity. It is perspectival arrogance of the ilk that Christopher Columbus expressed.

2. This was the response given to a European scientist when he queried an Asian-Indian woman about the nature of the universe. When she told him that the universe amounted to a great plate on the back of a giant tortoise, he cunningly asked what the tortoise stood on. She immediately responded that "it is turtles all the way down."

3. This turn toward non-Aristotelian aperspectivity is not at all limited to physics, but erupted in the twentieth century across disciplines. It was established in biology by Adolf Portmann's concept of "immanence"; in jurisprudence by Wolfhart Friedrich Burgi's queries into the concept of ownership, as in the ego-boundedness of "my own," and privatized property; Lani Guiner's critiques of majority rule, and already by Charles de Secondat Montesquieu's relativity of rights and responsibilities in *Cahiers* (1716–1755); in the eidetic sciences of Husserl (and especially his *Erfahrung und Urteil*, edited by Ludwig Landgrebe), and Ferdinand Gonseth; in social science by Georg Simmel, Romano Guardini, and Wilhelm Szilasi; in economics by Fritz Marbach; in history by Lecomte du Nouy, Henri Marrou, Andre Varagnac, J. R. von Salis, Walther Tritsch, and Arnold J. Toynbee; and in time studies by Henri Bergson, H. Hermann Minkowski, Constantin von Monakow and R. Mourgue, and Werner Gent.

4. The Forbidden City in Peking, Ankor Wat in Cambodia, the Pyramids of Tenochtitlan, and the earthworks built by the North American moundbuilders are examples of three-dimensional mandalas. They represent cosmological as well as spatial relationships.

5. For instance, both Immanuel Kant (1929) and Francis Bacon (1937) argued that there are two worlds, the phenomenal world of direct experience (the world of appearances), and the noumenal world of things-in-themselves or Being-as-it-is-in-itself, *ontos on*. *Episteme* is knowledge of the *ontos on*, while *doxa* conveys the relativity and indeterminateness which plagues the subjective vicissitudes of direct experience. Bacon referred to the idols of the cave, the tribe, the marketplace, the theater to express the sense that mortals, with their irregular sensory input, tendency toward group think, ego-interests, and so forth, do not have access to the Real, but instead only to the distorted phenomenal experience. But this raises a question that neither Kant nor Bacon explained, which is: If I only have access to information distorted by my less-than-perfect means of limited IQ, honesty, courage, and fallible sense organs, and have no access to Reality otherwise, then how can I do a comparison and thereby discover that in fact my direct experience is flawed? Hermeneuticians have argued that communication (especially language) offers a shared medium that enables dialogue and intersubjective challenge and agreement. But this still possesses problems for those who believe in absolute Reality, because even a grand consensus, such as the truth that the world is flat, has proven to be merely provisional.

REFERENCES

Alexandrov, E. B. (1993) *Interference of Atomic States*. New York: Springer.

Aristotle. (1938) *On Interpretation*. In Volume 1 of 23 of the Loeb Series. Cambridge, MA: Harvard University Press.

Bacon, F. (1937) *Essays, Advancement of Learning, New Atlantis and Other Pieces*. Garden City, NY: Doubleday, Doran & Company.

Birkhoff, G. D. (1923) *Relativity and Modern Physics*. Cambridge, MA: Harvard University Press.

Bohem, D. (1980) *Wholeness and the Implicate Order*. London: Routledge & Kegan Paul.

Bohr, N. (1987) *Essays 1932–1957 on Atomic Physics and Human Knowledge*. Woodbridge, CT: Ox Bow Press.

Bolyai, J. (1955) *Non-Euclidean Geometry: A Critical and Historical Study of Its Development*. New York: Dover.

Carnap, R. (1959) "The Elimination of Metaphysics Through Logical Analysis of Language." In *Logical Positivism*, edited by A. J. Ayer. Glencoe, IL: Free Press (pp. 60–81).

de Terra, H. (1939) *Studies on the Ice Age in India and Associated Human Cultures*. Washington DC: Carnegie Institute of Washington.

Durant, W. (1954) *Our Oriental Heritage*. New York: Simon and Schuster.

Durkheim, E. (1965) *The Elementary Forms of the Religious Life*. New York: Free Press.

Einstein, A. (1949) *The World as I See It*. New York: Philosophical Library.

Gamow, G. (1966) *Thirty Years That Shook Physics*. New York: Dover Publications.

Gauss, C. F. (1902) *General Investigations of Curved Surfaces of 1825–1827*. Princeton, NJ: Princeton University Press.

Gebser, J. (1985) *The Ever-Present Origin*. Athens: Ohio University Press.

Geertz, C. (1973) *The Interpretation of Cultures*. New York: Basic Books.

Gehlen, A. (1980) *Man in the Age of Technology*. New York: Columbia University Press.

Godel, K. (1953) *The Consistency of the Axiom of Choice and of the Generalized Continuum-Hypothesis with the Axioms of Set Theory.* Princeton, NJ: Princeton University Press.

Hall, E. T. (1966) *The Hidden Dimension.* New York: Doubleday.

———. (1976) *Beyond Culture.* New York: Doubleday.

———. (1983) *The Dance of Life: The Other Dimension of Time.* New York: Doubleday.

Hawking, S. (1988) *A Brief History of Time.* New York: Bantam.

Heisenberg, W. (1958) *Physics and Philosophy.* New York: Harper & Row.

Husserl, E. (1962) *Ideas.* New York: Collier.

———. (1970) *The Crisis of European Sciences and Transcendental Phenomenology.* Evanston, IL: Northwestern University Press.

Jordan, P. (1944) *Physics of the 20th Century.* New York: Philosophical Library.

Kant, I. (1929) *Critique of Pure Reason.* New York: St. Martin's Press.

Kramer, E. M. (1992) "Gebser and Culture." In *Consciousness and Culture: An Introduction to the Thought of Jean Gebser,* edited by E. Kramer. Westport, CT: Greenwood Press (pp. 1–60).

Kronig, R. (1960) "The Turning Point." In *Theoretical Physics in the Twentieth Century: A Memorial Volume to Wolfgang Pauli,* edited by M. Fierz and V. Weisskopf. New York: Interscience Publishers (pp. 5–39).

Kuhn, T. (1962) *The Structure of Scientific Revolutions.* Chicago: University of Chicago Press.

Landgrebe, L. (1981) *The Phenomenology of Edmund Husserl: Six Essays.* Ithaca, NY: Cornell University Press.

Levinas, I. (1987) *Time and the Other: And Additional Essays.* Pittsburgh: Duquesne University Press.

Lingis, A. (1983) *Excesses: Eros and Culture.* Albany: State University of New York Press.

Lobachevski, N. (1892) *Geometrical Researches on the Theory of Parallels.* Austin,: University of Texas Press.

Lovejoy, A. (1936) *The Great Chain of Being: A Study of the History of an Idea.* Cambridge, MA: Harvard University Press.

Lukacs, G. (1963) *The Meaning of Contemporary Realism,* trans. J. Mander and N. Mander. London: Merlin Press.

March, A. (1962) *The New World of Physics.* New York: Random House.

Mickunas, A. (1994) "The Terrible Beauty and Her Reflective Force." In *Ideals of Feminine Beauty,* by Karen A. Callaghan. Westport, CT: Greenwood Press (pp. 3–19).

Nietzsche, F. (1967) *On the Genealogy of Morals.* New York: Vintage.

Northrop, F. S. C. (1958) "Introduction." In *Physics and Philosophy,* by W. Heisenberg. New York: Harper & Row (pp. 1–26).

Pauli, W. (1994) *Writings on Physics and Philosophy.* New York: Springer.

Peirce, C. S. (1940) *The Philosophy of Peirce: Selected Writings,* edited by J. Buchler. New York: Harcourt.

Planck, M. (1949) *The Meaning and Limits of Exact Science.* Lancaster, PA: American Association for the Advancement of Science.

Reichenbach, H. (1944) *Philosophic Foundation of Quantum Mechanics.* Berkeley: University of California Press.

Riemann, B. (1923) *Uber die Hypothesen: Welche de Geometrie zu Grunde Liegen.* Berlin: Springer.

Rorty, R. (1991) *Objectivity, Relativism, and Truth.* New York: Cambridge Unversity Press.

Russell, B., and A. N. Whitehead. (1967) *Principia Mathematica.* Cambridge, England: Cambridge University Press.

Sapir, E. (1949) *Selected Writings in Language, Culture, and Personality.* Berkeley: University of California Press.

———. (1990) *American Indian Languages.* New York: Mouton de Gruyter.

Sartre, J. P. (1960) *To Freedom Condemned.* New York: Philosophical Library.

Schiller, F. (1910) *Literary and Philosophical Essays.* New York: P. F. Collier.

Schiller, H. I. (1993) ''Context of Our Work.'' In *Beyond National Sovereignty: International Communication in the 1990's.* Norwood, NJ: Ablex (pp. 464–470).

Schlegel, A. W. (1960) *Athenaeum.* Stuttgart: J. G. Cottasche Buchhandlung Nachf.

Spengler, O. (1926–1928) *The Decline of the West.* New York: A. A. Knopf.

Thoreau, H. (1981) *Works of Henry David Thoreau.* New York: Avenel Books.

von Neumann, J. (1955) *Mathematical Foundations of Quantum Mechanics.* Princeton, NJ: Princeton University Press.

von Weizsacker, C. F. (1975–1977) *Quantum Theory and the Structures of Time and Space.* Munich: C. Hanser.

Whorf, B. L. (1956) *Language Thought and Reality.* Cambridge, MA: MIT Press.

Wittgenstein, L. (1958) *Philosophical Investigations.* Cambridge, England: Basil Blackwell.

References

Abel, K. (1884) *Gegensinn der Urworte*. Leipzig: Friedrich Heitz.

Ackerman, D. (1990) *A Natural History of the Senses*. New York: Random House.

Adell, S. (1994) *Double-Consciousness/Double Bind*. Urbana: University of Illinois Press.

Adorno, T. W., and M. Horkheimer. (1972) *Dialectic of Enlightenment*. New York: Herder and Herder.

Alexandrov, E. B. (1993) *Interference of Atomic States*. New York: Springer.

Aristotle. (1938) *On Interpretation*. In Volume 1 of 23 of the Loeb Series. Cambridge, MA: Harvard University Press.

———. (1991) *Art of Rhetoric*. London: Harvard University Press.

Asante, M. K. (1987) *The Afrocentric Idea*. Philadelphia: Temple University Press.

Austin, J. L. (1962) *How to Do Things With Words*. Cambridge, MA: Harvard University Press.

Aveni, A. (1990) *Empires of Time*. London: I. B. Tauris & Company.

Bacon, F. (1937) *Essays, Advancement of Learning, New Atlantis and Other Pieces*. Garden City, NY: Doubleday, Doran & Company.

———. (1942) *New Atlantis*. New York: Classics Club, W. J. Black.

Bagdikian, B. H. (1990) *The Media Monopoly*. Boston: Beacon.

Baldwin, J., and M. Mead. (1971) *Rap on Race*. New York: J. B. Lippincott.

Bales, R. (1970) *Personality and Interpersonal Behavior*. New York: Holt, Rinehart & Winston.

Barthes, R. (1967) *Elements of Semiology*. New York: Hill & Wang.

———. (1982) *Mythologies*. New York: Hill & Wang.

Bataille, G. (1955) *The Birth of Art: Prehistoric Painting*. Lausanne, France: Skira.

———. (1989) *The Tears of Eros*. San Francisco: City Lights Books.

Bateson, G. (1951) ''Information and Codification.'' In *Communication and the Social Matrix of Pyschiatry*, with Jurgen Ruesch. New York: Norton (pp. 168–211).

Baudrillard, J. (1981) *Simulations*. New York: Semiotext(e).

Benjamin, W. (1969) *Illuminations*. New York: Schocken Books.

Bentham, J., and C. Ogden. (1977) *Bentham's Theory of Fictions*. New York: AMS Press.

Bestor, T. C. (1989) *Neighborhood Tokyo*. Stanford, CA: Stanford University Press.

Binet, A. (1913) *A Method of Measuring the Intelligence of Young Children*. Lincoln, IL: The Courier Company.

Birkhoff, G. D. (1923) *Relativity and Modern Physics*. Cambridge, MA: Harvard University Press.

Bohem, D. (1980) *Wholeness and the Implicate Order*. London: Routledge & Kegan Paul.

Bohr, N. (1987) *Essays 1932–1957 on Atomic Physics and Human Knowledge*. Woodbridge, CT: Ox Bow Press.

Bolyai, J. (1955) *Non-Euclidean Geometry: A Critical and Historical Study of Its Development*. New York: Dover.

Boorstin, D. (1964) *The Image: A Guide to Pseudo-Events in America*. New York: Harper & Row.

Bormann, E. (1985) *The Force of Fantasy: Restoring the American Dream*. Carbondale: Southern Illinois University Press.

Braverman, H. (1974) *Labor and Monopoly Capital*. New York: Monthly Review Press.

Broadhurst, A. R., and D. K. Darnell. (1965) "An Introduction to Cybernetics and Information Theory." *Quarterly Journal of Speech* 51, no. 4: 442–453.

Brown, L. et al. (1995) *State of the World: A Worldwatch Institute Report on Progress Toward a Sustainable Society*. Annual. New York: W. W. Norton.

Brown, T. (1995) *Black Lies/White Lies: The Truth According to Tony Brown*. New York: W. Morrow and Company.

Buber, M. (1970) *I and Thou*. New York: Charles Scribner's Sons.

Burke, K. (1941) *The Philosophy of Literary Form: Studies in Symbolic Action*. Baton Rouge: Louisiana State University Press.

———. (1950) *A Rhetoric of Motives*. Cleveland: World.

———. (1962) *A Grammar of Motives and a Rhetoric of Motives*. Cleveland: World.

Campbell, G. (1823) *The Philosophy of Rhetoric*. Boston: Charles Ewer.

Campbell, J., and B. Moyers. (1988) *The Power of Myth*. New York: Doubleday.

Carnap, R. (1959) "The Elimination of Metaphysics Through Logical Analysis of Language." In *Logical Positivism*, edited by A. J. Ayer. Glencoe, IL: Free Press (pp. 60–81).

———. (1963) *Philosophy of Rudolf Carnap*, edited by P. Schilpp. La Salle, IL: Open Court.

Cassirer, E. (1944) *An Essay on Man*. New Haven, CT: Yale University Press.

Chomsky, N. (1972) *Language and Mind*. New York: Harcourt Brace Jovanovich, Inc.

Chuang Tzu. (1974) *Inner Chapters*. New York: Vintage.

Codrington, R. (1841) Letter to F. Max Muller, quoted in G. van der Leeux, *Phanomenologie der Religion*. Tubingen: Mohr, 1933.

Coles, R. (1967) *Children in Crisis*. Boston: Little, Brown.

———. (1992) *Their Eyes Meeting the World: The Drawings and Paintings of Children*. Boston: Houghton Mifflin.

Comstock, G., S. Chaffee, N. Katzman, M. McCombs, and D. Roberts. (1978) *Television and Human Behavior*. New York: Columbia University Press.

Comte, A. (1865) *A General View of Positive Religion*. London: Trubner.

Cooper, J., F. Bloom, and R. Roth. (1996) *The Biochemical Basis of Neuropharmacology.* New York: Oxford University Press.

Covey, S. (1989) *The Seven Habits of Highly Effective People: Restoring the Character Ethic.* New York: Simon & Schuster.

Croce, B. (1960) *History: Its Theory and Practice.* New York: Russell & Russell.

Davis, P., and R. Hersh. (1981) *The Mathematical Experience.* Boston: Houghton Mifflin.

———. (1986) *Descartes' Dream: The World According to Mathematics.* Boston: Houghton Mifflin.

Deluze, G., and F. Guattari. (1983) *On the Line.* New York: Semiotext(e).

Derrida, J. (1973) *Speech and Phenomena.* Evanston, IL: Northwestern University Press.

———. (1976a) "Introduction." In *The Origin of Geometry* by E. Husserl. New York: Nicolas Hays.

———. (1976b) *Of Grammatology.* Baltimore: Johns Hopkins University Press.

———. (1978a) *Edmund Husserl's Origin of Geometry: An Introduction.* Stony Brook, NY: Nicolas Hays.

———. (1978b) *Writing and Difference* London: Routledge and Kegan Paul.

———. (1981) *Dissemination.* Chicago: University of Chicago Press.

de Saussure, F. (1974) *Course in General Linguistics.* London: Fontana.

Descartes, R. (1941) *A Discourse on Method.* London: J. M. Dent and Sons.

de Terra, H. (1939) *Studies on the Ice Age in India and Associated Human Cultures.* Washington, DC: Carnegie Institute of Washington.

Diamond, J. (1994) "How Africa Became Black." *Discover* 15, no. 2 (February): 72–81.

Drucker, P. (1942) *The Future of Industrial Man: A Conservative Approach.* New York: John Day Company.

Du Bois, W.E.B. (1989) *The Souls of Black Folk.* New York: Bantam.

Durant, W. (1954) *Our Oriental Heritage.* New York: Simon and Schuster.

Durkheim, E. (1965) *The Elementary Forms of the Religious Life.* New York: Free Press.

Eco, U., R. Rorty, and J. Culler. (1992) *Interpretation and Overinterpretation.* Cambridge, England: Cambridge University Press.

Edgerton, F. (1944) *The Bhagavad Gita: Translated and Interpreted.* Harvard Oriental Series, Vols. 38, 39. Cambridge, MA: Harvard University Press.

Einstein, A. (1949) *The World as I See It.* New York: Philosophical Library.

Eliade, M. (1963) *Myth and Reality.* New York: Harper and Row.

Ellison. R. (1952) *Invisible Man.* New York: Random House.

———. (1966) "Transcript of the American Academy Conference on the Negro American—May 14–15, 1965." *Daedalus* 95, no. 1 (Winter): 433–444.

Ellul, J. (1964) *The Technological Society.* New York: Vintage.

Fish, S. (1996) " 'Morphogenic Field' Day." *Newsweek,* June 3 (p. 37).

Fisher, W. (1987) *Human Communication as Narration: Toward a Philosophy of Reason, Value, and Action.* Columbia: University of South Carolina Press.

Forrester, J. (1961) *Industrial Dynamics.* Cambridge, MA: Wright-Allen Press.

———. (1968) *Principles of Systems.* Cambridge, MA: Wright-Allen Press.

———. (1971) *World Dynamics.* Cambridge, MA: Wright-Allen Press.

Foucault, M. (1970) *The Order of Things.* New York: Pantheon.

———. (1972) *The Archaeology of Knowledge and the Discourse on Language.* New York: Pantheon Books.

———. (1979a) *Discipline and Punish: The Birth of the Prison.* New York: Vintage.

————. (1979b) "What Is an Author?" In *Textual Strategies*, edited by J. Harari. Ithaca, NY: Cornell University Press (pp. 141–160).

————. (1980) *Power/Knowledge*. New York: Pantheon Books.

Fowles, J. (1992) *Why Viewers Watch*. Thousand Oaks, CA: Sage.

Frank, R., and P. Cook. (1995) *The Winner-Take-All Society: How More and More Americans Compete for Ever Fewer and Bigger Prizes, Encouraging Economic Waste, Income Inequality, and an Impoverished Cultural Life*. New York: Free Press.

Frazer, J. (1910) *Totemism and Exogamy: A Treatise on Certain Early Forms of Superstition and Society*. London: Macmillan.

Frazer, J. T., ed. (1981) *The Voices of Time*. Amherst: University of Massachusetts Press.

Frege, G. (1984) "On Sense and Reference." In *Readings in Semantics*, edited by F. Zabeeh et al. Urbana: University of Illinois Press (pp. 118–140).

Freud, S. (1918) *Totem and Taboo*. New York: Vintage.

————. (1943) *Gesammelte Werke chronologisch geordnet*. London: Imago.

Fukuyama, F. (1992) *The End of History and the Last Man*. New York: Free Press.

Gadamer, H. G. (1975) *Truth and Method*. New York: Seabury Press.

————. (1981) *Reason in the Age of Science*. Boston: MIT Press.

Gamow, G. (1966) *Thirty Years that Shook Physics*. New York: Dover Publications.

Gauss, C. F. (1902) *General Investigations of Curved Surfaces of 1825–1827*. Princeton, NJ: Princeton University Press.

Gebser, J. (1985) *The Ever-Present Origin*. Athens: Ohio University Press.

Geddes, P. (1911) *Evolution*. New York: Holt and Company.

Geertz, C. (1973) *The Interpretation of Cultures*. New York: Basic Books.

Gehlen, A. (1980) *Man in the Age of Technology*. New York: Columbia University Press.

Gigon, O. (1959) *Grundproblem der antiken Philosophie*. Bern: Francke.

Gilbreth, F. (1911) *Motion Study: A Method for Increasing the Efficiency of the Workman*. New York: D. Van Nostrand.

————. (1973) *Primer of Scientific Management*. Easton, PA: Hire.

Gilbreth, F., Jr. (1948) *Cheaper by the Dozen*. New York: T. Y. Crowell.

Gilroy, P. (1993a) *The Black Atlantic: Modernity and Double Consciousness*. Cambridge, MA: Harvard University Press.

————. (1993b) *Small Acts*. London: Serpent's Tail.

Godard, J. L. (1970) *See You at Mao* (U.S. title) [British title: *British Sounds*]. Kestrel Productions for London Weekend Television, London.

Godel, K. (1953) *The Consistency of the Axiom of Choice and of the Generalized Continuum-Hypothesis with the Axioms of Set Theory*. Princeton, NJ: Princeton University Press.

Grant, E. (1977) *Physical Science in the Middle Ages*. Cambridge, England: Cambridge University Press.

Gudykunst, W., and Y. Kim. (1992) *Communicating with Strangers: An Approach to Intercultural Communication*. New York: McGraw-Hill.

Gurwitsch, A. (1974) *Phenomenology and the Theory of Science*. Evanston, IL: Northwestern University Press.

Habermas, J. (1971) *Knowledge and Human Interest*. Boston: Beacon.

————. (1973) *Theory and Practice*. Boston: Beacon.

————. (1984) *The Theory of Communicative Action, Vol. 1: Reason and the Rationalization of Society*. Boston: Beacon Press.

———. (1992) *Postmodern Thinking*. Cambridge, MA: MIT Press.

Hall, E. T. (1966) *The Hidden Dimension*. New York: Anchor Books.

———. (1976) *Beyond Culture*. New York: Doubleday.

———. (1983) *The Dance of Life: The Other Dimension of Time*. New York: Doubleday.

Handlin, O. (1966) "The Goals of Integration." *Daedalus* 95, no. 1 (Winter): 279–290.

Hawking, S. (1988) *A Brief History of Time*. New York: Bantam Books.

Hayashida, C. T. (1976) *Identity, Race, and the Blood Ideology of Japan*. Dissertation for the University of Washington. AAC 7625413.

Hegel, G. (1953) *Reason in History: A General Introduction to the Philosophy of History*. New York: Liberal Arts Press.

Heidegger, M. (1962) *Being and Time*. New York: Harper & Row.

———. (1971) *On the Way to Language*. New York: Harper & Row.

Heisenberg, W. (1958) *Physics and Philosophy: The Revolution in Modern Science*. New York: Harper & Row.

———. (1970) *Natural Law and the Structure of Matter*. London: Rebel Press.

Henry, J. (1963) *Culture Against Man*. New York: Vintage.

Hobsbawm, E. J., and T. O. Ranger. (1983) *The Invention of Tradition*. New York: Cambridge University Press.

Hofstede, G., and M. Bond. (1984) "Hofstede's Culture Dimensions." *Journal of Cross-Cultural Psychology* 15, no. 4: 417–433.

Homans, G. (1954) "Social Behavior as Exchange." *The American Journal of Sociology* 62, no. 6: 597.

———. (1984) *Coming to My Senses: The Autobiography of a Sociologist*. New Brunswick, NJ: Transaction Books.

Hoy, D. C. (1978) *The Critical Circle*. Berkeley: University of California Press.

Hoyle, F. (1992) Essay in *Stephen Hawking's "A Brief History of Time": A Reader's Companion*, edited by S. Hawking. New York: Bantam Books (pp. 60, 61).

Humboldt, F. W. (1973) "On the Historian's Task." In *The Theory and Practice of History: Collected Manuscripts from 1829–1880*. Indianapolis: Bobbs-Merrill.

Hume, D. (1973) *A Treatise of Human Nature*. London: Oxford University Press.

Husserl, E. (1962) *Ideas: General Introduction to Pure Phenomenology*. New York: Collier.

———. (1964) *The Phenomenology of Internal Time-Consciousness*. Bloomington: Indiana University Press.

———. (1970) *The Crisis of European Sciences and Transcendental Phenomenology*. Evanston, IL: Northwestern University Press.

———. (1975) *The Paris Lectures*. The Hague: Nijhoff.

———. (1977) *The Origin of Geometry*. New York: Nicholas Hays.

Hyssen, A. (1987) "Foreword: The Return of Diogenes as Postmodern Intellectual." In *Critique of Cynical Reason*, by P. Sloterdijk. Minneapolis: University of Minnesota Press (pp. ix–xxxix).

Ikeda, R. (1992) *Ie to kazoku: A Shift in the Communication Pattern of the Japanese Family*. Master's thesis, University of Oklahoma.

Innis, H. (1950) *Empire and Communication*. Oxford, England: University of Oxford Press.

Jameson, F. (1972) *The Prison-House of Language*. Princeton, NJ: Princeton University Press.

Janis, I. (1982) *Victims of Groupthink: A Psychological Study of Foreign Decisions and Fiascos*. Boston: Houghton Mifflin.

Jordan, P. (1944) *Physics of the 20th Century*. New York: Philosophical Library.

Jung, C. G. (1956) *Symbols of Transformation*. Princeton, NJ: Princeton University Press.

Kant, I. (1929) *Critique of Pure Reason*. New York: St. Martin's Press.

Kaufmann, W. (1980) *Discovering the Mind, Volume Two: Nietzsche, Heidegger, and Buber*. New York: McGraw-Hill.

Kazinski, J. (1970) *Being There*. New York: Harcourt, Brace, Jovanovich.

Kierkegaard, S. (1944) *Either/Or*. Princeton, NJ: Princeton University Press.

Koestler, A. (1941) *Darkness at Noon*. New York: Bantam.

———. (1967) *The Ghost in the Machine*. New York: Macmillan.

Kramer, E. M. (1988) *Television Criticism and the Problem of Ground*. 2 Vols. Ann Arbor, MI: University Microfilms International, 8816770.

———. (1992) "Gebser and Culture." In *Consciousness and Culture: An Introduction to the Thought of Jean Gebser*, edited by E. Kramer. Westport, CT: Greenwood Press (pp. 1–60).

———. (1993a) "Investigative Journalism in Bulgaria: A Postponed Renaissance." In *Creating a Free Press in Eastern Europe*, edited by A. Hester and K. White. Athens: University of Georgia, The James M. Cox, Jr., Center for International Mass Communication Training & Research, The Henry W. Grady College of Journalism and Mass Communication, University of Georgia (pp. 111–159).

———. (1993b) "Mass Media and Democracy." In *Open Institutions: The Hope for Democracy*, edited by J. W. Murphy and D. Peck. Westport, CT: Praeger (pp. 77–98).

———. (1993c) "The Origin of Television as Civilizational Expression." In *Semiotics 1990: Sources in Semiotics, Vol. XI*, edited by J. Deely et al. Lanham, MD: University Press of America.

———. (1994) "Making Love Alone: Videocentrism and the Case of Modern Pornography." In *Ideals of Feminine Beauty*, by K. Callaghan. Westport, CT: Greenwood Press (pp. 79–98).

———. (1995) "A Brief Hermeneutic of the Co-Constitution of Nature and Culture in the West Including Some Contemporary Consequences." *History of European Ideas* 20, nos. 1–3: 649–659.

Kramer, E. M., and R. Ikeda. (1996) "Japanese Clocks: Semiotic Evidence of the Perspectival Mutation." In Press.

Krippendorf, K. (1975) "Information Theory." In *Communication and Behavior*, edited by G. Hanneman and W. McEwen. Reading, MA: Addison-Wesley (pp. 351–389).

Krober, A. L., ed. (1953) *Anthropology Today*. Chicago: University of Chicago Press.

Kronig, R. (1960) "The Turning Point." In *Theoretical Physics in the Twentieth Century: A Memorial Volume to Wolfgang Pauli*, edited by M. Fierz and V. Weisskopf. New York: Interscience Publishers (pp. 5–39).

Kuhn, T. (1962) *The Structure of Scientific Revolutions*. Chicago: University of Chicago Press.

Kula, W. (1986) *Measures and Men*. Princeton, NJ: Princeton University Press.

Landgrebe, L. (1981) *The Phenomenology of Edmund Husserl: Six Essays*. Ithaca, NY: Cornell University Press.

Landmann, M. (1974) *Philosophical Anthropology*. Philadelphia: Westminister.

Laertius. (1925) *Lives and Opinions of Eminent Philosophers*. New York: G. P. Putnam's Sons.

Leibniz, G. (1951) *The Monadology and Other Philosophical Writings*. London: Oxford University Press.

Lemelle, A. L. (1993) "Review of Ralph C. Gomes and Linda Faye Williams, *From Exclusion to Inclusion: The Long Struggle for African-American Political Power*." *Contemporary Sociology* 22, no. 1 (January): 60–78.

Levinas, E. (1961) *Totality and Infinity*. Pittsburgh: Duquesne University Press.

———. (1987) *Time and the Other: And Additional Essays*. Pittsburgh: Duquesne University Press.

Levi-Strauss, C. (1969) *The Raw and the Cooked*. Chicago: University of Chicago Press.

Lingis, A. (1983) *Excesses: Eros and Culture*. Albany: State University of New York Press.

Lobachevski, N. (1892) *Geometrical Researches on the Theory of Parallels*. Austin: University of Texas Press.

Lovejoy, A. (1936) *The Great Chain of Being: A Study of the History of an Idea*. Cambridge, MA: Harvard University Press.

Lovelock, J. E. (1979) *Gaia*. New York: Oxford University Press.

Luhmann, N. (1982) *The Differentiation of Society*. New York: Columbia University Press.

Lukacs, G. (1963) *The Meaning of Contemporary Realism*. London: Merlin Press.

Lyotard, J. F. (1984) *The Postmodern Condition: A Report on Knowledge*. Minneapolis: University of Minnesota Press.

———. (1993) *The Postmodern Explained*. Minneapolis: University of Minnesota Press.

Malebranche, N. (1992) *Philosophical Selections: From the Search After Truth*. Indianapolis: Hackett Publishing.

Mannheim, K. (1952) *Essays on the Sociology of Knowledge*. London: Routledge & Kegan Paul.

March, A. (1962) *The New World of Physics*. New York: Random House.

Marx, K. (1967) *Das Kapital, Vol. 1*. New York: International Publishers.

Maslow, A. (1968) *Toward a Psychology of Being*. New York: Van Nostrand.

McDaniel, A. (1995) "The Dynamic Racial Composition of the United States." *Daedalus* 124, no. 1 (Winter): 179–198.

McLuhan, M. (1962) *The Gutenberg Galaxy: The Making of Typographic Man*. Toronto: University of Toronto Press.

———. (1964) *Understanding Media: The Extensions of Man*. New York: Mentor Books.

McLuhan, M., and B. Powers. (1989) *Global Village*. New York: Oxford Unviersity Press.

Meadows, D. H., D. L. Meadows, and J. Randers. (1992) *Beyond the Limits*. Post Mills, VT: Chelsea Green Publishing.

Merleau-Ponty, M. (1962) *Phenomenology of Perception*. London: Routledge & Kegan Paul.

———. (1964) *The Primacy of Perception*. Evanston, IL: Northwestern University Press.

Mesarovic, M., and E. Pestel. (1974) *Mankind at the Turning Point*. New York: Signet.

Michard, J. G. (1992) *The Reign of the Dinosaurs*. New York: Harry N. Abrams.

Mickunas, A. (1978) personal conversation.

———. (1994) "The Terrible Beauty and Her Reflective Force." In *Ideals of Feminine Beauty*, by Karen A. Callaghan. Westport, CT: Greenwood Press (pp. 3–19).

Milgram, S. (1974) *Obedience to Authority*. New York: Harper & Row.

Monge, P. (1977) "The Systems Perspective as a Theoretical Basis for the Study of Human Communication." *Communication Quarterly* 25, no. 1: 19–29.

Monroe, C., D. Meekhof, B. King, and D. Wineland. (1996) "A 'Schrodinger Cat' Superposition State of an Atom." *Science* 272, May 24 (pp. 1131–1133).

Morris, D. (1967) *The Naked Ape*. New York: McGraw-Hill.

———. (1969) *The Human Zoo*. New York: Delta.

Morrison, T. (1970) *The Bluest Eye: A Novel*. New York: Holt, Rinehart and Winston.

Mudimbe, V. Y. (1988) *The Invention of Africa: Gnosis, Philosophy, and the Order of Knowledge*. Bloomington: Indiana University Press.

Mumford, L. (1963) *Techniques and Civilization*. New York: Harcourt, Brace and World.

Munsterberg, H. (1913) *Psychological and Industrial Efficiency*. New York: Houghton Mifflin.

Myrdal, G. (1944) *The American Dilemma: The Negro Problem and Modern Democracy*. New York: Harper & Brothers Publishers.

Nesson, R. (1980) "Now Television's the King-Maker." *TV Guide*, May 10 (p. 4).

Niehues-Probsting, H. (1979) *Der Kynismus des Diogenes und der Begriff des Zynismus*. Munich: W. Fink.

Nietzsche, F. (1966) *Thus Spoke Zarathustra*. New York: Viking Penguin.

———. (1967a) *On the Genealogy of Morals*. New York: Vintage.

———. (1967b) *The Birth of Tragedy*. New York: Vintage.

———. (1972) *Beyond Good and Evil*. New York: Penguin.

———. (1974) *The Gay Science*. New York: Vintage.

———. (1996) *Human, All-too-Human*. New York: Routledge.

Northrop, F. S. C. (1958) "Introduction." In *Physics and Philosophy*, by W. Heisenberg. New York: Harper & Row (pp. 1–26).

Noth, W. (1995) *Handbook of Semiotics*. Bloomington: Indiana University Press.

Ong, W. J. (1982) *Orality and Literacy: The Technologizing of the Word*. New York: Methuen.

Organ, T. (1970) *The Hindu Quest for the Perfection of Man*. Athens: Ohio University Press.

Palmer, R. (1969) *Hermeneutics*. Evanston, IL: Northwestern University Press.

Parenti, M. (1993) *Inventing Reality: The Politics of News Media*, 2d ed. New York: St. Martin's Press.

Parsons, T. (1951) *The Social System*. Glencoe, IL: Free Press.

Pathak, A. (1996) graduate student term paper, University of Oklahoma.

Pauli, W. (1994) *Writings on Physics and Philosophy*. New York: Springer.

Peirce. C. S. (1940) *The Philosophy of Peirce: Selected Writings*, edited by J. Buchler. New York: Harcourt.

Pestel, E. (1989) *Beyond the Limits to Growth*. New York: Universe Books.

Pilotta, J. (1992) "Media Power Working Over the Body: An Application of Gebser to Popular Culture." In *Consciousness and Culture: An Introduction to the Thought of Jean Gebser*, edited by E. Kramer. Westport, CT: Greenwood Press (pp. 79–102).

Planck, M. (1949) *The Meaning and Limits of Exact Science*. Lancaster, PA: American Association for the Advancement of Science.

Plot, R. (1677) *The Natural History of Oxford-shire*. Oxford, England: The Theatre.

Polak, F. L. (1961) *The Image of the Future*, 2 vols. Leyden, Netherlands: A. W. Sijthoff.

Polanyi, M. (1958) *Personal Knowledge: Towards a Post-Critical Philosophy*. Chicago: University of Chicago Press.

Popper, K. (1959) *Logic of Scientific Discovery*. New York: Basic Books.

Pribram, K. (1971) *Languages of the Brain: Experimental Paradoxes and Principles in Neuropsychology*. Englewood Cliffs, NJ: Prentice-Hall.

Rapoport, A. (1968) ''Foreword.'' In *Modern Systems Research for the Behavioral Scientist*, edited by W. Buckley. Chicago: Aldine (pp. xiii–xxv).

Rauch, J. (1992) *The Outnation: A Search for the Soul of Japan*. New York: Little, Brown and Company.

Rehorick, D., and W. Buxton. (1986) ''Recasting the Parsons-Schutz Dialogue: The Hidden Participation of Eric Voegelin.'' Paper presented at the International Society for the Sociology of Knowledge, New Delhi.

Reichenbach, H. (1944) *Philosophic Foundation of Quantum Mechanics*. Berkeley: University of California Press.

Reinach, S. (1939) *Orpheus: A History of Religions*. New York: Liveright.

Reingold, E. M. (1992) *Chrysanthemums and Thorns: The Untold Story of Modern Japan*. New York: St. Martin's Press.

Renyi, A. (1967) *Dialogues on Mathematics*. San Francisco: Holden-Day.

Ricoeur, P. (1965) *History and Truth*. Evanston, IL: Northwestern University Press.

———. (1974) *The Conflict of Interpretations*. Evanston, IL: Northwestern University Press.

———. (1981) *Hermeneutics and the Social Sciences*. Cambridge, England: Cambridge University Press.

Riemann, B. (1923) *Uber die Hypothesen: Welche de Geometrie zu Grunde Liegen*. Berlin: Springer.

Rifkin, J. (1987) *Time Wars*. New York: Henry Holt and Company.

Rorty, R. (1979) *Philosophy and the Mirror of Nature*. Princeton, NJ: Princeton University Press.

———. (1991) *Objectivity, Relativism, and Truth*. New York: Cambridge Unversity Press.

Ruesch, J., and G. Bateson. (1951) *Communication: The Social Matrix of Psychiatry*. New York: W. W. Norton & Company.

Russell, B., and A. N. Whitehead. (1967) *Principia Mathematica*. Cambridge, England: Cambridge University Press.

Russell, K., M. Wilson, and R. Hall. (1992) *The Color Complex: The Politics of Skin Color Among African Americans*. New York: Anchor Books, Doubleday.

Sagan, C. (1975) *Broca's Brain: Reflections on the Romance of Science*. New York: Random House.

Sapir, E. (1949) *Selected Writings in Language, Culture, and Personality*. Berkeley: University of California Press.

———. (1990) *American Indian Languages*. New York: Mouton de Gruyter.

Sartre, J. P. (1956) *Being and Nothing*. New York: Simon and Schuster.

———. (1960) *To Freedom Condemned*. New York: Philosophical Library.

Schiller, F. (1910) *Literary and Philosophical Essays*. New York: P. F. Collier.

Schiller, H. I. (1993) ''Context of Our Work.'' In *Beyond National Sovereignty: International Communication in the 1990's*, edited by Kaarle Nordenstreng and Herbert I. Schiller. Norwood, NJ: Ablex (pp. 464–470).

Schlegel, A. W. (1960) *Athenaeum*. Stuttgart: J. G. Cottasche Buchhandlung Nachf.

Schliermacher, F. (1961) *Ueder die Religion: Reden an die gebildeten unter ihren verachtern*. Hamburg: F. Meiner.

Schmidt, W. (1939) *Primitive Revelation*. London: Herder.

Schopenhauer, A. (1966) *The World as Will and Representation, Vols 1 and 2*. New York: Dover Press.

Schramm, W. (1971) "The Nature of Communication Between Humans." In *The Process and Effects of Mass Communication*, edited by W. Schramm and D. Roberts. Chicago: University of Illinois Press (pp. 3–53).

Shannon, C., and W. Weaver. (1949) *The Mathematical Theory of Communication*. Urbana: University of Illinois Press.

Sloterdijk, P. (1987) *Critique of Cynical Reason*. Minneapolis: University of Minnesota Press.

Sollors, W. (1989) *The Invention of Ethnicity*. New York: Oxford University Press.

Sowell, T. (1994) *Race and Culture*. New York: Basic Books.

Spengler, O. (1926–1928) *The Decline of the West*. New York: A. A. Knopf.

Spiegelberg, H. (1982) *The Phenomenological Movement*. The Hague: Martinus Nijhoff.

Taylor, F. (1911, reprint 1996) *The Principles of Scientific Management*. Dusseldorf: Wirstschaft und Finanzen.

Terebessy, K. (1944) *Zum Problem der Ambivalenz in der Sprachentwicklung*. Trnava, Germany: Urbanek.

Thoreau, H. (1981) *Works of Henry David Thoreau*. New York: Avenel Books.

Thorne, K. (1992) Essay in *Stephen Hawking's "A Brief History of Time": A Reader's Companion*, edited by S. Hawking. New York: Bantam Books (pp. 70–73).

Todorov, T. (1982) *Theories of the Symbol*. Ithaca, NY: Cornell University Press.

Toffler, A. (1990) *Power Shift: Knowledge, Wealth, and Violence at the Edge of the 21st Century*. New York: Bantam.

Turner Broadcasting. (1995) *China: The Wild East*. Turner Broadcasting System.

Tylor, E. (1958) *Primitive Culture*. New York: Harper.

Vico, G. (1974) *Opere giuridiche: il diritto universale*. Firenze, Italy: Sansoni.

von Bertalanffy, L. (1968) *General Systems Theory: Foundations, Development, Applications*. New York: Braziller.

von Neumann, J. (1955) *Mathematical Foundations of Quantum Mechanics*. Princeton, NJ: Princeton University Press.

von Weizsacker, C. F. (1949) *The History of Nature*. Chicago: University of Chicago Press.

———. (1975–1977) *Quantum Theory and the Structures of Time and Space*. Munich: C. Hanser.

Walker, N., and P. Shaver. (1994) "The Importance of Nongenetic Influences on Romantic Love Styles: A Twin-Family Study." *Psychological Science* 5, no. 5, September (pp. 268–274).

Waters, M. (1994) "The Social Construction of Race and Ethnicity: Some Examples from Demography," Proceedings from the Albany Conference, "American Diversity: A Demographic Challenge for the Twenty-First Century," April 15–16.

Watzlawick, P., J. Beavin, and D. Jackson. (1967) *Pragmatics of Human Communication*. New York: Norton.

Weber, M. (1949) *The Method of the Social Sciences*. Glencoe, IL: The Free Press.

Weiner, M. (1994) *Race and Migration in Imperial Japan*. London: Routledge.

West, C. (1993) *Prophetic Reflections*. Monroe, ME: Common Courage Press.

———. (1994) *Race Matters*. New York: Vintage.

Whorf, B. (1956) *Language, Thought, and Reality*. Boston: MIT Press.

Wiener, N. (1948) *Cybernetics: Or, Control and Communication in the Animal and the Machine*. Cambridge, MA: MIT Press.

Will, G. (1996) ''Communication and Science.'' *The Norman Oklahoma Transcript*, no. 323 (May 30, 1996): 6.

Willis, J., ed. (1985) *Slaves and Slavery in Muslim Africa*, 2 Vols. London: Frank Cass & Co.

Wittgenstein, L. (1958) *Philosophical Investigations*. Oxford, England: Basil Blackwell.

———. (1969) *On Certainty*. Oxford, England: Basil Blackwell.

———. (1971) *Prototractatus*. London: Routledge & Kegan Paul.

———. (1974) *Philosophical Grammar*. Oxford, England: Basil Blackwell.

———. (1975) *Philosophical Remarks*. Oxford, England: Basil Blackwell.

Woody, C. (1986) *Neural Mechanisms of Conditioning*. New York: Plenum Press.

Wright, L. (1992) *Clockwork Man*. New York: Barnes and Noble.

Wundt, W. (1926) *Wilhelm Wundts Werk: ein Verzeichnis seiner samtlichen Schriften*. Munich: Vittorio Klostermann.

Name Index

Subject Index

About the Author

ERIC MARK KRAMER is Assistant Professor of Communications at the University of Oklahoma. Among his earlier publications are *Consciousness and Culture*: *An Introduction to the Thought of Jean Gebser* (Greenwood, 1992) and *Postmodernism and Race*, forthcoming from Praeger.

ISBN 0-275-95758-6

HARDCOVER BAR CODE